THE GENIUS OF ARAB CIVILIZATION
Source of Renaissance

BRITISH MUSEUM

2 3 NOV 2001

EDUCATION SERVICE
LIBRARY

THE GENIUS OF
ARAB CIVILIZATION
Source of Renaissance

JOHN S. BADEAU · MAJID FAKHRY · OLEG GRABAR · SAMI K. HAMARNEH
DONALD R. HILL · MOUNAH A. KHOURI · IBRAHIM MADKOUR
RAGAEI EL MALLAKH · DOROTHEA EL MALLAKH · F. E. PETERS
ALI JIHAD RACY · ABDELHAMID I. SABRA · BAYLY WINDER
JOHN R. HAYES, EDITOR

SECOND EDITION

Eurabia (Publishing) Ltd
A member of the Eurabia group of companies
London, England

Second edition, 1983.
Published in USA and Canada by MIT Press.
Published in Europe, North Africa and the Middle East by Eurabia (Publishing) Ltd.

Library of Congress Cataloging Data.
Main entry under title:
The Genius of Arab Civilization.
Bibliography: P. 247–250. Includes indexes.
1. Civilization, Islamic. 1. Hayes, J.R. (John Richard) 1933 –.
DS36.85.G46 1983   909'.04927   83–922

MIT ISBN 0–262–08136–9   Eurabia ISBN 0 946598 00 2(Hard back)
ISBN 0–262–58063–2(pbk.)   ISBN 0 946598 01 0(Soft back)
ISBN 0 946598 02 9(Stud. Edition)

Original English edition published by Mobil Middle East Affiliates,
New York University Press and Phaidon Press, 1975.
First Arabic and paperback English edition published by MIT Press, 1978.

English and Arabic Copyright © Mobil Oil Corporation, 1975, 1978, 1983.
Printed in England by Westerham Press Limited.
Designed by Walter Ferro.
All rights reserved.

Contents

10477

BM 8 (GEN)

Monographs

Illustrations

Editor's Note

The transliteration system employed throughout this volume was devised with particular regard for readers who are not familiar with the Arabic language. In their interest an effort has been made to avoid overburdening the text with symbols that would be meaningless to them.

The Arabic consonants 'ayn (') and **hamzah** (') (medial and final) have, of course, been indicated. However, diacritical marks (for example, those used to differentiate between velarized and nonvelarized consonants and to distinguish long from short vowels) have been omitted on the assumption that they would be more confusing than helpful to non-Arabists, while readers proficient in Arabic would not be deprived by their absence and, hopefully, would understand.

Most Arabic place names have been transliterated from the original, but Western usage has been retained for those place names commonly known to Western readers in other forms (for example, Cairo, Kairouan, Damascus).

Following the Romanization system adopted and used by the United States Board on Geographic Names, the Arabic word for "son" is transliterated to conform with the Arabic spelling: ibn initially and bin when it occurs within a name. The abbreviation b. has not been used on the grounds that it would be unpronounceable to readers unfamiliar with Arabic.

Whatever the merits or demerits of this system may be, the editor accepts full responsibility.

In addition to the authors of the text, who gave so generously of their time and talent, we are grateful to many others who have helped in this effort: to W. E. MacDonald for his encouragement and support; to Philip Hitti, Jamal Sa'd, Mohamed Habib, George Lenczowski, Dr. C. Knipp, F. Vittor, W. Jack Butler, M. M. Ameen, S. G. Marzullo, Hassan Abul Naga, A. Y. Sakr, M. Mourad, P. R. Chase, Diana Sawma, James C. G. Conniff, and the Islamic Council of Cairo for their advice and guidance; to Esin Atil, Francis Maddison, Filez Cagman, Michael Bates, Neil MacKenzie, Richard Wormser, F. E. Peters, and Nawal Hassan and the staff of the Center for Egyptian Civilization Studies for their help with the selection and identification of illustrations; to Walter Ferro, the designer, Janet Dewar, who combined the roles of Assistant Editor and Picture Editor, Claire Cook, who copyedited the original manuscript, Deborah Urso, who assisted in the production of the first edition, and James Amanna, who helped make the second a reality.

Special acknowledgement is also owed to the many museums and libraries around the world who granted permission to reproduce objects and manuscripts from their collections. Details are provided in the Credits and References section at the back of the book.

And, most importantly, it is acknowledged that The Genius of Arab Civilization was made possible by a grant from Mobil Oil Corporation.

J. R. H.

Foreword

Bayly Winder

A second edition of *The Genius of Arab Civilization* is clearly in order. In the seven years since the first edition appeared, it has been reprinted, published in the United Kingdom as well as in the United States, and in addition has been translated into Arabic in a version of some 15,000 copies which have all disappeared. This new edition enlarges the scope of the original work by giving coverage to the performing arts. The new section on Arabic music, highlighted by Dr. Ali Jihad Racy's essay, thus goes far toward broadening the picture of Arab culture. There are other refinements. Most authors have made minor corrections, others have revised their sections more extensively on the basis of new research.

This new edition, then, is better able to achieve the objective of the old – that is, to create an opulent book which would introduce the general reader to the cultural achievements and heritage of the Arabs while satisfying the specialist as to its accuracy and quality. The text has been written by a group of outstanding authorities on the various subject areas. They represent, incidentally, a diversity of individual backgrounds that is worthy of the ethnic diversity seen during the high points of Arab-Muslim cultural achievement. It is noteworthy that seven of the eleven main chapters are by scholars of Arab background. Each author has, of course, reduced to a few thousand words a body of material that could, and has, filled volumes. The novice will appreciate the fact that the material has been simplified but not popularized; the initiate may be interested in seeing how each of the specialists approached his task. Throughout the text, the authors have called attention to the contributions made by the Arabs and Islam to the civilization of East and West. Particular emphasis has been placed on the role of classical Arabic civilization as a link between the Hellenic and Hellenistic past and the Renaissance future. The obvious debts in such areas as philosophy, medicine, and mathematics are easily acknowledged, and less obvious interrelations in such fields as literature, technology, and trade and commerce are explored. It is, perhaps, an unexpected bonus to see how interestingly such themes can be developed in a survey study, the author of each chapter fitting the data of his field into the general observations made by the writers of the introductory and concluding essays.

In order to infuse more life and color into a subject that might seem distant or unreal to readers who have little or no firsthand knowledge of the Arab world, the editor hit on the innovative idea of including twenty-six illustrated "monographs" on important people, places, and things. In selecting the subjects for the monographs, the objective was to convey some idea of the enormous wealth of material that awaits anyone who chooses to pursue Arab studies in greater depth. Each monograph might have been a book, and in fact books have been or are being written on the subjects of most of them. If this selection leads some readers to wonder if better choices might have been made or provokes other readers to look more deeply into the life of an al-Jahiz or the mystery of an Alhambra, the monographs will have more than served their purpose. In the expectation that curiosities will be further aroused, the new edition concludes with an expanded discursive bibliography. Although a considerable amount of history is woven into the text, the serious novice would do well to look into one or more histories of the period.

One of the most attractive features of *The Genius of Arab Civilization* is the display of magnificent illustrations including three maps. All of the scenic photography, many of the illustrations of art objects, and many of the objects themselves appeared in *The Genius of Arab Civilization* in color for the first time. The appeal of these beautiful reproductions, collectively and individually, to all readers of whatever degree of knowledge will surely be immediate.

One of the hallmarks of civilized man is knowledge of the past – the past of an individual's own family, tribe, nation, or culture; the past of others with whom one's own culture has had repeated and fruitful contact; or the past of any group that has contributed to the ascent of man. The Arabs fit profoundly into both of the latter two categories. But in the West the Arabs are not well known. Victims of ignorance as well as misinformation, they and their culture have often been stigmatized from afar. By providing us with knowledge of the Arab past, *The Genius of Arab Civilization* makes us all more civilized and more understanding. It is an eloquent statement about a people who have made great contributions to mankind in the past and who fully share now in an intellectual partnership with other peoples of the West and the East that should, *in sha' Allah* (*deo volente*), benefit all of us in the future.

Introduction

John Stothoff Badeau began his career in the Middle East in 1928 and subsequently served there as Professor of Philosophy, Dean of the Faculty of Arts and Sciences, and President of the American University at Cairo and as United States Ambassador to the United Arab Republic (1961–1964). In the United States, he has been a member of the faculties of Columbia University (New York) and Georgetown University (Washington, D.C.), and he is now Professor Emeritus of Columbia University. He is author of *East and West of Suez*, *The Emergence of Modern Egypt*, *The Lands Between*, and *The American Approach to the Arab World*.

The Arab Role in Islamic Culture

John S. Badeau

The Arab world is both a new and an old world.

The modern Arab world is new in time, having emerged only fifty years ago from the ruins of the defeated Ottoman Empire. It is new in political identity and composition, being composed primarily of nation-states that did not exist before the First World War. It is new in its freedom to guide its own destiny without the restraints of colonialism. It is new in its social, economic, and cultural aims and institutions and in its rapid absorption of the ways of the scientific and technological world civilization.

In this exciting atmosphere of newness, with all its potential for future achievement, the Arab past may seem remote and irrelevant. Its achievements were made centuries ago in a world very different from the one we know today. "What has sped is dead!" (*Ma fat mat!*) an oft-quoted Arab proverb tells us. But this is not so. Man can no more deny his past than he can deny his heredity. The past lives on, not merely as history, but much more in the character and identity of a people, even if they are unconscious of it. The Arab past indeed "cries out," and in its cry are lessons to be learned and resources to be used in the modern age. In a very real sense, the past is a source of renaissance.

CONQUEST AND CULTURE

The Arab conquest of the ancient world in the seventh and eighth centuries produced two momentous and enduring effects. The more immediate and dramatic was the creation of a new world state in the Mediterranean Basin and the Near East. The second effect, less rapid and tumultuous but no less important, was the development of a new world culture within this state. The impact of both the conquest and the culture has deeply influenced the shape of modern times.

The Arab world state was launched as an imperial system with a rapidity seldom matched in history. Within a century of their appearance on the world scene, the Arabs held sway from the Pyrenees on the border of France to the Pamirs in Central Asia. Spain, North Africa, Egypt,

5

the Byzantine territory south of the Taurus Mountains, and the Persian empire in the east were welded together into an imperial realm that rivaled that of Rome at its peak.

The new realm did not remain either imperial or Arab permanently, however. Stretching across 3,000 miles from east to west and embracing a great diversity of regions and peoples, it proved impossible to rule from a single seat of power by a single dynasty. For a little over a century the Arab conquerors were able to hold their subject lands together. After that, territories began to break away and non-Arab Muslims began to assert their right to a share in the rule of state and society. In the west, Spain, North Africa and, to a lesser extent, Egypt struggled against imperial control and finally went their own ways. In the east, Persia grew in power until it came to be master of the eastern lands. By the time the Mongols of the thirteenth century overran the Muslim world, the original Arab empire had long since ceased to exist. In its place stood a bewildering array of petty states, regional powers, and contending dynasties, few of them ruled by Arabs.

In effect, the Arab empire of the first conquests was transformed into the Muslim world of the Middle Ages. It was a *world* and not an empire—a political realm containing separate and often warring states, yet conscious of a common identity that distinguished it from other regions. It was *Muslim*, not solely Arab, built upon the community of faith rather than the exclusivism of racial and tribal bonds. As the Arab monopoly of power declined, Persians, Berbers, Seljuks, and other client peoples became the rulers and leaders of their own segments of a multiracial Muslim world.

It was within this Muslim setting that a new world culture, the second momentous result of the Arab conquest, was created. "Created" is the precise and proper term. For what happened was not the imposition of a foreign culture by invasion, not the same process that carried Western civilization to the East during the period of European colonialism. The Arab conquerors came with impressive military strength, but the culture of their desert home was simple and unsophisticated. Nothing in their culture, not even their language at the beginning, compared or competed with the classical and Hellenistic heritage of the lands they overran. The distinctive and richly hued civilization that characterized the Muslim world at its height was formed "in situ." It came into being within the new state, giving identity and character to the new order that resulted from the conquests of Islam as it spread among alien peoples. Its major components were at hand within the varied life and traditions of the subjugated people —classical literature, Hellenistic thought, Byzantine institutions, Roman law, Syriac scholarship, Persian art.

At first these resources were appropriated directly, with little reshaping. Before long, however, they were more selectively utilized, combined into novel patterns that served as both resource and stimulus to creative Muslim scholarship. The result was not simply a montage of bits and pieces of disparate culture. It was a new creation with its own distinctive pattern, infused with a new spirit and expressing a new social order.

This development of a distinctly Islamic culture reached full stride about the time that the Arab leadership of the empire began to wane. At first the conquerors were chiefly absorbed in the tasks of consolidating their rule and buttressing their position. The establishment of the

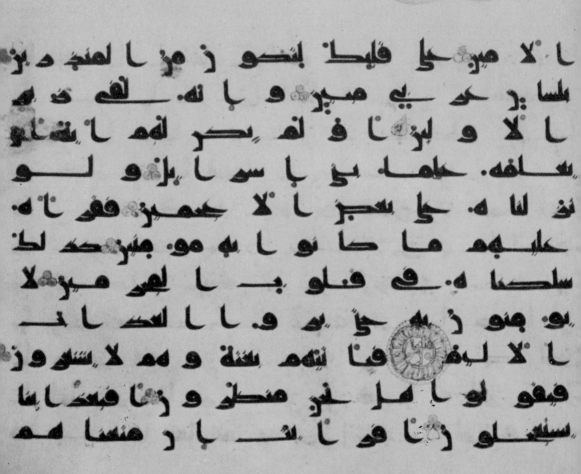

Early Qur'ans were written in angular Kufic script with illuminated roundels separating the verses.

new state, the maintenance of public order, the strengthening of military organization, and the collection of taxes were their major concerns. The daily business of government and administration was left to the existing bureaucracies. The Arab elite tended to live apart from their subjects, at first in military encampments and then in garrison cities.

This was obviously not a situation that stimulated much cultural absorption or creativity. Only when the conquest had settled into an accepted and permanent order and its exclusive monopoly of power had given way to a broader rule did the new culture develop rapidly. With the rise of the Abbasid dynasty in 750, convert Muslims and client peoples who were living on the fringes of the new society moved to its center, bringing with them their own heritage of culture and civilization.

In this setting the outstanding achievements of Muslim culture appeared. Arab literature reached its peak; the great codes of Canon Law were formulated; philosophy, science, and medicine were taken over from the ancients and given new dimensions and content. Muslim civilization—rich, sophisticated, varied—became the mark of the societies of the Islamic world and took its place among the great cultural achievements of human history.

THE ARABS AND ISLAMIC CULTURE

In the colorful tapestry of Muslim culture there are many threads of Arab weaving. In every field—literature, theology, philosophy, science, geography, architecture—there are notable Arab names and notable Arab achievements. But the Arab contribution goes far beyond the roles played by individual scholars and the significance of specific achievements. The exigencies of history are as nebulous as those of personal life; yet from the record it seems clear that the fact of an *Arab* conquest was definitive in determining the cultural development that followed. We have only to recall that the Mongol invasions, so similar on their surface to the Arab conquest, produced very different results. An ephemeral Mongol empire was created, but no new or significant civilization arose from it. When the Mongol hordes finally receded to their homes in the Gobi Desert, they left behind them little but ruin and destruction. It was not so with the Arabs. To their conquest of territory they brought constructive forces of their own, forces that set the stage for, and shaped the framework of, the civilization that finally emerged.

THE FACT OF EMPIRE

The first of these forces was the fact of empire itself. It might have been expected that the Arab invaders would be only desert raiders in the traditional pattern of the tribal foray, content to plunder and then to vanish. But this was not so. The Arabs explained their conquests by saying they were made "in the path of God," *fi sabil Allah*. By this they meant that a new social order was to be established among men and that their conquest was to be the tool of its creation. The empire that resulted from the invasion was thus conceived as both a permanent and a self-perpetuating realm, not merely a collection of subjugated territories to be held together only so long as they could enrich their conquerors.

8

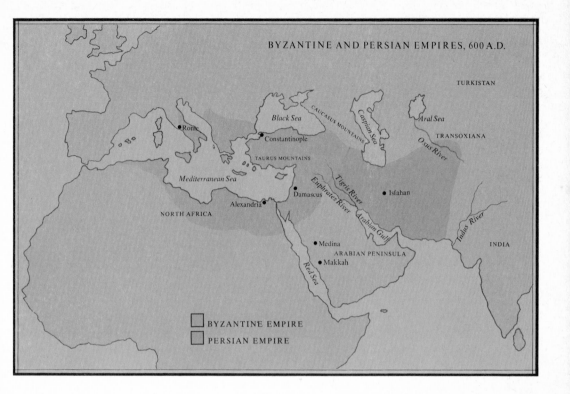

BYZANTINE AND PERSIAN EMPIRES, 600 A.D.

BYZANTINE EMPIRE

PERSIAN EMPIRE

The fact and vision of empire created both the need and the setting for a new social and cultural order to express the identity of the new realm. Those who had been Spaniards, Greeks, Egyptians, Syrians, and Persians, each with a separate history and tradition, were now subjects under one rule with a new, if as yet undefined, character. Inevitably, the creation of a new world state paved the way for the emergence of an imperial culture.

Within this new empire the diverse cultures and societies of the ancient world were shaken out of their regionalism and forced into new and fruitful interaction. The Arab conquerors themselves quickly responded to contact with the civilizations they overran. Once the initial absorption in conquest was relaxed, they "sat as pupils at the feet of the people they subdued— and what acquisitive pupils they proved to be," as Phillip K. Hitti has observed. Before the end of the first Arab dynasty, that of the Umayyads, classical works were being translated into Arabic, impressive buildings inspired by classical designs were being built, and Arab scholarship in grammar and literature, influenced by Greek patterns, began to flourish. By the time the Arabs lost their preeminence in rule, non-Arab materials had been established in the life and thought of the Islamic community.

At the same time, the diverse subject peoples shared in and absorbed one another's cultures. Barriers to travel through the Mediterranean and eastern lands were broken down, and subjects flocked from the provinces to the heart of empire, where they met and mingled in a

9

new relationship. Moreover, their contact with Arabs produced many Muslim converts and many intermarriages. Inevitably the emerging Islamic order became both multicultural and intercultural, drawing on a prolific and varied stock of traditions to create a new civilization.

THE FAITH OF ISLAM

That this interaction resulted in an impressive civilization with a unique character was due in large part to the second force let loose by the Arabs in their conquest—the faith of Islam. The Arab invaders brought Islam with them. Islam was a decisive factor in the process of cultural creation, and Islam was basically and peculiarly an Arab achievement.

The significance of this becomes apparent when we remember how often foreign conquerors have been absorbed into the people they subjugated. Successive invaders of China (the Mongols and the Manchus, for example, ruled "the Heavenly Kingdom," but in the end they became Chinese in language and culture, almost indistinguishable from their subjects.

This might have been so with the Arab invaders. Unfortified by a literate culture deeply rooted in history, confronted with civilizations much more sophisticated and rich than any they had known, they might have been expected to capitulate to the civilizations they overran, even while continuing to rule them. The result would have been either an indiscriminate synthesis of subject cultures, lacking distinctive character, or the fragmentation of the new realm into separate cultural components that shared nothing in common but imperial rule.

That the Arab conquest was Islamic as well as military prevented this kind of cultural formlessness. Once a territory had been subjugated, it became part of the "Abode of Islam" (*dar al-Islam*), a society under Muslim rule in which Muslims could practice their faith without hindrance. At the outset this did not mean that all the subject people, or even a majority, became Muslims. It did mean, however, that the Islamic way was to be the accepted institution of state and society.

Islam envisioned itself as an all-embracing framework of human life. No activity of the individual or community was alien to it. Its vision of God and man and society was definitive and rested upon divine authority—the "given" of human experience—which stood at the center and passed judgment on all that men might do. It is significant that, as Islam elaborated, it was Canon Law (*Shari'ah*) rather than theology that was most rigorously protected and applied. Men had to live within a Muslim society to be fully Muslim, not simply to profess Islamic beliefs in any society in which they might find themselves.

What shape and content Muslim society should have in the foreign world of the Arab conquests had to be worked out. In the new lands, the Arabs encountered conditions, problems, and materials that were unknown to the tribal life and that were often in apparent opposition to the unbending Islamic principles and obligations. In the interaction between these elements, it was the Islamic claim that had priority. Although Muslims might, and did, freely appropriate Greek, Byzantine, Hellenistic, Syriac, and Persian materials to construct their new civilization, the appropriation was under Islamic auspices and was meant to serve Islamic purposes. On the surface Muslim culture might appear to be highly eclectic; yet in fact and in substance

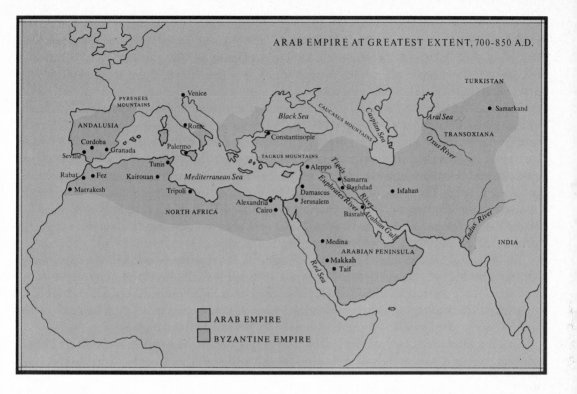

ARAB EMPIRE AT GREATEST EXTENT, 700-850 A.D.

TURKISTAN

PYRENEES
MOUNTAINS

Venice

ANDALUSIA

Rome

Black Sea

CAUCASUS MOUNTAINS

Caspian Sea

Aral Sea

Samarkand

TRANSOXIANA

Cordoba

Palermo

Constantinople

Oxus River

Seville

Granada

Tunis

TAURUS MOUNTAINS

Aleppo

Rabat

Fez

Kairouan

Mediterranean Sea

Tigris River

Samarra

Baghdad

Isfahan

Marrakesh

Tripoli

Euphrates River

Damascus

Indus River

Alexandria

Jerusalem

Arabian Gulf

Cairo

Basrah

INDIA

NORTH AFRICA

Medina

ARABIAN PENINSULA

Red Sea

Makkah

Taif

☐ ARAB EMPIRE

☐ BYZANTINE EMPIRE

it was selective and discriminating, including and excluding materials in terms of their compatibility with the nature and ends of an Islamic society.

Islam itself was influenced by this process. As a full-blown medieval intellectual system, it incorporated many elements of Neoplatonic philosophy, Aristotelian logic, and Roman law—to name some major influences. Yet this did not alter the fact that in substance, in character, and in origin Islam was *Arab*. The initial vision of Islam was seen and given to the world by an Arab prophet. Its central emphasis on community was rooted in immemorial Arab tribal life. Its fundamental concepts were expressed in the vocabulary of Arab experience. Whatever non-Arab materials might be used in the elaboration of Islam as a system, the character of Islam as an Arab view of life and faith was never lost, and never could be. Arab rule could fade and Arab preeminence in the medieval Muslim world could recede, but the Arab impact on Islam could not be obliterated. By their faith the Arabs made an enduring and irradicable contribution to both Islamic and world culture.

THE LANGUAGE

Closely related to the influence of an inclusive empire and an exclusive faith was a further contribution of Arabs to the rise of a new culture—their language. How inextricably Arabic

11

permeated the development of Muslim culture is shown by the fact that the system that finally evolved is still referred to as "Arab civilization" and "Arabic thought," despite the fact that many of its great cultural achievements did not take place under Arab auspices. Non-Arabs and even non-Muslims made important contributions, but they made them in the Arabic language, whatever their ethnic community.

That the language of the Arab invaders assumed this role may appear strange. The Mediterranean world was rich and old in its own classical tradition of language and literature. Greek, the most universal of the ancient tongues, still was used in Byzantine lands, and its classical literature was cherished. In comparison, the language of the conquering tribesmen of the desert seemed both alien and primitive. The Arabs had a tradition of oral poetry, but only one book—the Qur'an. Their grammar was yet to be explored, and the canons of their literature remained to be developed. The vocabulary of Arabic reflected the simple and limited experience of desert people and had yet to prove capable of expressing foreign ideas, abstract concepts, and the literary interests of a sophisticated society.

Yet Arabic overcame these handicaps and quickly became the dominant language of culture and scholarship in the rising Muslim world. It was able to do this partly because it was the language of both conquest and faith. Those who had business to do with Arabs or who sought to ingratiate themselves with their new rulers could not escape the use of Arabic. And no one could become a Muslim without some understanding of the Arabic language.

This fact of Islam as a vehicle for Arabic was preponderant. The Qur'an, source of all belief and piety, was in Arabic and could not be translated into any other tongue. Ritual prayers and public worship were in Arabic. Exegesis of the Qur'an called forth some of the first Arab scholarship, and the fact that God had chosen Arabic as the language of revelation made the study of its grammar and usage a religious necessity.

Yet it was more than conquest and religion that raised Arabic to its preeminent place in Muslim culture. Despite its original character as a desert tongue, Arabic displayed a remarkable potential as a medium of sophisticated and complex communication. It had the strongly marked structure of Semitic languages, in which the parts of speech are closely and clearly related. It could create new words out of existing verbal forms, and its ability to compress shades of meaning into a single dramatic expression made it a vivid and exact language. Elaborated by its grammarians and stimulated by the challenge of new horizons, it became a superb tool for thought and scholarship. Had it lacked an inherent quality of greatness, even the pressure of conquest and the benediction of religion would not have given Arabic its commanding position in the far-flung, multilingual Muslim world.

The effects on culture of the dominance of Arabic were profound and enduring. Arabic provided the inclusive medium of communication that translated the political intermixture of diverse peoples into a commonly shared culture. As Latin did in medieval Europe and as English did in British India, Arabic in the new state overarched local languages and literature to create a new and universal intellectual realm where Persian philosophers, Arab theologians, Jewish and Christian physicians, and Indian mathematicians could not only speak a common language but also have a sense of sharing in a common intellectual order.

12

Moreover, the use of Arabic and the adoption of its alphabet by non-Arab Muslim languages formed a kind of cultural frontier that demarked the Muslim world from other civilizations. The traveler from Europe or the East knew at once as he passed through the Muslim world that he was in a different culture, one whose language and writing were not related to anything he had known. The same linguistic frontier turned the Muslim people themselves away from their own past cultures and gave them a sense of identity and an awareness of their difference from other people.

Arabic had a further effect on the growth of Islamic culture, although it is an elusive one and difficult to define. Today we are only beginning to understand and measure something of the relatedness of "medium and message," but we now know that the very form of a language shapes and gives character to the ideas expressed in it and to the minds that use it. The highly distinctive qualities of Arabic, the richness and content of its vocabulary, its particular mode of expressing an idea, and its propensity for meter and rhyme—all placed an imprint on scholarly productions and scholarly minds and hence on the "flavor" of the Islamic intellectual world. Thus the unique character of medieval Muslim culture is partly due to the fact that it did its work in Arabic. Like the contribution of Islam, the penetrating influence of language ensured the Arabness of the medieval world far beyond the period of Arab political rule.

The Dome of the Rock in Jerusalem is the earliest example of Islamic architecture.

Literature

Mounah A. Khouri is Professor of Arabic Language and Literature at the Department of Near Eastern Studies of the University of California, Berkeley, where he formerly served as Chairman of this Department and as the U.S.A. Director of the Center for Arabic Study Abroad which operates in Cairo under the sponsorship of an 18-American University Consortium. Before his appointment at Berkeley Dr. Khouri taught at the American University of Beirut and Georgetown University. He is co-author of *Elementary Standard Arabic*, *Advanced Readings in Modern Arabic: The Novel and the Short Story* and *An Anthology of Modern Arabic Poetry, 1945-1970*. He is also the author of several works in the fields of Arabic studies in general and modern Arabic literature in particular. In Arabic these include a study of *Toynbee's Theory of History* and *The Literary Criticism of T.S. Eliot, Archibald MacLeish and I.A. Richards*. In English he has written *Poetry and the Making of Modern Egypt, 1882-1922*, and is currently preparing a "Critical Study of the Major Contemporary Arab Poets" which is intended to appear in both Arabic and English.

Literature

Mounah A. Khouri

Most general readers in the West, if they know Arabic literature at all, know only *The Thousand and One Nights*, and usually by an incorrect title, *The Arabian Nights*. Moreover, even the few who have industriously gleaned the available translations and the scholarly works of distinguished orientalists remain ignorant of many Arabic masterpieces. The reason for this is that most Western authorities have tended to identify Arabic literature with the general history of Arabic thought and culture and have therefore concentrated on those works, such as scientific and philosophical treatises, that have been deemed historically and culturally "important." As a result, the creative achievements of the Arabs in "belles lettres," their artistic prose and poetical productions, have remained for the most part insufficiently known and appreciated in the West. In an attempt to correct this deficiency, we shall focus attention here on Arabic literature in its restricted sense as the verbal art of the Arabs, with emphasis on its unique features and universal contributions.

Our starting point is the language itself. Arabic, first and foremost, gives the literature its unique quality. Although the leading literary figures within the Islamic empire represented a diversity of ethnic and cultural backgrounds, the non-Arabs among them had lost their national tongues and had adopted the language of the Qur'an as their universal medium of expression. Their literary art was shaped by the special genius of Arabic.

As an artistic medium, the Arabic language is most notable for its regularity. Like other languages from the ancient Semitic family, of which it is both the youngest and the most widespread offspring, Arabic is built on a system of triconsonantal roots. For example, from the root *KTB*, which conveys the idea of "writing," are formed such words as *kataba*, "to write"; *kitab*, "book"; *kutubi*, "bookseller"; *kuttab*, "Qur'an school"; *kitabah*, "script"; *maktab*, "office"; *maktabah*, "bookstore"; and *mukatabah*, "correspondence." In each case here, other sounds, chiefly vowels, have been added to *KTB*, the triconsonantal root, according to a pre-established pattern, to create variations on the fundamental idea that the root conveys. What gives Arabic its regularity is the fact that the same, or nearly the same, pattern of variations is applied to large groups of triconsonantal roots. The process of applying the pattern to create new words from existing triconsonantal roots, known as "analogical derivation," has historically been the most important method for the development of the language. What this means is that there are uniform families of words in Arabic, following the same patterns and differing in sound

17

The formal perfection of the Arabic language is made visual in the art of Arab calligraphy.

and structure only in the three consonants that are the heart of a word's meaning.

Because of this high degree of regularity in the shape of Arabic words, the language naturally lends itself to the creation of harmonious patterns, and a rich elaboration of rhyme and rhythm is an essential part of Arabic style and Arabic literary tradition. Arabic permits rhetorical effects that could never be achieved in any European language. Partly because of this intrinsic potential, Arabs have customarily considered their language a perfect instrument of concision, clarity, and eloquence. The validity of this view is clearly confirmed by pre-Islamic poetry and is even more evident in the Qur'an, which is viewed by all Muslims as literally the word of God, its divine origin being demonstrated by the beauty and inevitability of its language. This belief in Arabic as a perfect and potentially divine medium is further supported by the classical literary and philological tradition, and it inspired most of the great masterpieces of Arabic literature, which share the common ideal of formal perfection as the distinctive mark of aesthetic authenticity and creative achievement. This great emphasis on *formal perfection*—on concision, clarity, and eloquence as well as on musicality, embodied above

18

all in poetry—is the feature of Arabic literature that places it among the least translatable languages in the world.

The literature of the Arabs has some similarities with the literature of the West, but the origins and the details of composition are unique. The birthplace of Arabic literature is the sandy plain of central and northeastern Arabia. Except in the few oases, this region was unsuitable for settled communities. Its inhabitants were nomads, who moved about in search of water and fresh pasturage, living an austere, monotonous life enlivened only by the frequent tribal raids and the occasional pleasures of security and peace. The physical setting shaped the modes of thought and expression; it also restricted the scope of ideas and religious speculations. The desert Arabs' view of life in pre-Islamic times was summed up in a few maxims, and their religion was polytheistic.

The Arabian poet was the chief spokesman of his tribe. He did not compose poetry for poetry's sake; rather he was the propagandist, journalist, preacher, entertainer, and political representative of his people. As the image maker of his community, its moralist, and often the embodiment of its ideals, he enjoyed a status comparable in cultural importance with that of Homer among the ancient Greeks or with that of the *Beowulf* poet among the Anglo-Saxons. Just as the Arabian warrior defended his people with his sword, the Arabian bard defended the rights and honor of his tribe with verses immortalizing their glorious deeds and defaming their enemies. He performed both locally and at the famous poetic tournaments that were held periodically in conjunction with the popular intertribal fairs and pilgrimages.

Although the function of the pre-Islamic Arabic poet may be compared with that of Homer or the *Beowulf* poet, the form and content of his poetry are unlike anything in Western literature. Its origins are obscure, but the earliest forms may have been fountain songs, war chants, and hymns to idols. It is generally agreed, however, that around 500 A.D. there emerged in northern Arabia a large number of accomplished poets reciting to appreciative audiences either short pieces (*qit'ahs*) or long odes (*qasidahs*), with the longer form perhaps growing out of the shorter. The long poem, which runs to some seventy or eighty pairs of half lines (each half line being equivalent in length to a line of European poetry), recounts incidents from the poet's own life and that of the tribe, sometimes dramatically and sometimes with an epic flavor. But the whole poem is never a continuous narrative, and the mode may loosely be called lyric—although it contains eulogy and satire (or invective) as well as elegy, with descriptions of love affairs and beautiful women as well as of battles, storms, camels, horses, and desert scenes.

Because literacy was extremely rare during this period and writing materials very scarce and expensive, pre-Islamic poetry was for the most part composed, transmitted, and preserved orally for at least two hundred years before it was written down toward the end of the seventh century. During the following century Arab scholars collected and collated the odes and shorter compositions that had survived in the memories of professional reciters, who were called *rawis*. The efforts of these scholars produced the primary sources of ancient Arabic poetry, including collections of individual poets, tribal collections, and various anthologies.

Knowledge of this background is essential to an understanding and appreciation of Arabic literature. Not only are the best pre-Islamic poems the preeminent classics of Arabic literature, but also almost the entire body of Arabic poetry since the early period has been composed in conformity with the rhythmical patterns used in the pre-Islamic ode form. At the root of these prosodic patterns, or meters, are three strokes, or beats (*dá, dadá, dadadá*), that were traditionally juggled and transposed to form eight basic rhythmic units, or feet. By repeating a definite number of identical feet (*AAA* or *BBB* or *CCC*, for example) or by alternating different ones (*ABAB*), lines of verse equally divided into hemistichs (half lines) are formed within a given meter. There are sixteen metrical schemes, and the rhythmic patterns they produce are further reinforced by the monorhyme that occurs as the last syllable of each pair of half lines throughout the poem. Neither the rhythms nor the monorhyme can be successfully imitated in Western languages; and since most of the ancient poems were sung, exerting their magic power on the sensibility of their audience mainly through their heightened musicality, it becomes clear why Arabic poetry, which derives most of its evocative effect from its formal and rhythmic qualities, cannot be translated without losing its essential quality. For this reason the few available translations of classical Arabic poetry usually impress Western readers as bare and monotonous. It is as if they were obliged to examine a black-and-white reproduction of a colorful masterpiece or the crude underside of a luxurious Persian rug. Fortunately, this situation has improved somewhat in regard to modern Arabic poetry, which places greater emphasis on content than on form and can therefore be translated more successfully.

Despite the relative youth of the Arabic language as part of the Semitic family, it has a surprisingly vast and rich literature. The language has changed comparatively little since the Arabic of the Qur'an was adopted as the fixed standard; its literature has, therefore, accumulated over a period of fourteen hundred years. Arabic literary history is generally divided into six periods: the Jahiliyyah, or pre-Islamic (500–622); the early Islamic and Umayyad (622–750); the Abbasid (750–1258); the Hispano-Arabic in Muslim Spain (750–1492); the post-Abbasid (1258–1800); and the modern renaissance (1800 to the present).

THE PRE-ISLAMIC PERIOD

Outstanding among the pre-Islamic poets are the authors of the famous Golden Odes, known as the *Mu'allaqat*. These poets include the wandering king, Imru' al-Qays; the playboy, Tarafah; the moralist, Zuhayr; the black knight and Arab hero, 'Antarah; the centenarian, Labid; the regicide, 'Amr bin Kulthum; and the leper, al-Harith bin Hillizah. To these varied figures must be added the names of the professional panegyrist, an-Nabighah; the satirist, al-Hutay-'ah; the vagabond poet, ash-Shanfara; and the poetess, al-Khansa'.

Omar Pound has described the pre-Islamic poem "as a string of beads on which images are accumulated and juxtaposed one after the other without any seeming connection beyond that of a strict quantitative meter. The links are psychological and poetic: experiences held in common by poet and listener." Moreover, the themes of pre-Islamic poetry are limited and conventional, resembling medieval European religious art in that their merit lies primarily in the poet's ability to give a fresh treatment to fixed and stereotyped subject matter. The important thing is not *what* is said, which the audience already knew, but *how* it is said. Thus, although the poets differed widely as personalities, the *qasidah* tends to follow a standard outline, with three main thematic divisions.

First among these is a love prelude, in which the poet describes his visit to the deserted encampment of his beloved and his vain search for her and then laments her departure. This elegiac-erotic prelude may be the expression of the poet's true experience or simply a conventional opening intended to coax the listeners into the ceremony of the poem, perhaps based on the belief that "the song of love," as the ancient critic Ibn Qutaybah put it, "touches men's souls and takes hold of their hearts." Because of this poetic convention, the *ghazal* (love poetry) preludes never became a fully independent genre, but a number of the leading Arabian poets included fine pieces of love poetry in their compositions. The *Mu'allaqah* of Imru' al-Qays, for example, is notable for its lively descriptions of amorous adventures:

> Oh yes, many a fine day I've dallied with the white ladies,
> and especially I call to mind a day at Dara Juljul...
> Yes, and the day I entered the litter where Unaiza was
> and she cried, "Out on you! Will you make me walk on my feet?"
> She was saying, while the canopy swayed with the pair of us,
> "There now, you've hocked my camel, Imr al-Kais. Down with you!"
> But I said, "Ride on, and slacken the beast's reins,
> and oh, don't drive me away from your refreshing fruit.
> Many's the pregnant woman like you, aye and the nursing mother
> I've night-visited, and made her forget her amuleted one-year-old;
> whenever he whimpered behind her, she turned to him
> with half her body, her other half unshifted under me."
> (Translated by Arberry)

Recollecting in tranquillity the memory of a more idealized love, 'Abid bin al-Abras laments:

> ... my eyes seep sorrow,
> waterskins with holes
> (Translated by Omar Pound)

Second among the pre-Islamic *qasidah's* divisions is the journey theme, which includes praise of the poet's horse or camel for sharing the burden of his search and enduring the hardship of his exhausting journey. Thus Imru' al-Qays brings his steed to life in a famous passage:

> my horse short-haired, outstripping the wild game, huge-bodied,
> charging, fleet-fleeing, head-foremost, headlong, all together
> the match of a rugged boulder hurled from on high by the torrent....
> (Translated by Arberry)

The journey section may also include beautiful and vividly realistic descriptions of sandstorms, thunderstorms, and desert flora and fauna. Here, especially, the poem reveals its characteristic verbal concision, embodying a sharp picture in a few precise, concrete words. The Jahiliyyah poet's language is always remarkable for its concretization of the abstract. Because these concise images are complete in themselves, Arab critics have traditionally pointed to the perfection of individual lines to demonstrate a poet's skill, rather than to unity of structure.

The third section is the main theme of the poem, which the poet might devote either to extolling his own virtues or to glorifying his tribe and deprecating its enemies. The qualities that most inspired praise were honor, loyalty, generosity, courage, justice, hospitality, and tribal solidarity. Wherever his people might go, the desert Arab was pledged to follow. One poet expressed the prevailing attitude when he said:

> I am of Ghaziyya: if she be in error then I will err;
> And if Ghaziyya be guided right, I go right with her!
> (Translated by Nicholson)

Other collective values of the period included endurance in misfortune, persistence in revenge, protection of the weak, and defiance of the strong. The tribal code of conduct shaped the personal qualities praised by the pre-Islamic poet, and his poetry in turn reinforced the code.

A number of Arabian poets broke free of the bonds of tribal norms, however, and led the life of rebels, brigands, and outlaws. Chief among these was ash-Shanfara, who described his own heroic character and his feelings as follows:

> And somewhere the noble find a refuge afar from scathe,
> The outlaw a lonely spot where no kin with hatred burn.
> Oh never a prudent man, night-faring in hope or fear,
> Hard pressed on the face of earth, but still he has room to turn.
> (Translated by Nicholson)

Torn between the compelling need to conform to the strict tribal code, on the one hand, and the strong desire to pursue his own pleasures, on the other, Tarafah, the Arabian poet who died in the prime of life, described his wild and profligate style of life:

> Unceasingly I tippled the wine and took my joy,
> unceasingly I sold and squandered my hoard and my patrimony
> till all my family deserted me, every one of them,
> and I sat alone like a lonely camel scabby with mange....
> (Translated by Arberry)

Rationalizing his chosen mode of existence on the basis of the brevity of life and the inevitability of death, Tarafah sought to transcend the absurdity of the human condition through the pursuit of his own happiness. This he found in three pleasures—wine, love, and self-sacrifice on the battlefield:

> But for three things, that are the joy of a young fellow,
> I assure you I wouldn't care when my deathbed visitors arrive—
> First, to forestall my charming critics with a good swig
> of crimson wine that foams when the water is mingled in;

second, to wheel at the call of the beleaguered a curved-shanked steed
streaking like the wolf of the thicket you've startled lapping the water;
and third, to curtail the day of showers, such an admirable season,
dallying with a ripe wench under the pole-propped tent,
her anklets and her bracelets seemingly hung on the boughs
of a pliant, unriven gurn-tree or a castor-shrub.
So permit me to drench my head while there's still life in it,
for I tremble at the thought of the scant draught I'll get when I'm dead.
I'm a generous fellow, one that soaks himself in his lifetime;
you'll know to-morrow, when we're dead, which of us is the thirsty one.

(Translated by Arberry)

Even the warrior-poet 'Antarah, who later became an Arab folk hero, had something of the outcast about him—though he was an outcast who won glory for himself. The son of an Arab father from the tribe of 'Abs and a black slave mother, he was rejected in his youth by his father and later on by his uncle, whose daughter he loved passionately but was forbidden to marry. 'Antarah had the opportunity to display his prowess in an internecine war, also described by Zuhayr, between the tribes of 'Abs and Dhubyan. Through his exploits on the field of battle, the valiant black knight was able to achieve the status of a pure-blooded Arab and became the legendary hero of the celebrated popular epic entitled *Sirat 'Antar*.

Vaunting his prowess on the battlefield, 'Antarah sings in his ode:

Those who were present at the engagement will acquaint you
how I plunge into battle, but abstain at the booty-sharing.
Many's the bristling knight the warriors have shunned to take on,
those not in a hurry to flee or capitulate,
to them my hands have been right generous with the hasty thrust
of a well-tempered, strong-jointed, straightened spear
giving him a broad, double-sided gash, the hiss of which
guides in the night-season the prowling, famished wolves;
I split through his shielding armor with my solid lance
(for even the noblest is not sacrosanct to the spear)
and left him carrion for the wild beasts to pounce on,
all of him, from the crown of his head to his limp wrists.

(Based on a translation by Arberry)

The Arabian bard immortalized
the heroes of his tribe.

23

THE EARLY ISLAMIC AND UMAYYAD PERIOD

For all its technical virtuosity and artistic power, pre-Islamic Arabic poetry is marked by a simplicity and a purity of feeling that were shaped by the harsh environment, which fostered both fierce loyalty and rugged individualism. The literature that followed was the product of a more complex and more civilized era. Within a hundred years of the advent of Islam early in the seventh century, the Arabs had conquered the Sassanid empire, expelled the Byzantines from Syria, Egypt, and North Africa, and occupied most of southern Spain. These conquests and territorial expansion brought about radical transformations in the Arab world. Along with the impact of the Qur'an as a literary monument, the major changes affecting the literature of this period were the emergence of politico-religious parties, which based their conflicts on the issue of succession to the caliphate, and the growth of wealth and luxury in the main cities of the empire. Notwithstanding the development of Islamic oratory and pious poetry, which derived their cadence, imagery, and sonorous vocabulary from the Qur'an, it was mainly political poetry and love lyrics that most eloquently expressed the spirit of the age.

The preeminent position of the Qur'an in the Muslim world led to the creation and development of various Qur'anic disciplines, such as lexicography, biography, theology, philology, and law. Owing to the Prophet's hostile attitude toward the pagan code of ethics and the polytheistic system of belief, the poetic tradition that had reached its peak in the Golden Odes suffered a temporary decline during the early years of Muhammad's mission. But in time leading Arabian poets, such as Hasan bin Thabit and Ka'b bin Zuhayr, converted to Islam and gave their support to the Prophet and his new religion in their famous eulogies. These men were recognized as Muhammad's followers and court poets, and consequently poetry regained its former prestige and reassumed its vital role in reflecting and directing the various currents of the time.

Although several poets who flourished during this period advocated the ideologies of the Umayyad, Shiite Zubayrid, and Kharijite parties, the most prominent representatives of the major political trends were the three professional Iraqi poets—al-Akhtal, Jarir, and al-Farazdaq. Less concerned with verbal virtuosity than with the total evocative effect of their poetry, they dedicated their panegyrics to different masters and patrons, shifting their affiliations and loyalties in the direction of the highest reward.

Al-Akhtal, a Christian Arab from the tribe of Taghlib, was a fervent supporter of the Umayyads and especially of the Caliph 'Abd al-Malik bin Marwan, to whom he dedicated one of the most celebrated poems of this period. Al-Farazdaq, of the Tamim tribe, was characterized by his critics as thoroughly unprincipled. However, one of the best eulogies of the Shiite 'Ali bin al-Husayn is attributed to him. Jarir, who belonged to a branch of al-Farazdaq's tribe, the Bani Kulayb, was the court poet of al-Hajjaj, the dreaded Umayyad governor of Iraq. He also became the official poet of the Caliph 'Abd al-Malik, allegedly winning this position by addressing these lines to him:

> Are you not the best of those who on the noblest of mounts ride
> More open-handed than all in the world beside?
>
> (Translated by Nicholson)

Equally important for the study of the political history of this period are the biting attacks that al-Akhtal, Jarir, and al-Farazdaq launched against the enemies of their tribes or of their masters and against one another in the famous exchanges of poetical invectives called *naqa'id*. Also noteworthy are the politico-religious poems of such Kharijite writers as at-Tirimmah and 'Imran bin Hattan, who revealed their revolutionary and egalitarian beliefs and called for martyrdom for the sake of their principles.

It was also during the early Islamic and Umayyad period that the Arab way of life began to change from the nomadic mode of existence to a more sophisticated and refined urban style. The cities of Makkah and Medina became important cultural centers that attracted wealth from all over the empire, and with this increased wealth came the inevitable rise of an aristocratic leisured class. This in turn led to indulgence in such sensual pursuits as music and dancing, to which poetry now allied itself. Poetry, accompanied by or set to music, was sung by women in accordance with Greek and Persian practices of the time. Governed by musical considerations, the poetic form was simplified: the complex and highly refined meters of the traditional Arabian poetry were replaced by shorter, freer meters that are adaptable to music. Poetry and music became inseparable, as is shown by hundreds of examples from the famous *Kitab al-Aghani*, or *Book of Songs*. The language of the poems was also simplified in order to achieve a more conversational, less erudite idiom suitable for singing. Love poetry thrived in this setting.

Two schools of *ghazal* poetry flourished during this period: the Hijazi school of realistic, sensuous, urbane love poetry led by 'Umar and including, among others, al-Ahwas and al-'Arji; and the idealized, melancholic, pure and sublime 'Udhri school, represented most notably by Jamil, Qays bin Dharih, and the possibly apocryphal Qays bin al-Mulawwah.

Despite the differences between them, both these schools have their origins in the pre-Islamic *ghazal* tradition reflected in the *ghazal* preludes of Imru' al-Qays's *Mu'allaqah*. However, whereas pre-Islamic love poetry was only a transitional part of the *qasidahs*, Umayyad *ghazal* poetry became an independent genre entirely devoted to love and romance.

The Hijazi 'Umar bin Abi Rabi'ah lived for the pursuit of amorous adventures and sang with enchanting grace and naturalness of the noble ladies he had courted and won. His approach to love was sensuous and uninhibited, and he displayed a sensitive eye for physical detail. As the romantic hero of the Hijazi *ghazal*, 'Umar used the dialogue form to recreate vivid exchanges:

> She said: "Do not come to our house; our father is a jealous
> man. Do you not see the gate barred between us?"
> I said: "I shall spring over it."
> She said: "The castle stands between us." I said: "I shall
> climb in from the roof."
> She said: "The lion is up there." I said: "My sword is sharp
> and cutting."
>
> (Translated by M. Jones)

Like Catullus, 'Umar displayed an extraordinary ability to mold refined speech patterns to a metrical scheme with no loss of directness and naturalness. 'Umar's poems are short scenarios that freely and simply convey his delightful love experiences. His poetry is expressive of the social realities of the Hijaz, but it is more playful and personal than anything in the earlier period. The poet is now no longer the official spokesman of the tribe.

If the Hijazi school suggests the lyrics of Herrick, the 'Udhri school recalls those of Petrarch. It appears as though the harshness of the Bedouin environment has taken its toll of the poets in this second school of *ghazal*. The paternalistic policy of sexual repression led Jamil, for example, to escape, not into free love, but into spirituality. His frustrated love of Buthaynah drove him to extremes of passion, and all he could do was suffer, despair, and idealize his beloved in the platonic manner:

> *I loved you before you were born,*
> *And when we die, I shall hear your echoes.*

A Bedouin tradition of self-denial, worship of the loved one, and a hopelessness compounded by the prohibition of love outside the law led the 'Udhri poets to become martyrs to love.

The most extreme form of this genre is found in the poetry of Qays bin al-Mulawwah, whose unrequited love in an entirely unsympathetic environment drove him to madness. "My love-sickness is beyond all cure," he wrote, and "when I pray, I turn my face towards her, though the right direction be opposite." According to the legend, he ended his days pathetically wandering the desert in the vain hope that the sun would burn away the memory of his beloved but unapproachable Layla.

This second *ghazal* tradition, especially as reflected in the idealized love passion of *Qays* and *Layla*, left a deep mark on the classical love lyrics of Persia and ultimately manifested itself in the works of such prominent modern Western writers as the French poet Louis Aragon.

THE ABBASID PERIOD

With the rise of the Abbasids to power in Baghdad in the middle of the eighth century, there began a new era, unique in the history of Islamic civilization—the golden and silver ages of the Abbasid empire. The first of these lasted into the eleventh century, when the Abbasids began to lose full control of their empire. The later Abbasid period, the silver age, lasted until the empire fell into the hands of the Mongols in 1258.

Built in 762 by the Caliph Abu Ja'far 'Abdallah al-Mansur, Baghdad grew under the Abbasids into the great cultural and commercial center of medieval Islam. This happened largely through the support of the Persians, whose influence increased greatly, while the Arab dominance that had characterized the rule of the Umayyads diminished. The golden age, which reached its apogee under the reigns of Harun ar-Rashid and his son al-Ma'mun, witnessed the full development of Islamic society, with its universal character, its immense economic resources, and its sophisticated intellectual life, enriched by the encounter of Arab thought and culture with the Hellenistic, Indian, and Iranian civilizations. No longer did the Arabian Peninsula set the dominant tone of Arabic culture.

The Abbasid revolution that initiated these radical changes was primarily a triumph for Islam and the party of religious reform. Accordingly, the native Islamic disciplines were developed during this period, together with the related foreign sciences. It was Abbasid scholars who produced most of the fundamental sources and classical works in the fields of Qur'anic studies, jurisprudence, scholastic theology, grammar, lexicography, rhetoric, and literature, as well as in philosophy, science, medicine, geography, astronomy, and music. Although the Abbasid caliphate in Baghdad had lost much of its temporal authority long before the middle of the eleventh century and although a number of independent dynasties had been formed in Syria, Iraq, Eastern Persia, Egypt, North Africa, and Spain, Islamic culture continued to prevail throughout the realm of the Muslim conquests until the thirteenth century.

As part of the Abbasid culture, Arabic literature during this period changed significantly in its sources of inspiration, its themes, and its modes of expression; the nature of its audience also changed, in taste, sensibility, and expectations. Abbasid authors in the spheres of prose and poetry not only contributed immensely to the splendor of their age but also left their mark on several aspects of the European Renaissance.

Prior to this period, Arabic prose literature had essentially consisted of the Qur'an, for virtually the only prose that came down to the seventh century was in the form of brief proverbs and oracular utterances. Yet the Qur'an, despite its evocative power, could not serve as a model for later Arabic prose. To Muslims it was the Word of God and therefore inimitable;

Frontispiece of an early fourteenth-century Qur'an, the only known surviving example of the work of Muhammad bin al-Wahid, one of the most famous of Arab calligraphers.

The hare meets the king of the elephants in an illustration from a Persian translation of Kalila and Dimna.

moreover, its style was too heightened and poetic to satisfy the manifold needs of literary prose. Only slowly, however, after more than a century, did a more functional and flexible form of prose develop. It may be significant that this style arose in Iraq, in the hands of a largely Persian secretarial class still inspired by the customs and literature of the Sassanids, though often well versed in Arabic. The greatest representative of this class was Ibn al-Muqaffa', a convert to Islam, who died in 757. Most famous for his translations from Pahlavi, the classical Persian language, he wrote the book of *Kalila and Dimna*. This didactic narrative, in which moral exhortations and practical advice are offered by two jackals, is written in a simple and direct style. It was derived ultimately from the Sanscrit *Fables of Bidpai*, which eventually entered Europe and helped inspire such works as La Fontaine's *Fables*.

It was Abu 'Uthman 'Amr bin Bahr al-Jahiz (776–869), who brought Arabic prose to the heights of concision and clarity. Al-Jahiz, the grandson of a black slave, grew up in humble circumstances but still managed to gain a wide education in his native Basrah. His wit and learning made him one of Baghdad's leading intellectuals. Of the more than two hundred works that he composed, the most famous were his *Kitab al-Hayawan* (*Book of Animals*), an anthology of animal anecdotes; the *Kitab al-Bayan wa at-Tabyin* (*Book of Elucidation and Exposition*), a study in rhetoric that covers history, natural science, and much more besides; and

28

Dimna, the jackal, engages in courtly intrigue with his majesty, the lion, in a thirteenth-century Arabic copy of Kalila and Dimna.

the *Kitab al-Bukhala'* (*Book of Misers*), a witty and insightful study of human psychology. In all these works al-Jahiz reveals a lively wit; he pokes fun at himself as well as others, seeking to educate as he entertains. His comments on innumerable aspects of natural phenomena, human nature, and knowledge mark him as one of the most versatile and stimulating writers in all Arabic literature. He also wrote essays on—among other topics—the relative merits of blacks and whites and the charms of slave girls. He gave his work the stamp of refinement and molded Arabic prose into a vehicle of precision and elegance.

The *Kitab al-Aghani* (*Book of Songs*) of Abu al-Faraj al-Isfahani (died 967) almost equals the writings of al-Jahiz in breadth and merit and, lacking al-Jahiz's individualistic touch, perhaps provided an even better prose model. This impressive collection of some twenty-four volumes is essentially an anthology of songs and poems popular in Baghdad at the time of the Caliph Harun ar-Rashid. It contains much valuable information on the lives of Arab poets and musicians, on legends and battles of pre-Islamic times, and on the manners and customs of the Umayyad and Abbasid courts. The *Book of Songs* is almost a compendium of Arabic culture as known in its author's time. In it Abu al-Faraj, like al-Jahiz, seeks to educate and entertain at the same time, and to this end he employs a clear, generally simple style that avoids the ornamental excesses and the preciosity of later authors.

29

فقلت له بعد الدا يشيخ النارُ وزاملة العارُ فما متلك في طلاوة علانيك وخبیَّه

نبیَّك لا مثل رَوْن مضض او کیف میبضر ثم تفرقا فانطلقتُ ذاتَ اليمین

Virtuosity in prose writing has long been attributed to two later writers, Badi' az-Zaman al-Hamadhani (died 1008) and al-Hariri (died 1122). The former invented and the latter practiced the genre known as *maqamat* (assemblies)—dramatic anecdotes narrated by a witty vagabond in an exquisite, elaborately wrought form of rhymed prose. Basing the incidents on his own experiences as a wanderer in Persia—where he had mixed with all types of people, beggars as well as literati and courtiers—al-Hamadhani composed some four hundred *maqamat*, of which fifty-two survive; and on these his fame rests. In these sketches a roguish narrator describes the exploits of an equally unscrupulous rogue and cynic, Abu al-Fath. They reveal much of contemporary life and manners and poke fun at the idiosyncrasies of all classes, especially the elite. Clever and lively as these stories are, their main appeal to later readers springs from the extraordinary command of language that they display. Playing with rare and difficult words and making the most of the newly popular style of rhymed and balanced prose, which exploits the unique regularity of the Arabic language, al-Hamadhani made his *maqamat* a model of high Arabic prose, in which content, though not by any means lacking, is less important than verbal virtuosity.

In this respect his imitator, al-Hariri of Basrah, went still further, using the same format and inventing his own narrator and roguish hero, who meet in cleverly contrived circumstances and in the most unlikely disguises. But al-Hariri's stories are not so witty or original as those of his predecessor, for he was almost excessively concerned with demonstrating his ability to play with Arabic. He combined an inexhaustible vocabulary with the most farfetched verbal conceits and tricks; in one *maqamah*, for example, he used only words in which the letters are undotted or unjoined. With the *maqamat* of al-Hariri Arabic prose reached a formalistic extreme almost verging on Dadaism; thereafter it declined, as ever greater emphasis was placed upon embellishments and devices and less and less upon content. Slowly high Arabic came, if not full circle, at least to a point where it failed to be functional and to serve the needs of ordinary educated thought and discourse.

In the sphere of poetry two major trends, represented by the modernist and neoclassical groups of poets, developed under the Abbasids. The modernist school was largely made up of non-Arab or half-Arab poets who were profoundly influenced in both outlook and method by the diverse cultural atmosphere and the universal character of their age and who rejected a slavish devotion to the pre-Islamic and Umayyad poetic traditions. In their revolt they turned away from the rigid, archaic, and conventional style in favor of a simple, spontaneous, and immediate mode of expression that addressed itself directly to the masses. Like their contemporaries of the neoclassical school, the modernists were not above composing panegyrics in the conventional style for the Abbasid elite, but they were primarily inspired by their own unique circumstances and preoccupied with the expression of individual attitudes and experiences. This modernizing trend produced the sensuous love lyrics of Bashshar, the introspective and analytical verse of Ibn ar-Rumi, the didactic and religious poetry of Abu al-'Atahiyah, and the gay, cynical, and philosophic wine songs of the greatest figure among them, Abu Nuwas.

Half-Persian in origin, Abu Nuwas (died about 810) lost his father while still very young and was deserted by a neglectful, poor mother a few years later. Nonetheless he was well

A funeral ceremony from the Maqamat *of al-Hariri,*
a collection of essays that reveal much about life in medieval Baghdad.

educated among the learned circles of Basrah and Kufah. After living for some time in the desert among the Bedouins, where he acquired an excellent command of what was still regarded as the best and purest Arabic, he moved to Baghdad and joined the court of Harun ar-Rashid and his son al-Amin, who made him his favored poet and companion. A flagrant immoralist, Abu Nuwas was at his best in his wine poetry, in which he humorously described his drinking adventures and frankly confessed his sins. Boasting of his love of wine, he sang:

> Ho! a cup and fill it up, and tell me it is wine,
> For never will I drink in shade if I can drink in shine.
> Curst and poor is every hour that sober I must go,
> But rich am I whene'er well drunk I stagger to and fro.
> Speak, for shame, the loved one's name, let vain disguises fall;
> Good for naught are pleasures hid behind a curtain-wall.
>
> (Translated by Nicholson)

Relying on God to forgive his sins, Abu Nuwas told his critics:

> ...The world could end tomorrow
> with you regretting purity,
> while I will surely be
> worthy of His clemency
>
> (Translated by Omar Pound)

To those moralists who reproached him for his unorthodox way of life and his vain attempt to work out his salvation and transcend the absurdity of the human condition, he directed this simple question: "Fools, why not let me be?"

Representing a reaction to the modernists' mode of thought and expression, the poets of the neoclassical school addressed themselves to a select audience. Tradition-oriented, they tried to revive the sonority of ancient Arabian poetry and reinforce it with artistic ornamentation. Among the leading neoclassicists was Abu Tammam, who was historian to the Caliph al-Mu'tasim and who devoted several panegyrics to the caliph's victories over the Byzantines and the enemies of Islam. "Caliph of Allah," he wrote, "may Allah reward your strivings on behalf of the roots of the faith and Islam and honor." Abu Tammam's fellow Syrian and disciple al-Buhturi also pictured the disastrous events of his day, recalling in a serenely tragic mood the murder of the Caliph al-Mutawakkil. Stylistically he was able to combine tradition with innovation and produce smoother and less difficult verse than Abu Tammam had.

The neoclassicist par excellence, Abu at-Tayyib Ahmad al-Mutanabbi, appeared in the early decades of the tenth century. Born in Kufah but educated in Syria, al-Mutanabbi reached the height of his fame at the Court of Sayf ad-Dawlah, the Hamdanid ruler of Aleppo and patron of the arts, to whom he dedicated his finest panegyrics. His style was a blend of the simple and the contrived, and he is, in the judgment of many critics, the greatest of all the Arab poets. His proud and arrogant character and his glorification of the virtues of honor,

Abu Zayd before the Governor of Rahbah, a tale of hypocrisy and venality, from the Maqamat of al-Hariri, illustrated by Yahyah al-Wasiti.

loyalty, friendship, bravery, integrity, and chivalry revived the older Arab values that he lived, breathed, and sang. Al-Mutanabbi's philosophy of life is crystallized in his uncompromising motto: "Live honorably or die heroically."

The last great poet of the Abbasid period is Abu al-'Ala' al-Ma'arri (973–1057). Reflecting the pessimistic and skeptical mood of an age of anarchy, he nevertheless transcended his age to become one of the major figures of Arabic literature, as well as a special favorite of Western scholars, who find him profoundly modern in feeling. Blinded by smallpox early in life, al-Ma'arri compensated by developing a stupendous memory, and as a youth in Aleppo he enjoyed a reputation for scholarly and poetic attainments. At twenty, he returned to his native Ma'arrah and for fifteen years continued his studies in poetry, antiquities, and philology. His students spread the news of his abilities afar, and as his powers grew, he was induced to enter the intellectual ferment of Baghdad. This stay was decisive in its effect on al-Ma'arri's intellectual development, but for reasons that are not clearly known—his mother's illness, lack of funds, the ill treatment of a patron—he returned to Ma'arrah after only a year and a half and adopted an ascetic life, to which he adhered until his death. Years later, when the poet was seventy-five, the Persian poet and traveler Nasir-i Khusraw passed through Ma'arrah on his way to Egypt. Judging from al-Ma'arri's poetry, the Persian had expected to meet a miserable and dependent old man. On the contrary, the poet was the idol of the town. He had ample resources, and more than two hundred students attended his lectures on literature. Ten years later al-Ma'arri died, a spirit strangely ahead of his time.

We possess only three collections of al-Ma'arri's poetry. The first is *Saqt az-Zand*, alleged to contain the poems of his youth, though it clearly contains later compositions as well. The second is *ad-Dir'iyyat*, a brief collection of poems describing coats of mail (*dir'*). The third, the largest and the most important of the three, is the *Luzumiyyat*, written wholly in the ascetic phase of his career.

In the *Luzumiyyat* al-Ma'arri revealed a preoccupation with death, the most striking aspect of his poetry, and a deep pessimism and bitterness concerning the relative insignificance of man's existence and the reduction to nothingness of all that is in the face of eternity:

> I muse, but in my musing I recall
> The days of my iniquity; we're all
> An arrow shot across the wilderness,
>   Somewhere within the wilderness must fall.
>   (Based on a translation by ar-Rihani)

For al-Ma'arri nothing survives eternally; night is consumed by onrushing day, and even the heavens are impotent in the face of time. He decried with irony the pathetic attractiveness of mortal delights and the worthlessness of worldly gain in the face of death's destruction:

> Carouse, ye sovereign lords! The wheel will roll
> Forever to confound and console:
> Who sips today the golden cup will drink
> Mayhap tomorrow in a wooden bowl...

> And silent drink. The tumult of our mirth
> Is worse than our mad welcoming of birth:
> The thunder hath a grandeur, but the rains,
> Without the thunder, quench the thirst of earth.
>
> The Sultan, too, relinquishing his throne
> Must wayfayre through the darkening dust alone
> Where neither crown nor kingdom be, and he,
> Part of the Secret, here and there is blown.
>   (Translated by ar-Rihani)

Though not an unbeliever, al-Ma'arri derided religion's attempts to shield men from the brutal truth, mirrored in one another's being, when all humanity is bound to God's unchanging will:

> Now this religion happens to prevail
> Until by that one it is overthrown,
> Because men dare not live with men alone,
> But always with another fairy-tale.
>
> God is above. We never shall attain
> Our liberty from hands that overshroud;
> Nor can we shake aside this heavy cloud
> More than a slave can shake aside the chain.
>   (Translated by H. Baerlein)

Al-Ma'arri exuded contempt for what he sensed as men's selfish hypocrisy and their basically wicked character. Yet he understood that it is their desperation in the face of death that provokes such reprehensible behavior. He contemplated with a deep sense of irony the fact that, after a lifetime of avarice and envy, men would ask forgiveness in the hope of resurrection:

> I wheedle, too, even like my slave Zaydun,
> Who robs at dawn his brother, and at noon
> Prostrates himself in prayer—ah, let us pray
> That night might blot us and our sins, and soon.
>   (Translated by ar-Rihani)

Despite his black view of existence, al-Ma'arri expressed a loving compassion for mortal suffering, which he would relieve through recognition of a common truth, that the destiny of men, being the same for all, unites them in a bond of brotherhood:

> To humankind, O brother, consecrate
> Thy heart, and shun the hundred Sects that prate
> About the things they little know about—
> Let all receive thy pity, none thy hate . . .
> For my religion's love, and love alone.
>   (Translated by ar-Rihani)

When, finally, the poet turned to himself, he accepted his fate almost gratefully, as a natural course, discouraging any futile thoughts of delay or escape; and in the final liberation of this acceptance he vowed to outwit death by refraining from perpetuating life's anguish by the conception of another human being. He wished the following verse to be his epitaph:

This wrong was by my father done
To me, but ne'er by me to one.
(Translated by Nicholson)

Despite his dark and cynical mood, there is a faint aura of spirituality beyond al-Ma'arri's fatalism—a negation of death's finality and a desire to transcend man's mortal existence on earth. His *Luzumiyyat* ends with these lines:

Howbeit, my inner vision heir shall be
To the increasing flames of mystery
Which may illumine yet my prisons all,
All crown the ever living hope of me.
(Translated by ar-Rihani)

Many critics like to confer on al-Ma'arri the title of "philosopher," an irrelevant honor that misleads those who would understand him. He was simply interested in transforming his emotional and intellectual experiences into a disciplined literary excellence. Major questions of "what is" and "what ought to be" challenged him. His answers to them—no matter how uncertain they are—reveal insights that neither pure reason nor positive science are able to give, an intuitive knowledge that uncovers the incoherent structure of a unique age.

No less important than al-Ma'arri's poetry are his prose writings, and especially his masterpiece, *Risalat al-Ghufran* (*The Epistle of Forgiveness*), which many Western critics believe was a precursor of Dante's *Divine Comedy* and perhaps one of its sources of inspiration.

Although some aspects of Sufi or mystical literature may be traced back to the early Islamic and Umayyad periods, it was during the late Abbasid and post-Abbasid periods that the greatest Arab mystic poets and writers flourished. Foremost among these are al-Hallaj (died 922) and Ibn al-Farid (died 1235) in the east and Ibn al-'Arabi (died 1240) in Muslim Spain. Ibn al-'Arabi's account of Muhammad's ascent to Heaven, together with other contemporary popular accounts in Latin and French based on Arabic sources, closely parallels the structure of Dante's *Divine Comedy*, which it may have influenced.

THE HISPANO-ARABIC PERIOD

Muslim rule in Spain lasted from 711, when the Arabs and Berbers invaded and expelled the Visigoths, until 1492, when the Castillian Christians in turn expelled the Muslims from their last strongholds there. Throughout this lengthy period, Islamic culture and the Arabic language gradually spread across Andalusia, developing slowly because of internal conflicts and the distance from the eastern cultural center but ultimately gaining a special strength and significance because the Muslims replaced a barbarian rule. Andalusian, or Hispano-Arabic, poetry began in imitation of eastern models and did not strike out fully on its own until around the eleventh century. But the uniquely Hispano-Arabic forms that did develop are of peculiar importance to the West, because it was in Andalusia that Arabic and European literatures merged, with a resulting influence on Western styles and modes of feeling. Though the subject still requires much further exploration, there is a considerable likelihood that the Andalusian *zajal* and *muwashshah* were the precursors of the songs of love and chivalry of medieval Europe.

Andalusian poets during the early centuries of Arab rule imitated the neoclassical school exemplified by al-Mutanabbi. The first example of belles lettres is a work by Ibn 'Abd Rabbihi (died 940) that borrowed heavily from the encyclopedic collections of al-Jahiz and Ibn Qutaybah. Later there were also imitations of the *maqamat* and anthologies. However, the popular *zajal*, composed most notably by Ibn Quzman (died 1160), and the more courtly *muwashshah* were new and lively creations that rose from the fusion of Arabic and Provençal cultures. Both were based on a refrain for a chorus and therefore were meant to be sung; Arab music and European popular songs played an essential part in the cross-fertilization. The *muwashshah*, which is usually a love poem—though the mystics also adopted it—consists of rhymed Arabic strophes joined by a recurrent two-line *kharjah*, or envoi, which is usually in Romance or pungent, colloquial Arabic. Among its greatest practitioners were at-Tutili (died 1126), Ibn Baqi (died 1145), Ibn Sahl (died 1251) and Ibn al-Khatib (died 1374). The love traditions of Jamil and 'Umar thus made their way into Provençal courtly love, and it is even possible that the word *TRou-Badour* derives, via the Provençal *TRoBar*, from the Arabic root *TaRiBa*, which conveys the idea of joy and song. An innovator in this field and one of the most original minds in Muslim Spain, Ibn Hazm of Cordoba (died 1064), is famous for his *Dove's Necklace*, an essay on the psychology, anatomy, and manifestations of love in joy and sorrow. This pioneer work on chivalric love contains a number of parallels with Andreas Capellanus' *The Art of Courtly Love* (published 1185), and it is universally recognized as one of the greatest classics of medieval literature.

The Muslim courts of Spain also included centers for the translation of Arabic into Latin. As early as the twelfth century, scholars from France, England, Italy, and Germany came to Spain in pursuit of knowledge and became conversant with Arabic culture through these translation centers. Hispano-Arabic civilization had already involved the synthesis of many diverse cultural elements, and through this synthesis Spain was able to serve as a bridge between the Orient and the West. Though the Arab impact on the European Renaissance has long been recognized, the role that Arabic literature played in the medieval East-West synthesis has yet to be fully acknowledged and explored.

The Folkloric Tradition

The standardization of written Arabic that resulted from the adoption of the Qur'an as the linguistic criterion, together with the vast expansion of the Islamic empire, led to the phenomenon of *diglossa*, or the separation of Arabic into written and spoken languages. The classical

A public storyteller in Morocco helps to perpetuate an ancient Arabic literary tradition.

written texts were inaccessible to the illiterate masses, and a separate body of oral narratives, in the Arabic dialects or in a mixed language, had existed since the early days of Islam.

The most popular form in the folkloric tradition is the *sirah*. *Sirah* means "life" or "biography," and the stories that go by this title recount adventures and achievements of tribal or national heroes. Since by nature the *sirah* is lacking in high style, it is less close to the epic than to the popular romances of the Middle Ages, and in Western descriptions the term "romance" has often been assigned to it.

In his *Manners and Customs of the Modern Egyptians*, an account of Cairo in the mid-nineteenth century, Edward Lane described how professional storytellers rendered three of these works, *Sirat Bani Hilal*, *Sirat Baybars*, and *Sirat 'Antar*. Performing in the coffeehouses of the day, the narrators would recite at breakneck speed and, in hopes of increasing donations from the audience, would embellish the tales with witty asides and fresh anecdotes. In this way the tales grew into their present form after hundreds of years of oral transmission.

At least one of the *sirahs*, *Bani Hilal*, is still recited, with improvisations, in the coffeehouses of North Africa. This narrative recounts the saga of the Bani Hilal, an Arabian tribe that migrated to Egypt and North Africa. It focuses on the life and deeds of a fictitious tribal leader, Abu Zayd, the black son of a tribal prince who becomes a hero and leader in exile, unknowingly does battle against his own father (an incident that recalls the Persian epic *Shah-Nameh*), and lives on for hundreds of years to lead his people successfully through many vicissitudes. *Sirat Bani Hilal* embodies the spirit of nomadic life, in which family and tribal loyalties are foremost.

Sirat Baybars, which was compiled by the sixteenth century, is based on the life of the historic general and ruler Baybars I, who ruled Egypt and Syria in the thirteenth century, but the *sirah* romanticizes history and interweaves a rich tapestry of magic and superstition. Centering on medieval city life, it portrays Baybars as a champion of the common people against officials and soldiers, who are seen as rogues and oppressors, and gives an attractive picture of street life and a slightly cynical one of the court.

Popular since the eighth century and most famous among the *sirah* works is *Sirat 'Antar*, which comes closest to being an Arab national epic and epitomizes the chivalric ideals that prevailed among the early nomadic Arabs of the desert. *Sirat 'Antar* is based on the legend, surrounding the life of the pre-Islamic hero and poet 'Antarah, whose life we have already briefly touched on. Like the fictitious Abu Zayd of *Sirat Bani Hilal*, 'Antarah was a black man who overcame his low status and became a leader through personal heroism. His story represents the triumph of the underdog, a persistently appealing theme in this popular genre. As in the Western chivalric romances, 'Antarah wins his beloved, 'Ablah, by enduring a series of tests, presented in the repetitive episodes that are characteristic of oral literature. The *sirah* widens in scope by including a series of Syrian, Iraqi, Persian, and even European adventures, which represent successive additions to the oral tradition.

Out of a similar oral tradition and for the same popular audience there developed the single Arabic work that is by far the best known and most read in the West: the *Alf Laylah wa Laylah* or *The Thousand and One Nights*. The present forms of *The Nights* have been traced to a now lost fifteenth-century composite that contained three major strains: Persian stories with

39

Indian elements adapted into Arabic in the tenth century; stories composed in Baghdad between the tenth and twelfth centuries; and stories composed in Egypt, mostly between the thirteenth and fourteenth centuries. Perhaps the most famous element is the frame tale of the clever Shahrazad, who saves herself from execution by the misogynistic King Shahriyar by telling a seemingly endless series of entertaining stories. This device had its origin in India, which is also presumed to be the source of the frame-tale idea employed in *The Canterbury Tales* of Chaucer and the *Decameron* of Boccaccio.

The *Alf Laylah wa Laylah* was first translated, with astounding success, in the early eighteenth century by the French scholar Antoine Galland. His freely edited version, in a simple, elegant French, was published serially in little duodecimo volumes, the eighteenth-century equivalent of pocketbooks, and they caught on so well that in a short time all Europe was reading "M. Galland's tales." And in a sense they were his, first, because his native storytelling skill and his sense of the taste of the time made the translation a success and, second, because he added from an oral source outside *The Thousand and One Nights* collection some of the stories that became most famous—those of Ali Baba, Sindbad, and Aladdin, for example. Nearly a score of subsequent translations into European languages have failed to top Galland's version in general appeal or appropriateness of style.

Westerners at first regarded the collection as pure entertainment, but it soon began to influence European literary taste. It was largely responsible for the moral tales with oriental backgrounds that were popular throughout the eighteenth and much of the nineteenth centuries. Samuel Johnson's *Rasselas* and Voltaire's *Zadiq* are the most famous of these. Persian and Turkish story collections were also translated in the wake of the *The Thousand and One Nights*' popularity. This popularity was not, of course, an isolated phenomenon. It was simply one outstanding example of the Western taste for orientalia that developed after the great European voyages of discovery. This infatuation with the exotic East reached its high point in the pseudo-oriental chinoiserie craze in art, architecture, and decoration that occurred during the mid-eighteenth century. *The Thousand and One Nights*, being a blend of Greek, Chinese, Indian, Turkish, Persian, and Arabic sources and details, might be considered the literary equivalent of chinoiserie, without, of course, being pseudo-oriental.

Although the stories were introduced in Europe as adult fare—and their frank sexuality makes some of them less than wholly suitable for children—bowdlerized texts became a fixture in the nursery, and a variety of watered-down versions exist today in America and Europe. It may be assumed that every major English or French writer of the eighteenth or nineteenth century had some contact with *The Thousand and One Nights*, usually at an early and impressionable age. The book has been a source of inspiration for writers and poets from Byron and Wordsworth to Barth and Borges.

In view of the greatness of Arabic culture as a whole, it is ironic that *The Thousand and One Nights* should have become that culture's primary representative in the West. The oral creators of *Alf Laylah wa Laylah*, though obviously gifted, were only semiliterate, and the language of their tales is a mixture of the classical and the vernacular. This blend has been purified in modern Arabic versions because the original style was regarded as too inelegant by Arab

The accuracy of William Harvey's illustrations gave readers of Edward William Lane's translation of The Thousand and One Nights *an unusually realistic impression of this romantic classic.*

critics. In fact, although *The Thousand and One Nights* was the object of a brief fad among educated Arabs during the Abbasid period, the work was rarely mentioned, and then only with disfavor, by Arab authorities until recent times. Since the 1950's Arab scholars have increasingly recognized the *Nights'* importance as folklore, but this has largely been a delayed response to Western influence. Oddly enough, the translation's popularity misled Westerners into believing that the Arabic original was a revered classic, when traditionally quite the reverse was true.

THE POST-ABBASID AND MODERN PERIODS

From the middle of the thirteenth century to the late nineteenth century, Arabic literature suffered a long period of decline. There were a few exceptional writers, but, in general, this period was marked by an absence of those creative institutions and outstanding individual talents that had produced the great tradition of classical Arabic poetry—the odes and chants of pre-Islamic Arabia; the religious, political, and amatory compositions of the early Umayyad poets; the lyrics of the Andalusians; the mystical poetry of the Sufis; and the great classics of the Abbasids. It was not until the latter half of the nineteenth century that Arabic poetry, along with other forms of Arabic literature, began to revive gradually in response to the stimulus of internal reform and the challenge of Western influence.

Among the specific forces of change within the Arab world in the early part of the modern period were the rise of the Wahhabi movement in Arabia and the Sanusi order in North Africa. Externally, the Napoleonic expedition to Egypt in 1798 marked the beginning of a new era of Western influence in the Arab countries, which brought problems and achievements. Throughout the nineteenth century and during the twentieth century prior to the Second World War, new intellectual forces were at work within Arab society. These included the spread of education and a subsequent increase in literacy, the growth of printing presses and journalism, the production of massive translations and adaptations from Western works, the growing influence of English and French liberal thought on Arabic writers, the emergence of a stream of Islamic thought aimed at restating the social principles of Islam, and the rise of nationalistic movements concerned with the separation of religion from politics and the creation of a secular society. At the end of the Second World War, a great paradox appeared: while differences between the Arabs and the West deepened and multiplied in the postwar period, resulting in a series of revolutions aimed at complete political emancipation from Western domination, contemporary Arabic thought and literature, whether unconsciously or by design, became increasingly subject to a mounting impact from the West. As a result of this paradox, new movements sprang up not only in politics but also in fiction, poetry, criticism, and the other arts.

When modern Arab writers adopted the forms of the novel and short story, they already had a vast and rich traditional legacy of narrative, much of which had only recently appeared in print. This heritage included a variety of forms that were to influence a new fiction: stories, fables, fantastic tales as in *The Thousand and One Nights*, biographies of the Prophet Muhammad, elaborated accounts of historical episodes, the highly stylized *maqamat* in rhymed prose, and extensive chivalric romances in both verse and rhymed prose.

Until the early twentieth century, most Arab novelists and short story writers consciously wrote in a highly refined, neoclassical style, often aiming at a display of recondite erudition and pompous, florid language. Some strove to reproduce the ornate rhymed prose of the classical *maqamat*, as did Muhammad 'Uthman Jalal in his rhymed prose translation of *Paul et Virginie*, by B. de Saint-Pierre, and Muhammad al-Muwaylihi in his brilliant satirical novel, *Hadith 'Isa bin Hisham*.

A wealth of Western fiction, translated into Arabic, was made available to Arab readers and firmly established the novel and short story as Arabic forms. The process of translation tended to temper the oriental extravagance of language and also to expand the range of expression. A stage beyond translation was the adaptation of European works into Arabic, with the characters, settings, and circumstances reproduced in Arab guise. In this art Mustafa Lutfi al-Manfaluti was remarkably successful.

Out of this background there finally emerged novels and short stories written in the increasingly flexible and straightforward prose style of the translators and journalists. Authors now drew upon Arab situations and sources for subjects and began to deal with Arab problems. The eighteen historical novels of Jurji Zaydan, written in functional, fast-moving prose, largely purged of ornamental devices, had the twofold purpose of educating the public to Arab history and culture and of recreating national pride in the glory of the Arab past. Another landmark, sometimes called the first Arab novel, is M. H. Haykal's *Zaynab*, the romantic tale of an Egyptian girl in a changing world.

Several Syro-American writers—in particular, Jubran Khalil Jubran, who possessed an intimate knowledge of American and English literature, and Mikha'il Nu'aymah, who was thoroughly familiar with Russian literature, as well as with American and English—produced novellas and short stories in a new, liberated Arabic style, dealing with crucial issues of the early twentieth century. Among the older generation, Taha Husayn most clearly exemplifies the Azhar-trained scholar who, after acquiring French sophistication from study at the Sorbonne, grappled with the problems of Egyptian life as well as themes from the Islamic past. Mahmud Taymur, who initially wrote in a strictly classical style, has developed, over the years, a considerably looser style, and his latest works even include colloquial Arabic. Tawfiq al-Hakim has introduced symbolism into Arabic literature in plots on traditional themes that illustrate philosophical truths. He has also composed works of incisive social and political comment. Al-Hakim's style has ranged from a well-pruned classical elegance to a literary Arabic that is close in structure and word choice to the spoken dialect. His play *as-Safqah* may be read either as literary or colloquial Arabic.

Of the middle generation of contemporary authors, Tawfiq 'Awwad uses a potent, concrete style and excels as a writer of short stories that display an intense social realism. The novels and short stories of Najib Mahfuz, which present a multitude of meticulously drawn characters who face the changes and challenges of twentieth-century Egypt, amount to a psychological analysis of the Egyptian people during the last fifty years.

Among the younger group of writers, Jabra Ibrahim Jabra, using a highly Westernized style, has produced novels and short stories of deep introspection, based on his personal experiences as a Palestinian. Yusuf Idris, sometimes writing in the vein of the absurd, portrays the intense psychological problems rising from the drastic changes taking place in Egyptian revolutionary society. Layla Ba'albaki writes of the modern Arab women seeking social emancipation in the modernized, considerably transformed Lebanese society of the present. She depicts the dilemmas of her heroine with such convincing actuality that her novel, *I Live*, was banned as too revolutionary.

In the sphere of poetry, the modern Arab renaissance witnessed the rise of five successive generations of writers—the neoclassicists, the Syro-Americans, the Egyptian modernists, the Apollo group, and more recently the poets of the free-verse movement. The classical tradition that directly or indirectly inspired the poets of the first of these schools far outweighed any Western influences on their writing. Nevertheless, with their relatively imposing standards of "good sense," "refinement," and "correctness" in structure and style and their tendency toward an emotional expression of patriotic and social themes, these poets revived a petrified poetic language, revitalized a dying aesthetic sensibility, appealed to a wide range of the general public, and in a substantial part of their poetry achieved an authentic expression of current ideas and aspirations. The other group of poets are linked together by a progressive shift from emphasis on form to emphasis on content and from a relatively detached portrayal of the outside world to a concern with expression of individual experience. Poets such as Jubran, Shukri, ash-Shabbi, as-Sayyab, Adunis, Hawi, 'Abd as-Sabur, Jabra, and Sayigh, to mention a few, responded creatively to the challenging impact of Western culture on their modes of thought and expression and produced for the first time in several centuries an extremely original type of Arabic poetry.

Especially in its dynamic free-verse form, this poetry, which rejects traditional metrics and lifeless poetic diction in favor of a looser, simpler poetic language, is capable of a vital expression of content through the intensity of the artistic process and the imaginative use of words, metaphors, symbols, imagery, mythological allusions, dramatic monologues, and other devices. This content ranges from universal philosophical questions about the human condition—life, death, love, and salvation—to the particular social and cultural issues and situations characteristic of the poets' own time, visions, and experiences. In their endeavors to pigeonhole the various groups of these modern poets, critics have called them "romantics," "social realists," "Eliotists," "Tammuzists," "existentialists," "Palestinian elegists," and other titles; these descriptions are merely inadequate attempts to tame the rebellious and to represent in straight lines a dynamic poetic current that has numerous curves and divergences. In fact, this poetic energy is characteristic of the nature and function of the new poetry and is commensurate with the sensibility of its creators, who, unlike their predecessors, feel that they are one with the complex world and its problems and are thoroughly steeped in the restless spirit of the period in which they live. Existentially they are committed as creative artists to enlarging their fellow man's sensibility, deepening his sympathies, and inducing some order, harmony, and vitality in his world.

SUMMARY

Arabic literature, as it developed from the pre-Islamic period to the present, is not only the crowning artistic and intellectual achievement of the Arabs but also the enduring monument of Arab-Islamic culture—a remarkable culture that has achieved, at different times and places and through the creative process of challenge and response, evident interactions and cooperations with other cultures, both in the East and in Western Europe. Unfortunately, however, although the influence of the West on the modern Arab renaissance is generally accepted in the Arab world today, the vital role played by the Arab-Islamic culture in the European Renaissance is inadequately appreciated, particularly in the field of belles lettres. The names of the pre-Islamic bards and "troubadours," of the Islamic courtly-love poets, of al-Jahiz, al-Mutanabbi, Ibn Hazm, Ibn al-'Arabi, al-Ma'arri, and many others should be added to those of the other Arabs of ancient times—the philosophers and scientists—whose deep impact on the European Renaissance is generally recognized.

Qanun player, The Thousand and One Nights.

45

Abu 'Uthman 'Amr bin Bahr al-Jahiz

(776–869)

In the year 255 of the Hijrah (868–869), Abu 'Uthman 'Amr bin Bahr al-Jahiz, aged about 93, reached for one of the books piled high around him in his study at Basrah, and they toppled over and crushed him to death. Whether the account is true or not, there is a fine sense of propriety about it. For, probably more than any other individual of his time in the world west of the Ganges, al-Jahiz lived by the written word. To have died by the written word would have struck him as singularly eloquent and apt.

Al-Jahiz was born around 776 in the southern Iraqi city of Basrah, the first city founded by the Arab conquerors. His family was quite likely of Abyssinian origin, attached as clients to the Arab tribe of Kinana, and their financial situation was probably far from comfortable. Physically, al-Jahiz was said to have been so ugly that in later life he was refused a position as tutor to the family of the Caliph al-Mutawakkil because his face frightened the children. "Al-Jahiz," is, in fact, a nickname meaning "the goggle-eyed."

None of these circumstances can in any way have inhibited his education, however. Over a period of some twenty-five years he acquired knowledge of truly encyclopedic dimensions, covering Arabic poetry and philology, the Qur'an and the traditions of the Prophet Muhammad, history and quasi-legendary accounts of the pre-Islamic Arabs and Persians, religious law, and theology. To this fund of learning he later added an acquaintance, through Arabic translations, with the scientific and philosophical works of the Greek and Hellenistic thinkers, particularly Aristotle.

Before leaving Basrah for Baghdad around 815–816 al-Jahiz had already drunk from the wellsprings of Hellenism. The Mu'tazilite movement, to which he had attached himself, advanced a highly rationalistic and rigidly puristic interpretation of Islamic doctrine. To defend the faith against polemical attacks from outside and ideological subversion from within, the Mu'tazilah developed a form of theological scholasticism that adduced its evidence almost exclusively from the Qu'ran and employed Hellenistic and early Byzantine techniques of speculative reasoning. Al-Jahiz produced a number of theological and religiopolitical tracts on behalf of the Mu'tazilite position and, also, of the new Abbasid dynasty. Unfortunately, the Mu'tazilah's intellectualist and intolerant brand of Islam earned them repudiation by the community at large and, around 849, suppression by the central government. Al-Jahiz's association with the Mu'tazilah was undoubtedly responsible for the suspicion with which later generations of orthodox Muslims tended to regard at least this portion of his work.

Such writings, however, accounted for far fewer than a third of al-Jahiz's almost two hundred known titles. With the exception of a few relatively straightforward historical, genealogical, geographical, and philological works, the bulk of his literary production—over a hundred titles—falls into a complex cultural genre known as *adab*. The literary manifestations of this genre generally took the form of tastefully selected poetical and prose passages, more or less skillfully arranged to serve as moral, practical, or rhetorical examples, to expand on a given theme or themes, to reinforce certain biases or points of view, or to provide evidence for or against particular positions. Al-Jahiz is considered, if not the founder of this genre, at least its earliest significant exponent, and certainly one of its most distinctive and versatile.

Up to the second half of the eighth century, Arabic prose writing had been dominated by two classes of professional literati. The first was made up of the governmental scribes and bureaucrats—the *kuttab*—who were probably the first to develop a viable form of written Arabic prose. They wrote largely for one another's consumption and edification, and their writings reflected a tradition that idealized literary virtuosity and courtliness, and whose roots are traceable to the earliest literate civilizations of the Near East, when the scribal class had held a near monopoly on literacy and the art of writing. The *kuttab* wrote Arabic because their livelihood and status depended on it, but they wrote it as they would have written Greek, Coptic, Syriac, or Middle Persian less than a century before—with elegance, serviceability, circumspection, formality, allusiveness, and an almost cryptic concision. The other class consisted mainly of the religious, legal, historical, and philological scholars of the early Islamic community, who had successfully contested scribal and bureaucratic hegemony over the written word. These authors apparently modeled their prose on a native Arabic tradition of oral narrative, but for purposes of definition and explanation they adopted a terse, abbreviated, technical style. Despite their respect—almost reverence—for literary Arabic and their careful use of it in composing their books, they often maintained the fiction that their sources were oral and that their own works were all dictated from memory. Writing, they claimed, was little

46

"Bridled Giraffe" from the Book of Animals.

more than a mnemonic aid; even at its best it must be considered an unreliable tool.

But by the end of the eighth century, several factors—among them the systematic standardization of Arabic grammar and lexicography and the introduction of paper manufacture into the Islamic heartlands on a wide scale—had combined to exert a revolutionary influence on the cultural life of the peoples under Islamic rule. The level of effective literacy reached in the urban centers of the empire, among most classes of the Muslim population, was probably higher and more broadly based than any other culture had achieved or would achieve until the late Renaissance.

As a professional writer, al-Jahiz deliberately addressed himself to this relatively new, but potentially unlimited, readership, as well as to the more established one of scribes and scholars. Not for several centuries and possibly never before had an author been confronted with *a general reading public*—one with diverse social, ethnic, and cultural backgrounds, but with a shared linguistic, religious, and educational foundation. Al-Jahiz seems to have been the first Arabic author of any importance to show himself acutely sensitive and responsive to the tastes, needs, and capacities of this public, and he was also fully aware of the uses and abuses, advantages and disadvantages of the written word. Interspersed throughout his available works are passing remarks, personal observations, and practical insights on almost every aspect of authorship and the book business; and long passages are devoted to ringing praise of books and writing.

The new audience called for a new approach to professional writing. A marriage of the two conventional approaches to Arabic prose—the Near Eastern scribal and the Arab-Islamic scholarly—might have begot an offspring suitable to al-Jahiz's purposes. In fact, al-Jahiz occasionally seems to have effected a union of precisely that sort: he wedded a clearly literary style, characteristic of scribal prose but shorn of its arcane preciosity, to themes, subjects, or anecdotes from the classicized Arabic heritage. One literary genre that he used, for instance—the so-called "rhetorical contest"—had been current as early as the scribal schools of Sumer and Akkad. It is represented in al-Jahiz's work by more than a dozen titles, including *The Superiority of Blacks over Whites*, *Agriculture versus Date Orcharding*, and *A Boasting-match between Winter and Summer*. Related to such contests are a number of paired essays in which al-Jahiz argued both sides of a question. Essays "in praise of" and "in condemnation of" were composed on such subjects as "wine," "booksellers," and "scribal bureaucrats."

Yet even in these literary tours de force the synthesis of styles, genres, and subjects effected by al-Jahiz was by no means simple. And in his larger *adab* works—for example, the voluminous, all-encompassing *Book of Animals*; the sophisticated *Clarity and Clarification*, a manual of composi-

tion, rhetoric, and fine style; or the delightfully wry, perceptive, pretension-pricking *Book of Misers*—he was obviously reaching out to an audience that gained something more from his books than from those of the scribes and the scholars. These readers relished, along with their instruction, amusement of a kind that none before al-Jahiz had so artfully and liberally afforded. Perhaps no work better exemplifies al-Jahiz's mixture of humor, personal opinion, and encyclopedic knowledge than the bizarre medley of satirical witticism and unanswered questions oddly entitled *Squaring and Circling*. In this work, as elsewhere, his impatient skepticism toward conventional "wisdom" is matched with a deep appreciation of the rich Arab-Islamic tradition whose champion he had become. He paid unfeigned tribute to this tradition more than once. In the *Book of Animals*, for example, he wrote:

> We rarely hear of a statement by a philosopher on natural history, or come across a reference to the subject in books by doctors or dialecticians, without finding an identical passage in Arab and Bedouin poetry, or in the everyday wisdom of those who speak our language and belong to our religious community.
>
> (Translated by D. M. Hawke from Charles Pellat's *The Life and Works of Jahiz*)

The *adab* work of al-Jahiz draws heavily upon the vast body of poetry, oratory, history, legends, and proverbial lore of the early Arabs—most of which had already been accorded a "classical" status by the philologists—and upon the Qur'an and the extensive religiolegal compilations of the early Islamic scholars. But to amplify and ramify the subjects he set forth himself, he readily turned to the Arabized versions of Sassanian imperial chronicles, manuals of court protocol, and wisdom literature. In addition, he regularly utilized the many translations of Greek philosophical and scientific works, for passing allusions, longer extracts, and conceptual principles. The wealth of information on persons, peoples, places, and things that also appears throughout al-Jahiz's *adab* works suggests that he had many other sources at his disposal—anthological miscellanies, perhaps, or technical handbooks, or even trained consultants. But possibly the most typical and original feature of his *adab* compositions is the smooth, unselfconscious manner with which he introduces facts, observations, and opinions avowedly derived from his own variegated social experiences. Few prose writers in the history of medieval Arabic literature have so openly and pervasively expressed *themselves* or relied upon their own experience as a resource on a par with that received through traditional channels. In the *Book of Animals* al-Jahiz described his approach:

> The only way I can hope to win your interest is to present [my book] to you in the most attractive form possible

and guide you through the by-ways of many different subjects, leading you from argument based on the wise Qur'an to memorable traditions, from traditions to genuine poetry, from fine poetry to current everyday proverbs, from proverbs to philosophical curiosities, marvels confirmed by human experience, revealed by critical scrutiny and disclosed by reasoning, and wonders beloved by the human heart and eagerly sought after by the human mind.

(Translated by Pellat/Hawke)

Few works of medieval Arabic literature speak so convincingly and idiomatically with the voice of their author as do those of al-Jahiz. His tone of irony, reasoned doubt, and exuberant delight in all phenomena and the casual precision of his Arabic diction and style impress us today just as they must have impressed his ninth-century readers. At the very outset of al-Jahiz's career, around 815–816, the Caliph al-Ma'mun highly commended some of al-Jahiz's religio-political tracts on the office of caliphate:

Here is a book which does not require the presence of its author [to be understood], and needs no advocate; the subject is conscientiously dealt with, and profound

thinking goes hand in hand with elegance and lucidity; its appeal is both to princes and the common people, to the elite and the masses.

(Translated by Pellat/Hawke)

Al-Ma'mun's commendation holds good for almost all that al-Jahiz wrote over the subsequent half century. Instead of confining publication of his works to editions intended only for the controlled, interpretive lecture, as did most of his professional contemporaries, or to a patron's personalized edition, al-Jahiz evidently delivered most of his literary progeny into the hands of the copyists, the booksellers, and the general reading public. He let his books fend for themselves in the cultural jungle of plagiarists, critics, and ignoramuses, with which he was only too familiar. In allowing his books a life of their own, al-Jahiz helped greatly to open up the multifarious world of Arab-Islamic literature, scholarship, culture, and science to the ordinary—and hitherto neglected—reader of Arabic. Not since the Holy Book itself—the Qur'an—had been revealed, had *books* in general been given the consideration, importance, and wide circulation that they received at the time of the goggle-eyed polymath from Basrah.

M. ZWETTLER

"Ostrich Sitting on Eggs" from the Book of Animals.

49

Abu at-Tayyib Ahmad bin al-Husayn al-Mutanabbi
(915–965)

In this day and age, with a cult of public humility in vogue and public figures placed on pillories instead of pedestals, few arts are less congenial to general taste than that of the panegyrist. Yet the successful panegyrist is much like the successful painter of portraits: he must bend his talents and master his medium to represent a patron in a manner calculated at once to improve that patron's public image, to earn for himself approbation and due reward, and to meet his own standards of excellence. Such a panegyrist was Abu at-Tayyib Ahmad bin al-Husayn al-Mutanabbi.

Born in Kufah in 915 the son of a water-carrier, he spent much of his youth among the Syro-Iraqi Bedouins. A body of these he led in a quasi-religious uprising that ended for him in a two-year prison term (933–935) and also, according to a questionable tradition, in the coining of the nickname by which he is known, *al-Mutanabbi*, "the would-be prophet." After several years as a roving panegyrist for a number of unimpressive individuals, few of whom find mention outside his verse, he was received as court-poet into the entourage of the Hamdanid emir at Aleppo, Sayf ad-Dawlah (948).

Sayf ad-Dawlah, who ruled northern Syria from 945 to 967, divided his activity mainly between waging incessant warfare with his neighbors—Byzantium especially, but the bordering Muslim principalities as well—and adorning his court at Aleppo with the literary and intellectual luminaries of his time. From our vantage point, his ability, perspicacity, and good sense seem far more evident in his role of patron of letters and science than in his role of military and political leader. For, with a fine instinct for public relations, Sayf ad-Dawlah lavishly maintained a stable of prize panegyrists who produced altogether well over 10,000 lines of poetry in praise of his warlike prowess, his statesmanship, his physical, moral, and intellectual perfection, and—of course—his liberal generosity. No mention is made of the major reverses he met in the field or of the extortionate levies he imposed upon his subjects in support of his *jihad*.

In this respect his investment in al-Mutanabbi yielded extraordinarily rich returns. The poet's panegyrics of Sayf ad-Dawlah during—and even after—his nine-year sojourn at the Hamdanid court constitute not only the largest and

the most masterful, memorable, and self-expressive portion of his own work, but also the highest and most sustained achievement of panegyric artistry in the entire history of Arabic literature.

Al-Mutanabbi's odes in praise of Sayf ad-Dawlah contain their share of exaggerated expressions of flattery and extravagant hyperbole—rainclouds and seas of generosity, lion-like valor and invincibility in battle, piled-up superlatives of every noble quality. But these are to be read as conventional usages, which, incidentally, by no means predominate here to the extent they do in the works of other panegyrists or in many of al-Mutanabbi's poems in praise of lesser men. In the Sayf ad-Dawlah poems, too, as throughout the poet's work, one meets with exuberant flights of verbal virtuosity and unexpected images of haunting beauty. The compliments that are the panegyrist's stock in trade flow freely and amicably from poet to prince as between friends and near-equals. But they are also accompanied by clever touches of irony, importunate demands for reward, attacks on Sayf ad-Dawlah's enemies, explicit declarations of the poet's own incomparability and indispensability, snide remarks about rival panegyrists, complaints and reproaches for lapses in the prince's patronage, even threats of leaving the court unless his poetic preeminence is duly recognized.

It is clear that al-Mutanabbi had great admiration and affection for "the emir of the Arabs," as he calls Sayf ad-Dawlah, and it is equally clear that he had no mean opinion of his own person and abilities. As he wrote in an early ode:

> Horsemen and nighttime and wilderness know me,
> the sword and the spear, pen and paper as well.

Certainly the poet's tone of independence and easy familiarity with the emir—sometimes approaching impudence—and his notorious but generally misunderstood penchant for self-acclaim stand out as the salient features of his poetry from this period. Yet these features—which were not merely tolerated, but apparently relished and encouraged by the emir—must represent a conscious stylistic technique and not just personal idiosyncrasy. By avoiding

An enthroned ruler, surrounded by courtiers and entertainers.

the language of unqualified adulation, subservience, and self-abasement that had tended toward overuse in panegyric verse up to that time, al-Mutanabbi created a radically new image for a professional panegyrist.

To offer praise to one's patron and, at the same time, convey the impression (true or not) that one is a close friend and peer and that one could if one chose do otherwise lends considerable credibility and strength to words of praise. Moreover, this effect would be heightened and the demand for a poet's products would increase to the extent that his audiences and patron could be persuaded of his intrinsic worth and incontestable superiority as a panegyrist.

Obviously a panegyrist who was at the top of the trade would have been a desirable commodity to a ruler like Sayf ad-Dawlah, engaged as he was in conflict not only with the Byzantine infidels but also with his Muslim neighbors, for the latter fought their battles as frequently with words as with swords. In this context al-Mutanabbi's liberties and licenses and his celebration of himself while celebrating Sayf ad-Dawlah enhanced the emir's prestige. For, in this way, the eminent praiseworthiness of the Hamdanid ruler and the majesty of his regime were published abroad not merely through the verses of a paid panegyrist but by a great poet who had *chosen* to devote himself and his talents exclusively to the service of Sayf ad-Dawlah. In his verses al-Mutanabbi gives us some idea of the role he fashioned for himself:

I am naught but a strong, supple spear borne by you;
displayed, it adorns, but strikes terror when aimed. . . .
Reward me when you're sung any verse! For my verse,
resounding, alone brings you poets with praise.
Ignore any's but my voice! Mine is the cry
that is copied, another's the echoed refrain.

In early 958 this seemingly ideal symbiosis between prince and poet ended under obscure circumstances. The carefully cultivated illusion of the panegyrist's intimacy with the emir and of his freedom of expression was shattered when al-Mutanabbi had to flee for his safety to the south. During the next seven and a half years, his reputation secure as the foremost panegyrist of his age, al-Mutanabbi plied his verses in the service of patrons from Egypt to Iran. But none of these—not the powerful black eunuch Kafur, who dominated Egypt, Palestine, and southern Syria (946–968) and whom the poet subsequently satirized with searing scorn, nor the Buyid prince 'Adud ad-Dawlah in Shiraz (949–983), who controlled the caliphate and fostered dreams of a restored Persian Empire, nor any other—could hold in al-Mutanabbi's art and inspiration the place once occupied by his "emir of the Arabs." His later poems are laced with allusions—sometimes affectionate, sometimes bitter—to his former patron, in whose service he had transformed the Arabic panegyric from a detached verbal offering of poetic flattery into a highly personal offering of the poet himself, as praiser.

Nostalgia, perhaps, or restlessness lured him from Shiraz back toward the west. It was between Kufah and Baghdad in August, 965, that al-Mutanabbi and his son, with a few retainers, were attacked and killed by a party of Bedouins, who were allegedly seeking, besides profit, vengeance for a verse attack on their leader's uncle. The poet's own much-annotated copy of his poems was scattered, it is said. But the poems themselves have survived and flourished, and the names that al-Mutanabbi exalted or defiled resound again today with each recitation, just as he himself would unblushingly have predicted.

M. ZWETTLER

Philosophy and History

Dr. Majid Fakhry is the Chairman of the Department of Philosophy at the American University of Beirut and is a Visiting Fellow at Princeton University. Previously he was a Lecturer at the London School of Oriental Studies and an Associate Professor at Georgetown University. More recently he was a Visiting Scholar at Georgetown University and a Visiting Professor at the University of California at Los Angeles. Dr. Fakhry has written *A History of Islamic Philosophy*, *Studies in Arabic Thought, Ibn Bajjeh, Opera Metaphysica, Ibn Rushd, Aristotle*, and *Islamic Occasionalism*.

Philosophy and History
Majid Fakhry

The cultural history of the Arabs virtually begins in the seventh century, which witnessed the rise of Islam and the northward expansion of Arab power—a power destined to dominate a large part of the inhabited world in less than a century.

Not only did the new religion provide the Arabs with a coherent world view and enable them to transcend the narrow confines of their tribal existence, but it thrust them almost forcibly upon the cultural stage of the ancient Near East, setting before them the dazzling treasures of older civilizations. The Arabs suddenly found themselves in possession of the chief monuments of ancient learning: Greek philosophy and science, Persian literary and political wisdom, Indian medicine and mathematics. Confronted with this rich and complex cultural legacy, they faced a major challenge—the need to reconcile Islam with the secular knowledge of their subject peoples and thus provide their faith with the same intellectual resilience that the two other great religions of the Near East, Judaism and Christianity, had achieved after centuries of strife.

Despite the numerous political and theological tensions that inevitably arose, we can see in retrospect that the Arabs were able, throughout a period extending from the downfall of the Persian and Byzantine empires in the seventh century to the early Renaissance in the fourteenth, to assimilate almost the whole of ancient learning, to integrate it into their own cultural life, and to raise the level of knowledge in the fields of mathematics, medicine, astronomy, and philosophy to unprecedented heights. In fact, they served for almost half a millennium as the sole custodians of Greek and other ancient learning, at a time when Western Europe was plunged in semidarkness, having severed all but the most tenuous connections with the cultures of the ancient world.

THE TRANSMISSION OF GREEK PHILOSOPHY AND SCIENCE TO THE ARABS

Philosophy, the disinterested and relentless search for truth, is a distinctive product of the Greek genius. The story of its wanderings across the international borders of the ancient and medieval worlds is one of the most fascinating chapters in the cultural history of mankind.

The conquest of the Near East by Alexander the Great in the fourth century B.C., and in particular the founding of Alexandria in 332 B.C., set the stage for the eastward migration of Greek philosophy and science. During the Ptolemaic period, Alexandria became the cultural center of the ancient world. Its capture by the Arab general 'Amr bin al-'As in 641 A.D. ushered in a period of Arab cultural domination in the Near East that lasted almost half a millennium. Other centers of Greek learning in Syria, Iraq, and Persia—such as Antioch, Harran, Edessa, and Jundi Shapur—served with Alexandria as the major channels for the transmission of learning to the Arabs.

The Umayyad caliphs, who reigned at Damascus from 661 to 750, did little to advance the process of cultural assimilation, but there is some evidence that the first medical, astronomical, and alchemical translations were made during their rule. Philosophical translations, although still shrouded in obscurity, must have been initiated during this period also, as is demonstrated by the intense dialectical activity at Basrah and Damascus, in which different groups of theologians—Qadarites, Jahmites, Murjiites and Kharijites—were engaged.

With the succession of the Abbasids in 750, the capital of the Muslim empire moved to Baghdad, and the first known translations of Indian and Greek works on medicine, astronomy, and mathematics date from the reign of al-Mansur (754–775), the second member of that dynasty. But it was al-Mansur's great grandson, al-Ma'mun (813–833), who made the most determined and systematic attempt to acquire and translate the chief monuments of Greek philosophy and science. The physical embodiment of this attempt was the House of Wisdom, a center of research and translation that he founded at Baghdad in 830. Its first head was the court physician and scholar Yuhanna bin Masawayh, teacher and mentor of Hunayn bin Ishaq, who died in 873.

Hunayn was the greatest scholar in the entire history of the translation movement in Islam and one of the most outstanding intellectual figures of his age. Improving on the translation procedure initiated by his predecessors, he placed it on a sound scientific footing. The group of scholars who worked under his supervision included his son Ishaq, his nephew Hubaysh, and his disciple 'Isa bin Yahia. Hunayn's medical and philosophical translations were made in accordance with the highest standards of philological criticism and analysis. An autobiographical note on his methods informs us that very often, prior to translating a Greek work, he collated numerous manuscripts in order to establish a sound basic text. He also gives us an inkling of the scope of his medical and philosophical interests: his translations included not only the complete medical works of Galen, the Alexandrian physician and philosopher, but also Galen's paraphrases of Plato's *Sophistes*, *Parmenides*, *Cratylus*, *Euthydemus*, *Timaeus*, *Statesman*, *Republic*, and *Laws*.

In addition, Hunayn made Arabic or Syriac versions of the following Aristotelian treatises: *Categoriae*, *Hermeneutica*, part of the *Analytica Priora*, part of the *Analytica Posteriora*, *De Generatione et Corruptione*, *De Anima*, *Metaphysica L.*, and *Physica B*. In many cases, he translated the Greek text of Aristotle into Syriac, which was then rendered into Arabic by one of his associates. In this way, Hunayn and his team were able to translate into Arabic the complete medical works of Hippocrates and Galen and almost all of Aristotle and were responsible as well for most of the Arabic translations of Plato's work.

The roster of translators included, in addition to Hunayn and the members of his school, such distinguished figures as Ibn Na'imah al-Himsi (died 835), translator of the pseudo *Theology*

A theology class at al-Azhar, Cairo.

of Aristotle; Abu Bishr Matta (died 940), the greatest authority on logic of his day; Qusta bin Luqa (died 912), Hunayn's only equal in vastness of learning and mastery of Greek; Abu 'Uthman ad-Dimashqi (died 910), an important late translator of Aristotelian works; and Thabit bin Qurrah (died 901), the Harranian philosopher-mathematician who excelled particularly in the fields of astronomical and mathematical translation and authorship.

THE IMPACT OF GREEK PHILOSOPHY

The introduction of Greek philosophy had a far-reaching impact on Islamic intellectual and cultural life in the ninth century. First, it generated the urge to humanize the Islamic and Arab conceptions of man and his relation to God and the universe by bringing the Islamic precepts of right and wrong into line with the universal principles of ethical and social conduct elicited by Socrates, Plato, Aristotle, Zeno, and Plotinus. Second, it gave fresh impetus to the scholarly examination of dogma, a process started at Damascus as a result of contacts with such Christian theologians as St. John of Damascus (died about 724) and his disciples, who had been influenced by Greek rationalism as early as the rise of Christianity. Third, it brought the Arabs into the mainstream of world culture, as was demonstrated by the subsequent transmission of Greco-Arab philosophy and science to Western Europe in the twelfth century.

The spiritual, political, and moral life of Muslims revolves around the Qur'an. Although not a philosophical document, its accounts of God's creation of the world, man's position in it, and the phenomena of moral responsibility and judgment have profound metaphysical and ethical implications, which have conditioned all philosophical and theological thought in Islam. The task of justifying the introduction of Greek philosophy into the culture of Islam and of underscoring its essential conformity with the Qur'anic world view fell, first, to Abu Yusuf Ya'qub al-Kindi (died about 866), a scion of the same central Arabian tribe that gave Arabic literature one of its greatest figures, the poet Imru' al-Qays (died about 540).

Al-Kindi, the first genuine Arab philosopher, distinguished himself both as a great champion of Greek learning and as a serious student of Plato, Aristotle, and Plotinus. Moreover, as the first great Muslim thinker to wrestle with the perennial question of the harmony of philosophy and dogma, he showed a moderation almost without parallel in the subsequent history of Islamic thought. Despite his profound philhellenic sympathies, he remained thoroughly committed to the Islamic system of beliefs, as interpreted chiefly by the rationalist theologians of the eighth and ninth centuries, the Mu'tazilah. Al-Kindi was virtually alone in attempting to give philosophical support to the fundamental Qur'anic concepts of the creation of the world ex nihilo, the validity of divine revelation, the resurrection of the body, and the ultimate destruction of the world by God. Later philosophers either sacrificed a large portion of Islamic beliefs in the interest of greater consistency, as did al-Farabi (died 950) and Ibn Sina (died 1037), or repudiated them altogether, as did ar-Razi (died 925), Ibn ar-Rawandi (died 911), and others.

Abu Bakr ar-Razi, a towering philosophical and medical figure, showed a far greater zeal for the cause of reason in general, and for Greek philosophy in particular, than had his great predecessor. But whereas al-Kindi tended to follow in the footsteps of Aristotle, whom he attempted to Islamize, so to speak, ar-Razi developed a metaphysical system along Platonic and Manichean lines. Postulating five coeternal principles, his system is clearly irreconcilable with the Qur'anic concept of a unique God who created the world entirely from nothing and who will bring the whole creation to judgment at the end of time. In the beginning, according to ar-Razi, nothing existed save the five eternal principles: God, the soul, matter, space, and time. The creation of the physical world resulted from the intervention of God in a strange predicament of the soul. The soul, having developed an irrational passion for a sister principle, matter, was unable on its own to achieve union with the object of its passion. God was eventually compelled to come to the soul's rescue by creating the material universe to serve as the stage upon which the drama of the soul's passion could be enacted. At the same time, according to ar-Razi, God created man and imparted reason to him "from the essence of His divinity," ensuring thereby that the soul would eventually be roused from its terrestrial slumber and would be reminded of its destiny as a citizen of the higher, intelligible world.

In this process, philosophy plays for ar-Razi a therapeutic role. It cures the soul of its pathological impulses and enables it to be released, as the old Pythagoreans had put it, from "the wheel of birth," the eternal cycle of reincarnations it is fated to go through in this lower world. Individual souls that fall short of this philosophical ideal continue to linger in this world until they discover the restorative function of philosophy and turn toward the intelligible world. When this goal has been attained and all the souls have returned to their original abode in heaven, this world will cease to exist, and matter, which God had forcibly chained to form, will return to its original condition of absolute purity, or formlessness.

Ar-Razi's grandiose concept of the cosmic destiny of the soul ran counter to Islamic teaching not only in challenging the unqualified uniqueness of God and the time-circumscribed creation of the individual soul but also in reasserting the Platonic-Pythagorean doctrine of the transmigration of the soul. On both scores, ar-Razi deliberately disassociated himself from accepted Islamic doctrine and stood outside the pale of orthodoxy. He further compromised his position as a Muslim by disputing the validity of the whole concept of divine revelation.

Among ar-Razi's immediate successors were a religiophilosophical fraternity of dedicated scholars that flourished in Basrah. Its members called themselves the "Brethren of Sincerity." To this group we owe an anonymous collection of fifty-two "epistles" covering the whole range of philosophical and mathematical sciences current in the tenth century. The Brethren of Sincerity had a more eclectic philosophical outlook than their predecessors had and a greater dedication to the study of mathematics, which they regarded as the key to the most profitable knowledge—knowledge of the self, which is a prelude to the highest knowledge, that of God. Like ar-Razi, they accepted the transmigration of the soul, but unlike him, they proclaimed in unqualified terms the unity of philosophical and religious truth, of Greek philosophy and Islam, and indeed of Judaism and Christianity. In the last respect, this Neopythagorean fraternity, which described itself as a group of fellow-seekers after truth, stands out as one of the most tolerant of religious and philosophical groups in Islam.

Al-Farabi (died 950) and Ibn Sina (died 1037), who was known in the West as Avicenna, developed a philosophical and ethical world view derived ultimately from Plotinus and Proclus, the last two great Greek philosophers of late antiquity. Under the influence of these two pagan Neoplatonists, al-Farabi and, a generation later, Ibn Sina formulated an emanationist theory of the origination of the universe, which is in direct conflict with the Qur'anic concept of creation ex nihilo. Describing the vocation of man in purely intellectual terms, they held man's ultimate goal to be "conjunction," or contact (*ittisal*), with the active intellect, a semidivine agency interposed between God and man. This "conjunction" would ensure for man a kind of spiritual immortality, a concept at variance with the Qur'anic doctrine of bodily resurrection.

THE SYSTEMATIC REFUTATION OF NEOPLATONISM

The more conservative theologians approached the study of philosophy with grave suspicion, and regarded its dissemination as a genuine threat to orthodoxy. Their frequent reproach to the more liberal or rationalist theologians of the early period was that they had "looked into the books of philosophy." Without considering the substance of the teaching of the philosophers, many of the conservative theologians condemned the study of philosophy in its entirety, either on the ground that its protagonists advocated a strictly rationalist approach to truth, which rendered revelation superfluous, or on the ground that it was a foreign importation rooted in paganism and consequently irreconcilable with Islamic doctrine. Until about the middle of the tenth century, there were few systematic attempts to spell out the orthodox grievances against philosophy. From that point on, however, the attacks against the Greco-Arab Neoplatonists became progressively more sophisticated.

The most devastating attack on Neoplatonism was launched by al-Ghazali (died 1111) toward the end of the eleventh century. This remarkable theologian and mystic addressed himself to this task with a perspicacity and singlemindedness worthy of the greatest apologists of history. After preparing the ground by undertaking a comprehensive exposition of Neoplatonic metaphysics and cosmology on the one hand and of Aristotelian logic on the other, he launched a direct attack on the leading philosophers of Islam and their major Greek masters. His declared aim was to show the internal "incoherence" (tahafut) of the philosophers, rather than to set forth in positive terms the true creed of Islam. He recognized, however, that a distinction must be made between those aspects of Greco-Arab philosophy that are not in conflict with religious truth, such as logic and mathematics, and those that are essentially incompatible with it, such as physics and metaphysics. He argued that the religious critic of philosophy who fails to make this distinction could do the cause of religious truth as much damage as its deliberate opponent.

In general, al-Ghazali argues against the Neoplatonic concept of a Supreme Being from whom the world emanates from all eternity. He reasserts the Qur'anic concept of an omnipotent Deity whose decrees are irreversible and inscrutable and who carries out His creative designs freely and imperiously in the world. Mysticism and Asharism had enhanced his sense of the ineffable mystery of God, beside whom no genuine reality or agency exists, and had convinced him of man's utter nothingness without God. According to al-Ghazali, the Neoplatonists had seriously jeopardized this mystery and challenged the uniqueness and transcendence of the Supreme Being by subjecting Him to the categories of human thought and interposing between Him and the world a whole series of subordinate agencies, called separate intelligences and invested with divine or semidivine creative powers. Their emanationist world view is not only contradictory to Islamic dogma but philosophically untenable. The arguments adduced by them in its support are logically tenuous and inconclusive.

The refutation of Neoplatonism embodied in the at-Tahafut (Incoherence of the Philosophers) is a signal episode in the long controversy between the theologians and mystics of Islam and the Hellenistically minded philosophers. Ibn Rushd's systematic and conscientious rebuttal of al-Ghazali's treatise a century later represents an equally signal episode.

POST-AVICENNIAN DEVELOPMENTS

Despite al-Ghazali's damaging attack on Islamic Neoplatonism, Ibn Sina, its chief protagonist, remained a central figure in the subsequent history of philosophical and theological thought in Islam. Most later developments can be properly understood only against the enduring background of Avicennianism. From the eleventh century onward, Avicennianism—with its genuine basis in al-Farabi, Plotinus, and Aristotle—served as the foundation for more complex and more sympathetic developments in many theological and philosophical quarters.

The latter phases of Ibn Sina's thought were characterized by a certain ambivalence—in particular, a certain hesitation in choosing between the direct, experiential path of mysticism and the discursive processes of Greek thought. This aspect of his thought is embodied in *al-Isharat* and in a cycle of mystical or allegorical writings that depict the soul's yearning for the open spaces of the higher, intelligible world. Here Ibn Sina expresses some dissatisfaction with the methods of Peripateticism and a predilection for the direct methods of speculative mysticism, which he associated with an ancient wisdom having its roots in the East and called accordingly "Oriental wisdom" or "illumination" (*ishraq*).

Ibn Sina, however, did not work out all the implications of his anti-Peripateticism. It was left to another great mystic and philosopher of the twelfth century, Shihab ad-Din as-Suhrawardi (died 1191), to exploit to the full this latent tendency in the thought of Ibn Sina. Within the *ishraqi* tradition, as-Suhrawardi is credited with having initiated the whole process of synthesizing the methods of discursive philosophy and experiential mysticism. This achievement is hailed as an epoch-making contribution in the history of philosophy, never equaled before or after.

What sets as-Suhrawardi and the other illuminationists apart from Ibn Sina and his brand of Neoplatonism is their unqualified belief in the unity of truth, as expressed in a perennial wisdom in which religious and speculative elements have been thoroughly incorporated. This wisdom was initiated by Hermes and transmitted over the centuries by Pythagoras, Plato, Aristotle, and Zarathustra; and its genuine inheritors in Islam are not the philosophers, but rather the Sufis. In fact, as-Suhrawardi often inveighs against the Muslim Peripatetics in the name of a pure Aristotelianism, which he claims they have either misunderstood or distorted. It is noteworthy, however, that it is the pseudo Aristotle, Plotinus, of the apocryphal *Theology* who is the prime target of as-Suhrawardi's reaction against Muslim Peripateticism.

IBN KHALDUN OF TUNIS, SOCIOLOGIST AND PHILOSOPHER OF HISTORY

Antiphilosophical reaction received support in the fourteenth century from an unexpected quarter. Ibn Khaldun of Tunis (died 1406), the founder of sociology and the philosophy of history in Islam, stands out as one of the major protagonists of anti-Hellenism in Islam, of whom al-Ghazali was the most eloquent. Somewhat like this illustrious theologian, Ibn Khaldun rejects the basic presuppositions of the Muslim Neoplatonists, especially al-Farabi and Ibn Sina, on religious grounds. Their doctrine of emanation, their ontology, their theory of knowledge, and their theory of human felicity are entirely groundless, according to him. Their adulation of reason and their use of the syllogistic method of proof are unavailing, insofar as they fly in the face of empirical evidence, which should guide us in our search for knowledge.

Ibn Khaldun's greatest contribution to Islamic thought, however, is his "positivist" philosophy of history and social evolution. His deference to empiricism enabled him to develop "a

كرّاسانِ وعَدَدُ أيامه تِسعَةٌ وعِشرونَ ولَيسَ فيهِ عيدٌ وصَومُ اليَومِ التّاسِعَ عَشَرَ

مِنهُ وفيهِ كَسَرَ موسى الألواحَ وفيهِ ابتَدَأَ أحصَنَ بَيتَ المَقدِسِ في الإنهِدامِ أيامَ بُختَنَصَّرَ

أيّامَهُم وفيهِ اتَّخَذَ صَنَمَ بَيتِ المَقدِسِ ووُضِعَ في المِحرابِ جُرأةً على اللهِ جَلَّ وطُغيانًا فيهِ

أُحرِقَتِ التَّوراةُ وفيهِ بَطَلَ القُربانِ

كرّاسانِ واحِدٌ وعَدَدُ أيّامِهِ ثَلثونَ وصَومُ اليَومِ الأوّلِ مِنهُ وهُوَ الَّذي ماتَ فيهِ

هارونُ بنُ عِمرانَ ورُفِعَ الغَمامُ الَّذي جُعِلَ كَرامَةً لَهُ وفي اليَومِ التّاسِعِ صَومٌ وفيهِ

أُخبِرَ وهُم في التّيهِ بِأنَّهُم غَيرُ داخِلينَ بَيتَ المَقدِسِ فأغتَمّوا وفيهِ فُتِحَ بَيتُ المَقدِسِ وخَلا حَضَرَ

وخَرِبَهُ بالحَريقِ وفيهِ خُرِّبَ بالبَيتِ خَرابَ الثّاني وحُرِثَ أيضًا وفي اليَومِ الخامِسَ

عَشَرَ صَومُ زَوالِ النّارِ عَنِ البَيتِ وهُوَ خُروجُ مُختَصَرٌ عَنهُ ورَفعُ الحَريقِ عَن خَزائنِهِ وهياكِلِهِ

وفي اليَومِ الثّامِنَ عَشَرَ مِنهُ صَومٌ شُبَّ اطفاءُ سِراجِ الهَيكَلِ بَيتِ المَقدِسِ في أيّامِ السّونِ النَّبَوّيَّةِ و

ذَلِكَ عَلامَةٌ لِغَضَبِ اللهِ عَلَيهِم

كرّاسانِ وعَدَدُ أيّامِهِ تِسعَةٌ وعِشرونَ ولَيسَ فيهِ عيدٌ وفي اليَومِ السّابِعِ مِنهُ صَومُ الخامِسَ

وهُوَ اليَومُ الَّذي رَجَعَ فيهِ الطّلاعُ إلى موسى وأخبَرَهُ بِالجَبّارينَ فإن غَتَمَ بَنو اسرائيلَ تبكَلُ

وكَذَبَ يوشَعَ بنَ نونَ فأثبَتَ لِذَلِكَ ومِنهُم مَن يَجعَلُ صَومَ هذا الشَّهرِ يَومَ الاثنَينِ والخَميسِ

science of civilization" without parallel in the history of ancient and medieval thought. The laws of this science are reducible, according to him, to a series of geographic, economic, and cultural patterns and to a certain "dialectic" of historical development, which is partly immanent, partly determined by the transcendent will of the Almighty. The positivist element in this dialectic, which has a modern ring about it, is thoroughly developed in the introduction (al-Muqaddimah) to his study of world history, a document unique in the history of Arabic literature. Although some of his predecessors, such as al-Mas'udi (died 956), al-Kindi, al-Farabi, and the Brethren of Sincerity, had touched briefly and incidentally on the topographical and demographic factors that determine the development of human character or political institutions, it is to Ibn Khaldun that we owe the systematic elaboration of a full-fledged theory of sociological determinism. His works had no parallel before the development, in relatively modern times, of those theories of historical evolution that we associate with such illustrious names as Giovanni Battista Vico (died 1744), Emile Durkheim (died 1917), and Arnold Toynbee.

THE HISPANO-ARAB INTERLUDE

During the ninth century, which witnessed the consolidation of Abbasid power in the east and the diffusion of Greek philosophy and science under the patronage of the early caliphs of Baghdad, there was a parallel development at a rival seat of power in Muslim Spain. Interest in philosophy and science began in the west during the reign of the fifth Umayyad ruler of Spain, Muhammad bin 'Abd ar-Rahman (852–886), but the process of assimilating ancient learning really got under way during the reign of al-Mustansir (961–976), who attempted to vie with his Abbasid rivals in the fine art of collecting books and patronizing scholars. Even before this, however, the political rivalries between the Umayyads of Spain and the Abbasids of Baghdad had not prevented scholars, such as Ibn Massarah (died 931) and al-Majriti (died 1008), from traveling east and bringing back with them books and ideas, thus ensuring what one may call the cultural unity of the Islamic world.

The first major writer on philosophical subjects in the west was Abu Bakr bin as-Sayigh, better known as Ibn Bajah, or Avempace (died 1138). This physician and philosopher impressed his contemporaries and disciples as an outstanding expositor of Greco-Arab philosophy, of which al-Farabi and Ibn Sina had been the great masters in the east. Enough of his work has survived to enable us to assess his role in disseminating Neoplatonic and Peripatetic ideas in the west. Although his Peripatetic learning appears to have been vast, his worldly and medical concerns apparently distracted him somewhat, for he was not always diligent in expounding philosophical doctrines. However, like Ibn Tufayl (died 1185), another major figure in the history of Hispano-Arab thought, he was certainly instrumental in stimulating the interest of his countrymen in the study of Greco-Arab philosophy. The problem that preoccupied both men was the mystical, or illuminationist, question that Ibn Sina had broached under the title Oriental Philosophy. Ibn Bajah and Ibn Tufayl wrote elaborate works setting forth the personal and social implications of this illuminationist philosophy. The prototype of the genuine philosopher, according to them, is the "solitary" man, who, though in the world, is not *of* the world

A page from The Chronology of Ancient Nations *by al-Biruni describing Nebuchadnezzar's destruction of Jerusalem.*
In the Chronology, *a comparative history of the religious and civil calendars of all the Near Eastern peoples,*
al-Biruni displays his knowledge of mathematics as well as the histories and cultures of other peoples.

and who strives constantly toward the only goal worthy of the true seeker after wisdom—"contact," or "conjunction," with the supermundane, or intelligible, world. In this contact—which is analogous to the mystic union of the Sufis, though clearly distinct from it—the soul fulfills its genuine vocation as a citizen of the intelligible world, from which it had been temporarily banished. Politically and socially, the philosopher, or solitary, can only grudgingly reconcile himself to life in a world in which he is forever a stranger. Contrary to the argument of Aristotle, political association is neither necessary nor natural for such men; it is at best a temporary misfortune that they must endure while continually struggling for deliverance.

If neither of these philosophers in the west attained the standing of their professed masters in the east, al-Farabi and Ibn Sina, the picture changed completely with the advent of Ibn Rushd in the twelfth century. Known in the West as Averroes, Ibn Rushd was probably the greatest and most faithful commentator on, and interpreter of, Aristotle between Theophrastus (died 287 B.C.) and St. Thomas Aquinas (died 1274 A.D.).

His philosophical career did not really begin until he was about forty. Introduced to the Caliph Abu Ya'qub Yusuf (1163–1184) by Ibn Tufayl, Ibn Rushd at once impressed that enlightened ruler. The caliph appointed him *qadi* (religious judge) of Seville and ordered him to comment on the works of Aristotle, which the caliph, an assiduous reader of philosophical books, had found difficult. Shortly thereafter, Ibn Rushd was made chief qadi and was attached to the court as royal physician. After a short period of estrangement during the reign of al-Mansur, son and successor of Abu Ya'qub Yusuf, Ibn Rushd was restored to favor, and the caliph, who had earlier issued an edict exiling Ibn Rushd and other scientists and philosophers, applied himself to the study of philosophy. Ibn Rushd died in 1198 at the age of seventy-two.

Although Ibn Rushd was the greatest philosopher of Islam since Ibn Sina, his only equal in the east, the differences between the two men are great. Both in their understanding of Aristotle and in their conception of the relation between philosophy and dogma, they are in radical disagreement. Ibn Rushd's religious functions, as qadi at Seville and subsequently as chief qadi at Cordoba, contributed in no small measure to his intense concern with the crucial problem of harmonizing philosophy and dogma. Whereas Ibn Sina had dealt casually, and often furtively, with this issue, Ibn Rushd wrote two of the most important works in Arabic on this perennial theme, *Fasl al-Maqal (Relation of Philosophy and Religion)* and *al-Kashf 'an Manahij al-'Adillah (Methods of Proof Concerning the Beliefs of the Community)*. To those two works must naturally be added his great philosophical rebuttal of al-Ghazali, *Tahafut at-Tahafut (Incoherence of the Incoherence)*, and his treatises on Maliki canonical theology and jurisprudence.

Al-Ghazali's attack on Muslim Neoplatonism had considerably sharpened the issue. Ibn Rushd's careful study and analysis of the Aristotelian texts had enabled him to appreciate the measure of Ibn Sina's departure from genuine Aristotelian teaching and consequently to assess the philosophical scope of al-Ghazali's onslaught. In *at-Tahafut* Ibn Rushd frequently concedes the justness of al-Ghazali's criticism and accuses Ibn Sina of having misunderstood or distorted the teaching of Aristotle. The chief deficiency of the Avicennian interpretation of Aristotle, as a matter of history, lies in the hopeless manner in which Aristotelian and Plotinian doctrine had been confused by the unfortunate influence of the pseudo *Theology*.

In general, it may be said that Ibn Rushd was primarily concerned in *at-Tahafut* with defending Aristotle, rather than Ibn Sina, against al-Ghazali. Thus, on the question of the origination of the world, he is unwilling to entertain either the Ghazalian thesis of creation in time or the Avicennian thesis of eternal emanation. The former thesis, he argues, is inconsistent with the fundamental Islamic concept of divine omnipotence, since it implies that God was able to create the world only at the given time He actually did so. The latter thesis is inconsistent with the fundamental Aristotelian dualism of form and matter and consequently is entirely alien to Aristotelian doctrine. In the Aristotelian system, the cause does not *produce* the effect out of nothing; rather, the cause *informs* the preexisting matter or, more accurately, brings the form and the matter together. As the Supreme Cause, God is simply the agent of this act of bringing together or compounding (*ribat* or *tarkib*) the two essential and eternally preexisting components of the universe, form and matter. But this act of bringing together is not an event in time; it is an eternal process, coeval with its Author, and consequently the world is the product of God's creation *ab aeterno*, from all eternity.

Unlike al-Ghazali, Ibn Rushd finds no inconsistency in the thesis of "eternal creation." Indeed, according to him, this thesis is in keeping with the concept of divine omnipotence and with those passages in the Qur'an that speak of God "ascending to the heaven which was made up of smoke" (Qur'an 41, 10) or "creating the heavens and the earth in six days, while His throne rested on water" (Qur'an 11, 9). For the first verse implies that God created the world out of a preexisting stuff, that is, smoke; the second that water, the throne of God, and the time that measures duration (six days) are eternal. The utterances of Scripture, when they do not actually corroborate the thesis of eternal creation, are at best ambiguous or equivocal. It belongs to the learned alone, as the Qur'an itself says (Qur'an 3, 5), to interpret them.

THE MIGRATION OF ARABIC PHILOSOPHY TO WESTERN EUROPE

Neither al-Ghazali's nor Ibn Rushd's strictures were able to dislodge Avicennianism completely in Muslim lands. The subsequent history of philosophy in the east, particularly in Persia, is essentially the history of illumination (*ishraq*) and of the incorporation of Avicennian ontological themes into the more philosophical forms of theology, by such theologians as Fakhr ad-Din ar-Razi (died 1209) and Nasir ad-Din at-Tusi (died 1274). Initiated by Ibn Sina, the *ishraqi* quasi-mystical current was developed by the last creative philosopher-mystic of Islam, as-Suhrawardi. The current that as-Suhrawardi unleashed continued to swell, particularly in Shiite circles in Safawid Persia. The founder of the Safawid dynasty, Shah Isma'il (1500–1524), who claimed descent from a Sufi order founded in the thirteenth century, undertook to enforce the Shiite creed throughout Persia. As a consequence, interest in philosophy and theology, which had declined during the Mongol period, revived during this reign and that of his successors. A number of scholars continued the *ishraqi* tradition during the sixteenth century— among them, Baha' ad-Din al-Amili (died 1621), Mir Damad (died 1631), and Mir Fendereski (died 1640). These men were the most important teachers of Mulla Sadra (died 1641), who is generally recognized as the greatest philosopher of Persia in modern times.

Mulla Sadra's philosophy, like that of as-Suhrawardi's, was essentially a blend of Sufism and Neoplatonism. It marked in many fundamental ways the culmination of the whole of Islamic thought, with its profound religious preoccupations, its impatience with the laborious and circuitous ways of the intellect, its predilection for the direct and secure path of mysticism, and finally its universal syncretism. Mulla Sadra's many disciples and successors attest to his influence and to the continuity of *ishraqi* thought in Persia.

It was in the Latin West that the anti-Avicennian movement championed by Ibn Rushd in the name of genuine Aristotelianism was destined to gain ground. By the end of the twelfth century, the Peripatetic and Neoplatonic legacies of the Arabs began to find their way into Western Europe. Many Hebrew scholars played the same role in transmitting the Arab heritage to the Latin West that the Syriacs had played in transmitting the Greek heritage to the Arabs in the ninth century. Most of Ibn Rushd's translators were Jewish scholars who had been drawn to the study of his writings by the high regard in which he was held by the greatest Jewish Aristotelian, Musa bin Maymun (died 1204), who is known in the West as Moses Maimonides. Most of Ibn Maymun's philosophical treatises (as distinct from his rabbinical works) were composed in Arabic, as were the works of Yahuda Halevi (died 1140), Salomon bin Gabirol (died about 1070), and others.

The Latin translations of Ibn Sina and Ibn Rushd, between the middle of the twelfth century and the beginning of the thirteenth, introduced the Christian Scholastic theologians to Greek learning, which had remained unknown in Western Europe from the time of Boethius. The rediscovery of Aristotle by St. Thomas Aquinas and his master, Albert the Great—which was due primarily to these translations—wrought a major intellectual revolution in Scholastic circles. The whole concept of Scholastic theology was bound up with this rediscovery; prior to the diffusion of Arabic Aristotelianism in the thirteenth century no genuine Scholastic synthesis would have been possible. The march of time, it is true, could not be halted. The Arabic Aristotle was soon to cede his place to the more venerable Greek. By the middle of the thirteenth century, St. Thomas, who felt the need for more direct access to the Aristotelian texts, commissioned William of Moerbeke to translate the works of Aristotle directly from Greek. On the basis of those translations, St. Thomas was to write extensive commentaries unmatched in their thoroughness except by the great commentaries of the Arabic Cordovese (or Cordobiensis), as Averroes of Cordoba is usually referred to in the Latin sources.

It is noteworthy, however, that St. Thomas—through his great teacher, Albertus Magnus of Cologne—had first come to know Aristotle in the Arabic interpretations of Ibn Sina and Ibn Rushd. Up to the sixteenth century the most important editions of Aristotle in Latin were not those of William of Moerbeke, but rather the older Latin-Arabic versions, often accompanied by the commentaries of Averroes (which have recently been reedited in Germany and the United States). During the thirteenth century, the golden age of Scholasticism, the whole intellectual scene in Western Europe was dominated by the controversies between the Latin Averroists and their opponents and between the Latin Avicennians and their opponents, as the writings of Roger Bacon (died 1294), St. Bonaventura (died 1274) and Duns Scotus (died 1308), clearly show.

The works of Arab philosophers played such a major role in the development of Western philosophy that the Renaissance painter, Raphael, in his School of Athens placed the Arab philosopher, Ibn Rushd (Averroes), among the masters of Hellenic thought. Ibn Rushd is shown at the upper left, wearing a turban.

Abu Yusuf Ya'qub al-Kindi

(801–873)

'Abdallah al-Ma'mun, the Caliph of Baghdad, lay restless in his royal chambers, brooding on his deep desire to have his reign remembered as a period of enlightenment, an era of unsurpassed scholars and great philosophers. He had almost completed plans for a magnificent House of Wisdom, a center of learning that would include a library, a translation bureau, and a school. It would be his monument, and all was finally in readiness for its construction. What was it, then, that disturbed him, now that his dream was about to become a reality? A nagging doubt kept him awake at night, an unanswered question prevented sleep: *Was his purpose truly worthy in the eyes of God?*

Was it right to spread ideas, to stimulate new thoughts, to revive the wisdom of the ancients, the Greek philosophies? Should he encourage the use of reason and logic to examine a world created by God? God's truth had been given to man by the revelations of the Prophet. But suppose reason and logic led elsewhere. If man could not prove the validity of supernatural mysteries, did that mean he disproved God? The caliph slipped into a troubled doze.

As he slept, he relaxed, the tenseness of his recent nights eased by a curious dream. Aristotle, smiling reassurance, appeared to him and touched his forehead with enlightenment. "There is no conflict," the Greek sage murmured gently. "Reason and religion are allies, not enemies." Al-Ma'mun awoke abruptly. His night visitor had disappeared, but the caliph felt a renewed confidence in his project and its value. He ordered construction of the learning center to begin immediately.

For such a caliph, at such a time, and in such a place there could probably have been no more congenial a philosopher than Abu Yusuf Ya'qub al-Kindi.

Baghdad during the reign of al-Ma'mun was perhaps the foremost cultural center in the world. Each week in the palace the caliph held scholarly sessions for the intellectuals of Islam. There they sat around a table, listening to one another's views, discussing the issues of the day, and sometimes reconciling their differences. One evening, the self-assured young philosopher al-Kindi strode into the meeting room, looked around him, then took a seat fairly close to the caliph. At that time, a man's place at the table indicated his status, and al-Kindi had placed himself in a position above a prominent theologian.

"How dare you sit above me?" complained the deeply affronted man. Al-Kindi shrugged.

"Because," he replied simply, "I know what you know, and you don't know what I know."

Al-Kindi was the first formal philosopher of Islam and the foremost philosopher of pure Arab ancestry. A devout Muslim, he felt it was his personal mission in life to try to reconcile the bitter disputes between theologians and philosophers that recurrently plagued the Arab-Islamic world. During a lifetime devoted to this cause, he learned that the role of arbiter or peacemaker can be a thankless one.

Al-Kindi defined *falsafah*, an Arabic word derived from the Greek word for philosophy, as "knowledge of things as they are in reality, according to human capacity." Truth, he claimed, is universal and supreme, and the truths of religion and philosophy are in accord.

In an effort to placate those theologians who viewed the aims of philosophy as essentially opposed to the dictates of faith and revelation, al-Kindi proposed that the holy scriptures be looked upon as allegories that can guide the thoughts of men of reason. He argued that revelation was intended for all men and that it offers ample truth to all men in accordance with their abilities to perceive and understand. The masses, he insisted, were given the gift of faith. The elite, the educated, were given the intellect to expand upon the words of revelation by applying logic and reason.

For example, al-Kindi pointed out, the Qur'an tells the Muslim that the sun, moon, stars, mountains, trees, and beasts "offer worship" to God. This is a true statement and an inspiration to all the Faithful. For the unsophisticated, however, the words evoke simply a poetic image of all creation bending in prayer, and for them that is enough. But, al-Kindi suggested, the scholar can view the universal phenomenon of worship as an obedience to the will of God. The behavior of all entities, both animate and inanimate, follows laws established by the Supreme Power.

Al-Kindi's tireless effort to make philosophy acceptable to the theologians eventually revitalized Islamic thought. But the difficulties he encountered along the way are reflected in the advice he offered to his students: "For a seeker of learning aspiring to be a philosopher," he said, "six prerequisites are essential: a superior mind, uninterrupted passion, gracious patience, a free-from-worry heart, a com-

The Great Mosque of al-Mutawakkil in Samarra, a royal city northwest of Baghdad, was built between 848 and 852. Its spiral minaret conforms to an ancient local tradition that was still popular as late as the twelfth century.

petent introducer, and a long, long time. Should one of these prerequisites be lacking, the student is bound to fail."

In his role as court physician, al-Kindi was apparently more prudent and less free of worry than he was in his tumultuous philosophical career. He advised his colleagues in the medical profession: "Take no risks, bearing in mind that for health there is no substitute. To the extent to which a physician likes to be mentioned as the restorer of a patient's health, he should guard against being cited as its destroyer and the cause of his death."

In the realm of science, al-Kindi did not produce much original work, but he did present an embryonic concept of psychophysics and wrote a series of astrological and astronomical works. An astrologer to three caliphs, he believed the science genuine, although he distinguished between true and false astrologers. Alchemists, however, he criticized, charging them with deceptive claims and vain get-rich-quick schemes. He was the first Arab writer to form a comprehensive and systematic classification of the sciences.

His ingenuity and inventiveness as a man of letters rested on his ability to coin phrases. Otherwise, his style was labored and long-winded, sprinkled with farfetched terms and idioms. He was a scholar, not a writer. He stressed the importance of using the intellect. The intelligent man who knows God and practices good works attains the highest possible good for himself, he said, since those caught up by

bodily pleasures could not achieve the perfect state. In his personal affairs, he is remembered as having been "thrifty." A contemporary, al-Jahiz, recorded his name in a *Book of Misers* written shortly before his death.

In his later life, al-Kindi fell victim to an unkind fate and to the machinations of jealous rivals. Three of the caliphs al-Kindi had served had supported philosophical thought, and he had flourished under their patronage. The unsympathetic attitude of a fourth caliph, however, brought about loss of popular prestige and personal fortune. The sixty-year-old al-Kindi suffered more when two competitors convinced the caliph that the philosopher was dangerous and untrustworthy. The ruler ordered the conspirators to confiscate the scholar's personal library, known to all of Baghdad as *al-Kindiyah*, and al-Kindi received fifty lashes. Although a friend managed to retrieve the library by means of subtle extortion, the public beating left a permanent mark on al-Kindi's spirit. He retired to his home, sad and sulky.

If pride bordering on arrogance and thrift bordering on avarice can be counted against al-Kindi, they were more than offset by his brilliance of mind and his many other virtues – intellectual courage, a love of truth, an open mind, abstinence, and patience. He viewed suffering and death as an inescapable part of human life, and he succumbed in silence and dignity. He died about 873 at the age of seventy-two.

M. A. Martin

Abu al-Walid Muhammad bin Rushd (Averroes)

(1126–1198)

"I believe the soul is immortal," declared Abu al-Walid Muhammad bin Rushd, the famed scholar, jurist, physician, and philosopher, "but I cannot prove it." This must have been a painful admission for him, for he was—above all—a supreme logician. Whereas other thinkers fell back on personal experiences and emotions to fill the gaps in their understanding, he relied on reason. Man's purpose is to discover truth, Ibn Rushd insisted, and the serious study of God and his works constitute the noblest form of worship. Scripture, properly understood, is in harmony with philosophy, properly understood. Almost all mysteries could be explained in Ibn Rushd's philosophy, and he specialized in making all things clear. His mind forged a vital link between the ancient Greek philosophies and the European Renaissance. But he could find no logic with which to prove or disprove the eternal existence of the soul.

In an age when philosophers tended to be arrogant, Ibn Rushd was humble and generous. When his friends criticized him for being charitable to his enemies, he countered easily: "There is no virtue in being generous to a friend. But he is virtuous who gives to an enemy." He did stand by his friends, however, and supported them and their reputations far more vigorously than he did his own interests. An insult to himself might pass unnoticed, but an unfair criticism of one of his friends elicited rage. Once, he soundly trounced a poet who had satirized a member of Ibn Rushd's circle.

A scholar and a perfectionist—the kind of man who would destroy the love poems he had composed in his youth because they struck him as frivolous in later years—he desired neither power nor possessions. The one strength he esteemed was learning. "In all his life he never missed an evening with reading or writing except the day he married and the day his father died," observed his biographer.

Born in Cordoba, Spain, in 1126, he came from a long line of distinguished scholars and jurists. He grew up during a golden era of Muslim culture and studied law and medicine. As an adult, he led a staid, scholarly life in Cordoba until the day his friend and mentor, Abu Bakr bin Tufayl, recommended him to the caliph at Marrakesh. Although he was a mature man of thirty-eight, Ibn Rushd was nervous in the presence of the exalted ruler. Why had he been summoned? What had Ibn Tufayl said about him? When the caliph began questioning him about philosophy, his nervousness turned to fear. Philosophy was a politically dangerous occupation. Was this a trap? Suppose he gave an improper answer?

Ibn Rushd was well versed in matters of philosophy, and as a doctor of medicine he had taken the position that scientific scholarship was not incompatible with theology and faith. "He who studies anatomy increases his belief in God," he had said frequently. But, terrified by the caliph's prodding, he denied all knowledge of philosophy. At last the caliph recognized his subject's discomfort and put him at ease. This was not an inquisition. Rather, the caliph wanted Ibn Rushd to undertake a project: to simplify philosophy and to provide a clear, accurate explanation of true Aristotelian thought. To help induce his compliance, the caliph appointed him religious judge of Seville.

Ibn Rushd composed his greatest works with the backing of this patron. He is best known for his commentaries on Aristotle, which approach the works of the master on three levels—for beginning, intermediate, and advanced students. The works ranged from simple paraphrases to line-by-line, in-depth treatments that were far longer than the Greek originals. These monumental studies by Ibn Rushd earned him the singular title "The Commentator." Translated into Latin a century later, his writings gave the Western world its first truly substantive introduction to Hellenistic philosophy.

In the great philosophical-theological disputes that raged in both the East and the West throughout the medieval period, the works of Ibn Rushd, along with those of Ibn Sina, were often condemned and banned from circulation. Nevertheless, these two giants of Arab scholarship provided the foundation on which later scholars were to build. In the West, their writings were the basic inspiration for such men as Duns Scotus, Albertus Magnus, Thomas Aquinas, and Roger Bacon.

At the age of sixty-eight, Ibn Rushd became the victim of political intrigues that resulted in the burning of his philosophical works and his banishment from court. Two years later, however, the decree against him was lifted, and he was called back to Marrakesh. He died in 1198 at the age of seventy-two.

M. A. MARTIN

ARISTOTELIS·
STAGIRITAE,
PERIPATETICORVM PRINCIPIS
DE ANIMA LIBER PRIMVS.

cum *Auerrois Cordubensis*
Commentarijs.

SVMMÆ LIBRI.　10

In Prima proponitur nobilitas, ac difficultas scientiæ
ipsius Animæ.

In Secunda Antiquorum narrantur opiniones de Animæ essentia.

In Tertia eædē confutantur opiniones: Adducunturq́
nonnullæ circa Animæ vnitatem quæstiones.

Summæ Primæ Caput Primum. Quas ob res Animæ cognitio & nobilis sit, & difficilis.

BOnorum, & hono　20
rabilium notitiam
opinantes , magis
autem alteram al-
tera, aut secundum
certitudinē , aut ex
eo quòd & melio-
rum, & mirabilio-
rū est : ppter vtra-
que hæc animæ hi-
storiam rōnabiliter vtiq; in primis ponemus. 30

QVoniam de rebus honorabilibus est scire aliquid de rebus, quæ differunt abinuicé,
aut in subtilitate, aut qa sunt
cognitæ per res digniores,&
nobiliores,necessariū est pro
pter hæc duo ponere narra-
tionem de anima positione precedenti.

Ntendit per subtilitatem confirmatio-　40
nem demonstrationis, Et intendit per
hoc,quod dixit aut quia sunt cognitæ
per res digniores & nobiliores, nobilitatem subiecti. Artes enim non differunt abinuicé,nisi altero istorum duo-
rum modorum,saut confirmatione demonstrationis,
aut nobilitate subiecti, aut vtroq;.v.g.quoniam Geometria excedit Astrologiam per confirmationem demonstrationis,Astrologia autem excedit illam nobilitate subiecti. Et dixit,necessarium est propter hæc
duo,&c,idest necessarium est,quia hæc duo inueniun-
tur in scientia de anima,vt procedat sermo de ea ante
alias scientias. Et manifestum est consyderantibus:　50
quoniam subiectum huius scientiæ est nobilius alijs:&
similiter demōstratio eius est magis firma. Et incæpit
sermocinari ita,Qm de rebus,&c.inducendo hoies ad
amorē sciæ,& sermo eius est in forma syllogistici cate-
gorici,& qsi dicit &, qa nos opinamur cp cognitio est
de rebus honorabilibus,& delectabilibus , & cp scientiæ superant se adinuicem,aut propter cōfirmationem

demonstrationis,aut propter nobilitatem subiecti, aut
propter vtrunq;,sicut inuenimus in scientia de anima,
scilicet quia superat in his duobus alias scientias, prę̄ter
scientiam Diuinam:necessarium est opinari cp scientia
animæ antecedit alias scientias : & ideo posuimus eam
inter omnia quæsita positione præcedenti.

Videtur autem & ad veritatem omnē cognitio ipsius multum conferre: maxime autem ad naturam . est enim tanquam principium animalium .

Et nos videmus etiam quód cognoscere
eam adiuuat magno iuuamento in omni ve-
ritate:& maxime in natura; est eni quási prin
cipium animalium .

Cùm demōstrauit causam,propter quam debet esse
hæc scientia magis honorabilis,& præcedéret alias scien
tias nobilitate,incæpit etiam demonstrare vtilitatem
huius scientiæ , dicendo Et nos videmus etiam quód
cognitio,&c. Et intendit per omnem veritatē scientias speculatiuas,& intendit per hoc,quod dixit & ma
xime in natura,i.& maxime in sciétia Naturali. Dein
de dedit causam,propter quā magis adiuuat Naturalé
scientiam qi aliam , dicendo est.n. * quasi principium
animalium.i.& causa l hoc est,quia cognoscere de animalibus est maxima cognitio partium naturaliū : &
anima est principium aīalium, vnde necessarium est vt
scire de aīa sit necessarium in cognitione animaliū, non
tantum vtile. Et debes scire cp iuuamentum scientiæ
animę ad alias scientias inuenitur tribus modis.Quoḿ
vnus est fm cp est pars illius sciétiæ:immo nobilissima
partium eius,sicut habet dispositionem cum scia Natu
rali.Aīalia,n.sunt nobilissima corporum gnabilium,et
corruptibilium , anima autē est nobilius omnibus, quæ
sunt in animalibus . Secundus est, quia dat pluribus
scientijs plura principia: vt scientiæ Morali, s. regendi
ciuitates,& Diuinæ. Moralis enim suscipit ab hac scia
vltimum finem hominis,in eo cp est homo, & sciétiam
suæ substantiæ,quæ sit. Diuinus autem suscipit ab ea
substantiam subiecti sui,hic enim declarabitur,qū for
mæ abstractæ sunt *intelligentiæ, & alia multa de cognitione dispositionum consequétium intelligentiam,
in eo cp est intelligentia, & intellectus . Tertius vero
est commune iuuamentum:& est facere acquirere con
firmationem in primis principijs . quoniam ex ea ac-
quiritur cognitio causarum primarū propositionum,
& cognitio alicuius per suam causam est magis firma,
quàm sui esse tantum.

Quęrimus autem contemplari,& cognoscere naturam ipsius, & substantiam : postea
quæcunq; accidunt circa ipsam: quorum alia
quidem propriæ passiones videntur, alia aūt
cōmunes,&animalibus propter illam inesse.

Et quæsitum est scire naturam,& substantiam eius:postea autem oia, quæ accidunt ei.
& existimatum est cp horum accidentiū quæ-
dam sunt passiones propriæ animæ, & quæ-
dam accidunt corpori propter animam.

Cùm demōstrauit vtilitatem huius scientiæ, incæ-
pi demonstrare intentionem suam dicendo, Et quæ-
sirum est,&c.i.& illud,quod quærendū est in hac scia,
& perscrutandum,est scię̄ animæ naturam,i. substantiam eius,deinde scire oia contingentia ei:sicut est de
alijs cōsyderandis in scia Naturali.*Cognitio, n.cuius-
libet generis,& spei nō complebitur nisi per cognitio-
nem

Vide cōtra-
dichōnl Zi
mare.

Dfia in no-
bilitate scię̄
tiarum.

Scia de aīa
ūs scias ex
cedit nobi
litate subie-
ti, & certi-
tudie demō-
strationis, ex
cepta Diui-
na.

* a.1. quod-
dam.

2

* a.1. q̄ddam

Documētū .
huiusmōram
sciæ aīæ ad
alias scias i-
uenit tribus
modis.

Idē.12. Me.
16.et.s.Cū
de et.1.hu
co.1.in latō
ne qōus ter
tiæ .
* a.1.intelli-
gentiæ.

3

a Cognitio
cuiusli ge-
neris,et spei
ei nō com-
plet nisl per
cognitiones

Latin translation of Aristotle's *de Anima* with *commentaries by Ibn Rushd*.

'Abd ar-Rahman bin Muhammad bin Khaldun
(1332–1406)

Every era is a modern era. Each generation of young people has no doubt that its way is the best way, that its methods are the most efficient, most up-to-date, ever devised. But, surprisingly, the roots of new ideas, the prototypes of modern concepts, often reach deep into a previous age or ages. Civilizations develop and decline, but at their height they often emulate the glory of the past.

As far as scholars are able to determine, this cyclical theory of society was first proposed by a fourteenth-century Spanish Arab, 'Abd ar-Rahman bin Muhammad bin Khaldun, who was born in Tunis in 1332. In addition to originating a philosophical approach to history, Ibn Khaldun fathered the sciences of economics, anthropology, and political science. But because he lived at a time when the Arab empire had passed its peak, his ideas were not absorbed by future generations, and his work was not carried on.

Indeed, by the time the writings of Ibn Khaldun were discovered by Western scholars, they no longer seemed new. During the European Renaissance and the European Enlightenment, other men, building slowly on the thoughts of one another, had devised similar theories and reached similar conclusions. Centuries after his death, with the social sciences already in bloom, his works were finally translated and read, and Western thinkers could only ponder in amazement his solitary achievements and wonder at the source of his genius.

In his youth Ibn Khaldun was an adventurer. A born opportunist and ambitious for fame and fortune, he was attracted to politics and had an extraordinary talent for getting in and out of trouble. In his early years he moved from court to court, involving himself in intrigues, and frequently found himself in danger and political disgrace. His wanderings gave him an opportunity to see firsthand much of North Africa, Egypt, and Spain. He studied his lords and masters from advantageous posts within their castles, as well as from their prisons and dungeons. Prompted by curiosity and blessed with an instinct for survival, he analyzed the social and political mechanics of cities, towns, and villages, trying to make sense out of apparent chaos.

By the time he was forty-five, his many enemies had seemingly put an end to his political career, and he was forced to seek asylum in the tiny village of Qal'at bin Sala-mah in Wahran (Oran) province. Middle-aged—even old by the standards of his day—he was entitled to slow down and rest. But a man has to do something with his time, even when living in seclusion.

By forcing Ibn Khaldun out of politics, his enemies had done him—and the world, as well—more good than had all his friends. As a secretary in important circles, he had established a new trend in royal correspondence, introducing eloquence and impressive rhetoric while maintaining a clear, comprehensible style. In exile he applied his talents to writing a history of the world, Kitab al-'Ibar. Al-Muqaddimah, the introductory volume, is perhaps his most penetrating composition.

The politician-turned-writer had noticed that the structured reasoning applied to theology, philosophy, and science had never been applied to history. "Why not?" he wondered, and he set himself the task of correcting this curious oversight. Surely he could show that historical events were interrelated and followed a cause-and-effect pattern. If he had once criticized philosophers for trying to explain the unexplainable and to make physical reality conform to logic, he was nonetheless confident that he could explain the science of civilization; for he had seen it all—on the battlefields, in the bazaars and villages, in the courts of the princes. His reasoning would be a posteriori.

He began by grouping historical events around peoples, dynasties, and rulers—a system that had been used to advantage by the tenth-century historian al-Mas'udi, although Ibn Khaldun was not aware of this. In analyzing society, however, the philosopher-historian did borrow an Aristotelian maxim as a starting point: Man is by nature a political animal, since he is unable to provide for his needs without the assistance of his fellow man. This dependence requires a ruler to protect the rights of individuals. A group of people bound together by common ties, such as a family, achieves its greatest strength when guided by a uniform code of beliefs. In this manner, a society is born.

Ibn Khaldun observed that a society flourishes for a period, then declines as a result of inefficiency, pomp, luxury, and corruption. A new order takes over, but the cycle continues. On explaining the downfall of societies, he suggested that civilization (urban life) corrupts an in-

A view of the medieval wall at Fez, Morocco. Ibn Khaldun's intimate knowledge of North Africa and Spain gave him a unique insight into the social dynamics of urban and rural life.

herently good or neutral human nature, and he tended to idealize "men of the desert" and their nomadic ways. "The ideal framework for Islamic life," he suggested, "is a holy city with a nomadic periphery, with the city representing the stronghold of learning and meditation and the nomadic 'hinterland' guaranteeing the constant influx of fresh elements [people unspoiled by urban culture]."

Ibn Khaldun further concluded that the manner in which people cling together or interact and the shaping of cultural character depend on such factors as climate, geography, economics, religion, and ecology—along with the revelations of God. These concepts led him to formulate a more concrete attitude toward city planning. Air pollution, physical layout, zoning, education, and city support for the arts and sciences—all these issues came under consideration. In regard to economics, commerce and inflation seemed as inevitably linked then as now. "The residents of Damascus could do without Chinese porcelain or Indian spices," Ibn Khaldun reflected, "but wealthy Damascenes will not do without them now that they are to be found in the bazaars.... A city with a large population develops a competition for goods, and the result is rising prices in the bazaars."

Closeted in a small village, Ibn Khaldun had a need that the local bazaars could not meet. His book had reached a point where he had to consult other sources, and he ventured back into Tunis. Here the sultan, now the mightiest ruler in North Africa, chose to offer him amnesty and patronage. Once again in favor, Ibn Khaldun revised part of his history and dedicated the volume to the sultan.

The past, however, repeated itself. Jealous courtiers schemed to discredit the prodigal philosopher and warned the prince to be on his guard against him. The wary sultan suggested that his protégé accompany him on his next military expedition. By this time Ibn Khaldun wanted only to live quietly and to finish his history of the world in peace. Suspecting a plot, he informed the sultan that he was preparing to embark on holy pilgrimage (this would have been a justifiable excuse from military service, had it been true) and boarded the first ship leaving the harbor. His next and last stop was Egypt, where he stayed for twenty-three years.

Although he served as a university professor, college president, judge, and diplomat (shortly before his death, he was lowered in a basket over the walls of Damascus as a member of a peace delegation to meet with the Tartar chief Tamerlane), the Egyptian people complained of his coldness, severity, ignorance of Muslim law, and pride.

Yet even his detractors had to acknowledge his eloquence and vast knowledge, particularly of affairs of state. He was a good essayist and a good critic of poetry (although his own poetic ability was limited). Overriding everything, he was an astonishing chronicler and philosopher of human events. Known to be an opportunist who changed loyalties with the swing of battle, he nevertheless recorded the cycle of his time with restraint and objectivity. Rarely flattering a personal friend or belittling an enemy, he presented an unbiased report. The new approach to history that he originated is known today as "the science of civilization." He died in 1406 at the age of seventy-four.   M. A. Martin

73

Architecture and Art

Oleg Grabar is the Aga Khan Professor of Islamic Art at Harvard University (Cambridge, Mass.). He has previously taught at the University of Michigan, where he was editor of *Ars Orientalis*. He has also served as Director of the American School of Oriental Research and of the Michigan/Harvard archaeological excavations in Syria. He is the author of *Coinage of Tulunids, Islamic Architecture and its Decoration, Sasanian Silver, The Formation of Islamic Art, City in the Desert,* and *The Alhambra.*

Architecture and Art

Oleg Grabar

From time immemorial the Arabs have been able to express their spiritual values and practical needs in visual ways that have symbolic and aesthetic qualities. Not much is known, however, about the characteristics of Arab architecture and art during the millennium that preceded the emergence of Islam in the seventh century.

We do know that the northern mercantile kingdoms of the Nabateans, of Palmyra, and of Hatra played an important role in international trade for many centuries. Their cities—Petra in Jordan, Mada'in Salih in Saudi Arabia, Palmyra in Syria, Hatra in Iraq—contain many striking sculptures and architectural monuments. But, despite a number of stylistic and functional idiosyncrasies, the aesthetic tastes of these cities came predominantly from the Hellenistic and Roman traditions of the Mediterranean or from the rich heritage of Iran.

The art of Yemen was more original, and the remains of its ancient palaces, holy places, and public works suggest a monumentality that has been preserved in Arab memory. Al-Hamadhani's *Iklil*, a tenth-century source, mentions the tall, towerlike palace of Ghumdan, with sculptures of roaring lions and a brilliantly decorated domed hall on the top. And the Ma'rib Dam was no doubt as great a work of engineering as later legend has it. But today too little is known to evaluate accurately the character of South Arabian artistic achievements.

Farther north, where the kingdoms of the Lakhmids in Iraq and of the Ghassanids in Syria were still flourishing a century before Islam, we also rely more on legends than on facts. The Lakhmid palace of Khawarnaq, for example, was celebrated by poets for many centuries. But the absence of excavations and surveys makes it almost impossible to find out whether these major centers of Arab culture before Islam had any buildings sufficiently important to deserve consideration as major works of art.

Our knowledge of Arab architecture and art improves greatly, however, with the formation of a universal Muslim culture in the seventh century. As Islam projected the Arab world from the steppes of Central Asia to the Pyrenees, artisans developed new techniques, architects created new types of monuments, older functions acquired new forms, and a new mood of visual expression permeated most of the Islamic empire. Much in this new expression had

77

earlier roots, of course. Iranian, Byzantine, Roman, Central Asian, and other motifs were adopted and used by the new civilization. But almost always these borrowings were modified and transfigured in a way that is remarkably consistent. Novelties and transformations acquired a life of their own. They grew, withered away, and revived over the centuries, becoming the visually perceptible fabric of the Muslim world. They provided the Faithful with a recognizable setting from Morocco to Indonesia and made non-Muslims aware of the presence of a unique phenomenon.

What are these novelties and transformations? How should we define their unique qualities? Can we explain them? Can and should we draw distinctions between what is Arab and what is Muslim? What forces over the centuries affected their development?

Before we probe for answers to these and other questions, one note of caution must be struck. The political, social, religious, and intellectual components of the Muslim world did not remain static over the centuries; generalizations or conclusions valid for one period or one area are not necessarily true for a later time or for another region. In the seventh and eighth centuries, a synthesis was created between the new needs and aspirations of Islam and the immensely rich artistic vocabulary of earlier civilizations. This synthesis can appropriately be called Arab because the dominant impetus for its creation lay in the taste and the requirements of the Arab leaders of early Islam in Syria and Iraq, even when newly converted non-Arabs or even non-Muslims were involved in its making. The geographical expansion of the Muslim world carried this Arab synthesis from Spain to eastern Iran; both the mosque of Cordoba and the ceramics of Nishapur illustrate its characteristics.

By the tenth century, however, all sorts of centrifugal forces had acted to break up the striking unity of earlier centuries. With the Iranian renaissance and, later, with the creation of a Turkified Anatolia and the growth of Berber dynasties in North Africa, ethnic distinctions appeared. These distinctions were at times tied to political and religious differences, although always under the broad umbrella of an Islamic way of life. The Arabic language remained the principal medium of intellectual discourse until well into the thirteenth century, but by the end of the tenth century literary creativity had already begun to develop in other languages, most significantly in Persian. As far as the arts are concerned, the developments that occurred in the Iranian world in the tenth century prefigure strictly Iranian developments, and the occasional appearance of these forms in the Arab world represents the influence of a related but different artistic tradition. From the tenth or eleventh century onward, Arab art flourished in a smaller area, approximating the region known as the Arab world today: the Fertile Crescent, the Arabian Peninsula, Egypt, North Africa, and, of course, Spain, the one major Arab center that was eventually lost to Islam.

After the destructive Mongol invasion of the thirteenth century, cultural differences within the Islamic empire became politicized. Baghdad and most of the Tigris valley became enmeshed in the complex dynastic struggles of Iran. The middle Euphrates valley became the easternmost outpost of the Mamluk world, which was centered on Cairo. Although practical leadership during the Mamluk centuries was in the hands of Turkic and Circassian emirs, the arts reflected a fascinating symbiosis of local Egyptian, Syrian, or Palestinian traditions and two

78

The facade of the Treasury Building at Petra, capital of the Nabatean Kingdom.

broader tendencies—the expression of Islamic ideals and the development of an aristocratic art of princes.

The Maghreb and Spain, of course, were not affected by the Mongol onslaught, but a number of other factors modified their character after the middle of the thirteenth century. In Spain, Christian pressures grew irresistible. Despite its brilliant culture, the last Arab kingdom of Spain survived until 1492 on only a minute segment of its former possessions. In North Africa, the ravage of Tunisia in the eleventh century made contacts with the east more difficult and less frequent. As a result local dynasties in Tunisia and in Morocco tended to develop within closed worlds of intense conservatism, limited in contacts with the outside world, endlessly refining the earlier cultural traits of the Muslim west. This interiorization of Maghrebi culture was perpetuated by the constant influx into North Africa of Andalusian Muslims, refugees from Spain, which was gradually being lost to the Christian reconquest.

The sixteenth century marks the end of this third period of Islamic-Arab history. The Ottoman Empire became the direct ruler, or at least suzerain, of the whole Arab world, except Morocco, and from Algiers to Baghdad its forms and ideas tended to be the most visible. Local traditions became restricted to the private art of houses and to the practices and techniques of artisans.

Altogether, then, there were four broad periods in the development of Arab art after Islam. The first lasted roughly until the early tenth century. It was characterized by Arab rule, and in this era it is almost impossible to make distinctions between what is Arab and what is Islamic. During the second period, from the tenth to the thirteenth centuries, Arab and other components can at times be separated from one another within a complex taste in which urban and feudal elements tend to dominate. Yet the preeminence of Cairo and of Baghdad

79

Early example (ninth–tenth century) of tin-glazed ceramic ware, Northern Iraq.

suggests that these predominantly Arab metropolises were still the intellectual and taste-making centers of a universal Islamic culture. From the late thirteenth to the early sixteenth centuries, the boundaries of the Arab world shrank approximately to what they are now, and —with a few brilliant exceptions in Spain and North Africa—its main centers were Egypt and the Mamluk provinces in Syria and Palestine. Finally, after the sixteenth century, the Arab world withdrew into its own shell, and its artistic development became very private or was relegated to folk techniques. Its architectural and artistic influence on the traditions of the lands it had occupied and on adjoining territories was, however, massive and irradicable. The Arab culture was and is a source of recurrent inspiration.

In many ways the impact of Arab-Islamic culture on other artistic traditions, especially in the West, reflected its own internal character. This was particularly so in the Middle Ages and in premodern times, when the Christian world was fascinated by the exotic quality of Islamic art. This fascination naturally expressed itself in imitation and in a serious and prolonged effort to duplicate technique. It took the West centuries to discover ceramic techniques that could match Iraqi or Egyptian creations, and until very recent times Near Eastern textiles were imported or imitated in the West. In the case of ivories, glass, or metalwork, certain types of objects—for example, the sculpted bronze animals known as *dinanderies*, Venetian inlaid metalwork, and the ceremonial ivory horns known as oliphants from southern Italy—owe many of their characteristics to Islamic models.

Along with adopting Arab techniques and types of objects, Western art also recurrently used Muslim motifs. The most obvious examples are ornamental. Imitations of Arabic writing adorn many medieval cathedrals and decorate the robes of the Virgin in countless Renaissance representations. But there are other examples as well, and it is not accidental that the Italian Renaissance used the term "arabesque" to mean intricate design. In a land like Spain, Islamic

A luster-painted ceramic jar of the Fatimid period, Cairo.

influences were immediate. Elsewhere in Europe almost all Islamic objects and a smaller number of specific motifs served for centuries as symbols of opulence and wealth. Although Westerners knew very little about the religious aspects of the art of Islam, they were remarkably aware of the Muslim world's fascination with luxury, and they were especially impressed by the means it had found to make beautiful things.

There is, however, another, perhaps subtler, and certainly much less investigated side to the impact of Muslim art and architecture on the West. During the last decades of the eighteenth century, cultivated travelers from Europe began to include Arab lands in their itineraries, and they were profoundly affected by the experience. In the writings of Victor Hugo we detect a romantic vision of the Arab world. In art the effect is at times sensuous, as in the odalisque paintings; at other times it manifests itself as a new and exciting vigor, as in some of Delacroix's paintings from Algeria. In the works of such architects as G. Jones, who made the first drawings of the Alhambra, or Bourgoin and Prisse d'Avesnes, who lived in Egypt, the Arab influence resulted in a whole new aesthetic perception that rekindled minds tired of the classical tradition. Exposed to new forms, new compositions of space, a geometric excitement, many of these men attempted, more in their teaching than in their actual buildings, to explain the meaning of Arab forms. They rarely understood these forms in their Islamic context, and they usually excerpted them from their setting. But they did incorporate them in Western architecture. The results can be seen even in early developments in American city architecture —for example, in the buildings of Louis Sullivan. The severity of American exteriors and the interest of American architects in long ornamental friezes owe something to the influence of monuments such as the *madrasah* (a religious school) of Sultan Hasan in Cairo.

The fascination with ornament and with the possibility of making objects beautiful as well as useful that characterizes so much of Western art during the late nineteenth and early twentieth centuries may not have been as immediately inspired by the Near East. But many of the ideas and motifs reflected in this period are identical with those that had for centuries inspired craftsmen in the Muslim world.

ARCHITECTURAL FUNCTIONS

The religion of Islam has neither a clergy nor a liturgy. Early Islam did not, therefore, require a holy place in which to worship. According to a celebrated tradition, wherever a Muslim is found, there is a *masjid* (literally, a place where one prostrates oneself to God, whence the Westernized word "mosque"). Only the *haram* in Makkah was truly sacred, because of its close associations with the prophetic tradition and because it indicated the *qiblah*, or direction in which to face for prayer.

Before the conquests, the very first Muslim community gathered for most occasions in the private house of the Prophet in Medina. On certain major feast days everyone went to a *musalla* (literally, a place for prayer), probably outside the town proper. In time, however, as Islam flourished and spread, Muslim communities felt an increasing need to formalize religious observances. Characterized by a cohesive sharing of common beliefs and by a carefully

82

The mihrab of the Sultan Hasan Madrasah in Cairo, an outstanding example of the use of interlocking marbles of different colors in Islamic decorative design.

regulated common way of life, Muslims demanded what we would call today "a community center"—a place in which they could pray together at appointed times; organize themselves under the leadership of the imam; pay the *zakat*, or poor tax; receive instructions in matters of faith or in practical matters, such as war or taxes; and communicate with one another on everything from gossip to political affairs. In Medina, itself, all these requirements were met in the house of the Prophet, which grew in size as the community expanded. In the lands conquered by Islam in the seventh century, every city set aside a *masjid al-jami'*, a place reserved for the whole community, and smaller *masjids* for secondary groups within the community, such as the tribes. Practically nothing is known about the latter, but the former became an essential requirement of any Muslim settlement. It served primarily as a place where all the Muslims in the community could gather together.

This functional need was the basis for the single most original creation of Arab Islam—the hypostyle mosque. At the outset, there were no obvious formal models for such large buildings, except for the public constructions of Roman times, which by the seventh century were mostly ruined and abandoned. Thanks to written records, however, it is possible today to reconstruct the process whereby the ancient hypostyle form was rediscovered and made to meet the new functions—the mapping out of a vast space, the construction of a covered area on the qiblah side, the creation of a portico around the rest of the building, and eventually the building of walls with large numbers of doors that made the mosque accessible from all directions. The earliest mosques were very simple buildings, and their artistic merits were not great. But the underlying conception of a large space, partly covered and partly open, flexible enough to suit the manifold needs of a whole community, was a strikingly contemporary idea.

The earliest functional development of the hypostyle mosque occurred primarily in the Arab settlements of Iraq, such as Basrah and Kufah. In the older cities of the Near East, most characteristically in Damascus, the simple hypostyle space that had been developed in Iraq was transformed into major works of architecture. The open space became a court, and the covered space acquired a facade fronting on the court. A higher central nave provided an axis to the composition of the mosque. The number of doors decreased, and the building lost some of its immediate accessibility. Decoration in expensive mosaics or cheaper stucco gave a new visual dimension to wall surfaces. And, most significantly, two ritually meaningful features were added: the *mihrab*, a niche in the qiblah wall of the mosque serving to commemorate the place of the Prophet and to indicate the direction of prayer; and the minaret, a tower used to call the Faithful to prayer and to symbolize the presence of the new faith.

Whether the responsibility for these developments is to be attributed to the patronage of Umayyad princes, to the tastes of new converts to Islam accustomed to settings more elaborate than the austerity of early mosques, or to changes within the community itself is a problem for arcane scholarship to investigate. What matters is that an organized, large, flexible design, featuring sunlit and shaded areas and a small number of precise symbols, spread from the Fertile Crescent, where it had been created by the Arabs of the early eighth century, to all parts of the Muslim world. This architectural form has survived as the most common type of Arab mosque until the present day, and it is also the type most commonly associated with

84

One of the finest examples of Islamic architecture,
the Kutubiyah Mosque of Marrakesh.

Islam in general. The first mosques of India and of Anatolia belonged to this type, even though Iran and, later, Turkey eventually created alternative forms.

The best-preserved examples of the Arab hypostyle mosque are the mosque of Cordoba (eighth to tenth centuries); the mosque of Kairouan (eighth to ninth centuries); the Amr, Azhar, and Hakim mosques in Cairo (seventh to eleventh centuries); the Aqsa mosque in Jerusalem (eighth to eleventh centuries, with many later changes); the mosque of Damascus (eighth century); and the great mosques in Samarra (ninth century). With a relatively small number of modifications, later mosques in Rabat, Fez, Marrakesh, Cairo (the mosques of Baybars and an-Nasir in the thirteenth and fourteenth centuries), Aleppo, and Mosul (as late as the twelfth and thirteenth centuries)—all belong to the same group; and until very recently many of them were still used for a whole range of social and pious activities, just as in early Islamic times. The differences between them involve details, such as the degree of architectural and decorative emphasis given to the area in front and around the mihrab. Kairouan and Cordoba, for example, exhibit unusually elaborate ornamentation.

Although the mosque was both functionally and formally the most distinctive and the most ubiquitous of Arab-Islamic monuments, it was not the only one with a primary religious significance. As early as the eighth century, an unusual type of building appeared, the *ribat*. The ribat was a religious institution constructed on the frontier of Islamic lands, where the military and missionary establishment defended the *dar al-Islam* ("abode of Islam") and converted non-Muslims. One celebrated example of the ribat can be found in Sousse, Tunisia. It is an austere square building with a large mosque inside and a high minaret. Other ribats exist in central Asia, but on the whole the ribat is not a very clearly differentiated form. As in the case of the later *khanqah*, an urban institution for members of religious communities, it is not easy to define.

Other types of religious buildings are far easier to distinguish, although their exact origins and at times their functions pose certain problems. Three of these are particularly noteworthy. One is the small mosque, the *masjid*, which frequently was sponsored by an individual or by a social subgroup, such as a quarter or a profession. From the tenth or eleventh centuries onward, small masjids began to proliferate in most Arab cities. At times, as in Cairo's Aqmar mosque, they are simply miniaturized hypostyle mosques. At other times, as in Toledo's Bab Mardum mosque, they are aberrant types based on one or more domed areas. When Islam was at the height of its influence, literally hundreds of these small mosques dotted the empire. Their primary importance lies in the fact that they reflected the growth of social differentiation within the Muslim world. In the history of architecture they are particularly interesting because they often exhibit innovative features, such as elaborate facades, fancy minarets, fountains, and other peculiarities that illustrate varieties of taste more personal than those found in large mosques.

Private taste and private ambitions also characterize the development of funerary architecture. Its origins in Islamic culture are rather complex, for in principle Islam prohibited any monumental commemoration of the dead as a violation of its basic egalitarianism. But a variety of factors led to a modification of this restriction. One factor was the growth of Shiism,

The interior courtyard of the Great Umayyad Mosque of Damascus.

a movement that emphasized the right to rule of the Prophet's direct descendants through his daughter Fatimah. Shiism's emphasis on a strict filiation in authority led to the appearance of cults around the direct descendants of 'Ali, a cousin and son-in-law of the Prophet. Another factor was the formation of mystical and other movements focused on holy or merely powerful individuals. To counteract the impact of Shiism and probably to redirect an endemic folk piety tied to traditional holy places, twelfth-century Sunni leadership began to encourage pilgrimages to sites related to Old Testament Prophets and to build them up. And, finally, there is little doubt that sheer human vanity played a part in the development of the mausoleum— architecture's greatest example of conspicuous consumption. The Arab world, however, never went to the extremes of Iranian and Indian Islamic architecture in the construction of funerary monuments. On the whole, the Arabs preserved a certain austerity and spiritual depth in the development of what has been called a "cult of the dead."

The groups of private mausoleums found at Aswan and in Cairo are the most noteworthy examples of monumental necropolises in the Arab world, and the sanctuaries of Abraham in Hebron and of Jonas in Ninevah are among the best examples of sanctuaries to Old Testament Prophets. The mausoleum of ash-Shafi'i in Cairo is an example of a monument built over the tomb of a religious leader. The great Shiite sanctuaries of Kerbela and Najaf are very much under Iranian influence. Royal mausoleums are found in Rabat and Marrakesh.

A unique example of commemorative building is the Dome of the Rock, the earliest (691) major work of Islamic architecture. Created as a monument to the Muslim presence in the holy city of Jerusalem, it acquired a succession of holy and mystical associations connected with the Night Journey of the Prophet to Heaven. The Haram ash-Sharif, the area surrounding the Dome of the Rock, is devoted to recollections of ancient prophets.

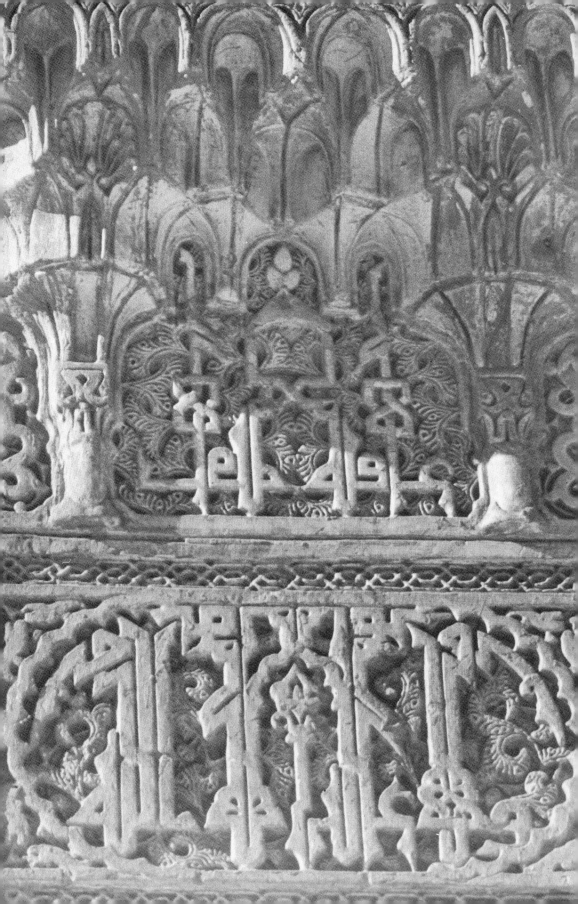

In addition to small mosques and mausoleums, Islamic piety developed a series of institutions that fulfilled socially useful purposes. Some are obvious enough, such as hospitals and schools. Others, such as the *madrasah*, are unique. The madrasah was an institution that trained spiritual and legal leaders according to the Sunni tradition. Its exact origins are still much debated, but by the twelfth century the madrasah had become one of the most typical institutions of the Muslim world. For reasons that are not entirely clear we find the largest numbers of these establishments in the cities of Syria and Egypt. They were most often privately endowed, and frequently the tomb of the founder adjoins the teaching part of the monument, thus playing down somewhat the impropriety of a separate mausoleum. The best examples are the great complexes of Qala'un, Sultan Hasan, Barsbay, and Qaytbay in Cairo. These madrasahs, constructed from the late thirteenth through the fifteenth centuries, illustrate the immense efforts made by the urban Arab world in devising unique blends of socially useful and at the same time conspicuously personal monuments. Formally most madrasahs are centered on a court with one or more *iwans*, large vaulted halls used for teaching. But their most important and most visible features are their portals and minarets, and today they compete visually with modern streets and skylines in much the same way that their founders competed to make history.

It is, of course, not surprising to discover a large number of monuments from medieval times serving a primarily religious purpose. What distinguishes these monuments in Arab lands is, first, that they were designed to serve an unusual variety of purposes and, second, that many of them fulfilled socially useful functions. The religious monuments of the Arab world reflect one of the most characteristic aspects of Islam, its emphasis on "public works," on the development of institutions designed to foster the successful operation of society.

The purely secular monuments of the Arab world have not been so well preserved. Admirable though they are at times, the city walls, gates, and citadels that protected medieval towns have frequently suffered the encroachments of growing metropolises. Still, the magnificent citadel of Aleppo, towering over the city, and parts of Cairo's and Jerusalem's walls testify to the quality of Arab military architecture, especially that constructed from the eleventh through the thirteenth centuries.

Even more original than defensive buildings are the monuments that served the peculiar needs of Middle Eastern cities. In addition to hospitals and schools, which were usually tied to religious endowments, the cities of the Arab world developed almost from the beginning a monumental architecture of trade. Recent excavation has proved that one of the earliest standing masterpieces of Islamic architecture, the large building of Qasr al-Hayr East in the Syrian Desert, was a caravanserai. All the major roads crisscrossing the Arab world were covered with these medieval equivalents of modern motels. Caravanserais also existed inside cities, usually connected with warehouses and covered bazaars. Baths were scattered throughout. Today, there are few sites where this complex combination of commercial buildings has been preserved in its entirety. But the Aleppo *suqs* (marketplaces), which enclose the congregational mosque on two sides, give us some idea what the medieval Arab city must have been like. The Arab world gave a monumental character to its economic activity centuries before the

A muqarna in the Alhambra.

The "arabesque" used as a decorative, architectural device above a portal of the Great Mosque of Cordoba.

same phenomenon appeared in Italian and northern European cities, and only the much earlier achievement of Rome is comparable to it.

A last group of architectural monuments involves royal and imperial functions. The only well-preserved royal monument is the Alhambra in Granada. Built in the fourteenth century, it consists of two main complexes of buildings, located around courts and surrounded by gardens. Regardless of its brilliance as a work of art, almost all that remain of the Alhambra today are the formal halls, which were used for a great many different purposes and endowed by poetic decorations with a complex symbolism. The Alhambra's living quarters have almost completely disappeared.

Nothing but descriptions is left of the great palaces of the Abbasid caliphs in Baghdad or of the Fatimids in Cairo. In Samarra, north of Baghdad, partial excavations provide a glimpse of the enormous ninth-century royal cities-within-a-city that are mentioned in the stories and legends surrounding Harun ar-Rashid. Unfortunately not much can be said about their specific characteristics.

Excavations in Syria, Jordan, and Iraq have brought to light a special category of palatial buildings, the so-called desert palaces of the Umayyads, which date from the first half of the eighth century. Long thought to be retreats for hunting and pleasure, they are now looked upon as residences varying in luxury and quality in the midst of agricultural latifundia. The architectural forms of such palaces as Khirbat al-Mafjar, Qasr al-Hayr West, Mshatta, Qusayr Amrah, and Ukhaydir in Iraq (second half of the eighth century) derive from Roman and Sassanian times. Their main interest lies in two features: many of them are lavishly decorated

90

with paintings, sculptures, and mosaics, thus illustrating the amazing wealth of early Arab princes; and they are almost the only existing examples of a private manorial architecture between the villas of Rome and the country palaces of the Renaissance.

CONSTRUCTION AND DECORATION

The technical vocabulary of construction and decoration used by Muslim Arabs derived almost entirely from the rich repertoire of the ancient Near East and especially of Mediterranean Roman art. Only in a few practical details, such as dams and canalizations, is an Arabian impact detectable, although further explorations may modify this judgment.

The basic forms were few and tended to be the same for religious and secular functions. The courtyard, usually porticoed, served as the center of most compositions. The main supports consisted of walls and of columns and piers surmounted by arches. Walls were made of stone throughout the Arab world, except in Iraq and, during earlier centuries, in Islamic Egypt, where brick was preferred. Wooden ceilings were common in large buildings, especially mosques, and in private dwellings, but vaults and domes predominated in military and commercial architecture from the earliest times and took over most monumental architecture from the twelfth century onward. Roofs were usually tiled. There were few formal gates and portals during the early centuries, but they increased both in number and in quality as the centuries passed. Most of them were covered with elaborately decorated half domes.

The main techniques of decoration were traditional: stone and wood sculpture, painting, and mosaics, although the latter declined quite rapidly, except in Jerusalem. In addition, however, the Islamic world adopted the Mediterranean stucco sculpture previously characteristic of lower Iraq and Iran, and stucco was a ubiquitous technique from Umayyad times onward. A more original technique, known first in the decoration of the mihrab area of the Kairouan mosque, consists of glazed and lustered ceramic plaques that give particular brilliance to the wall. Although never equaling the extraordinary quality of Iranian uses of color in architectural decoration, tiles later became typical of many Spanish and North African monuments.

With the exceptions of stucco and the occasional use of color, none of the decorative, compositional, and constructional techniques employed by the Arabs appears particularly original. Yet the collective impression of thousands of monuments, spread over 3,000 miles and built during seven centuries, clearly distinguishes Arab architecture from earlier architecture and from contemporary architecture elsewhere, even in neighboring Muslim provinces.

Of the many distinguishing characteristics of Islamic architecture in Arab lands, two in particular may be singled out. The first is a tendency toward interior refinement. Despite some striking exceptions—for example, the madrasah of Sultan Hasan in Cairo, the unique Dome of the Rock, and such details as minarets—most Arab-Islamic monuments must be seen inside for proper appreciation. The Alhambra is perhaps the most remarkable example of a monument whose exterior blandness in no way prepares the visitor for the subtle proportions, the constantly shifting effects of light and shade and of fullness and void, and the orgy of simultaneous impressions that characterize the interior.

The same wealth of unsuspected effects and contrasts strikes the visitor entering the large mosque of Damascus or the small Aqmar mosque in Cairo or the funerary ensembles in the Qarafah cemetery. It is as though the whole point of these major architectural constructions was to provide a sense of peace and quietude, or merely of otherness, of something apart from the clamor of the street. This invitation to privacy and personal fulfillment is found in architectural compositions that, almost secretively, lead through bent passages to another world. It occurs also in the modifications wrought in very traditional forms of construction. The most characteristic example is the *muqarnas*, or stalactite, a ubiquitous feature of Islamic architecture. Muqarnas cover an entire cupola in the Alhambra; zones of transition and portals in most Cairene monuments; and pilasters and capitals almost throughout.

The origin of the muqarnas is not yet known, but its basic character is fairly clear. It consists of an assemblage of small three-dimensional units with a curved section that is almost always seen as segments of vaults. Depending on the manner of assembly, it may take the form of an overhanging full or a complex void penetrating into the masonry. But in either case, even in its simplest forms, it is a fully logical, symmetrical assemblage that is, at the same time, totally arbitrary. The muqarnas is arresting because, while not seeming necessary, it captivates the attention of the viewer by its precise logic. Even in its most monumental forms, it compels the eye to stop and look deeper into the detail of the monument's very fabric.

Effects similar to that of the muqarnas are produced by the breakup of arches found in the mihrab of Cordoba's mosque, by the subtle alternation of stones of different colors found in so many Syrian and Egyptian monuments, and by the geometric subtlety of Spanish tilework. Many explanations can be provided for the fascination with interiors that is so characteristic of Islamic architecture. Perhaps it is best explained simply as an attempt to create a setting that is sufficiently different from a natural one to intimate another world—at times the mystical world of the faithful, at other times a sensuous world of pleasure.

This notion may be strengthened by consideration of the second major characteristic of Arab architectural tradition: its fascination with ornamental calligraphy and decorative design. Except in the case of very early monuments, which were still strongly influenced by classical motifs, two themes dominate most architectural decoration. The first is writing—at times small inscriptions woven into ornament, at other times boldly stated proclamations surrounding a whole monument. The inscriptions are usually either religious quotations, primarily from the Qur'an, or proud lists of princely titles. The second theme consists of designs that sometimes emphasize a specific architectural element and at other times seem purely arbitrary. These designs frequently incorporate vegetal motifs; but their dominant feature is a strong geometry, and the vegetal elements are rarely copied directly from nature. Even the baroque minarets of late Mamluk times maintain the linear geometry of carefully studied patterns. Both writing and geometry are viewed as arbitrary conventions, intellectual devices that can be manipulated to lead the viewer to a set of values other than those of the world that surrounds him. Writing leads to God or to an appreciation of princely power. Geometry is the basic but invisible skeleton of reality. The whole thrust of the decorator's talents leads him to create for man a setting other than his own, to make man think of other worlds.

Resting travelers from the Maqamat *of al-Hariri.*

Thus a curious paradox emerges. On the one hand, Islamic architecture was eminently practical. It performed the functions for which it was created. On the other hand, its decorative and expressive intent was often arbitrary and unnecessary. But the paradox may exist only if one looks at Islamic architecture through non-Muslim eyes. It dissolves if the viewer focuses on a central idea of classical Islam: the obligation to do good deeds on earth and the awareness that no reality exists outside of God. The coincidence of this obligation and this awareness is superbly illustrated by the architecture of Islam.

PAINTING AND DECORATIVE ARTS

Reflection on works of Islamic art other than buildings generally produces two immediate impressions: the virtual absence of representations of living forms and the predominance of useful and frequently luxurious objects—textiles, ceramics, glass, and metalwork. Both impressions are correct, but if they are not studied carefully they may also be misleading.

Representation of Living Forms
Neither the Qur'an nor very early Muslim practice in Arabia itself indicates the existence of a Muslim doctrine on representation of living forms. It seems that the question never really arose, for images rarely appeared in Arabia. There were a few idols, rejected by Islam as idols but not as representations, and a few imported luxury objects decorated with representations, which never seemed to have disturbed anyone. In other words, although Islam asserted with full force that only God is the Creator and only He is to be worshipped, neither one of these basic tenets was associated with the matter of representation of living forms.

93

Attitudes changed considerably, however, when the Muslim conquest brought the Arabs into immediate contact with the Mediterranean and Iranian worlds. These cultures had unusually rich histories of painting and sculpture representing virtually every imaginable subject in dozens of different styles. Moreover, the seventh century was a unique period in the history of the arts. More than in any other recorded period of history, images and representations played an essential part in the affairs of church and state. Icons abounded. People at almost all levels, from pious folk to sophisticated intellectuals, were accustomed to equating art subjects with art objects in terms of both value and effectiveness. The state, for its part, had developed an extremely complex iconography of power, whereby a sophisticated system of signs could serve an immense number of internal and external purposes.

The Arabs were clearly fascinated and tempted by this world of virtually operational representations. As Muslims they rejected the worship of images, and as still unsophisticated egalitarians they regarded elaborate ceremonies and official symbols as vain and pompous nonsense. The extent of the temptation is revealed most clearly in the Umayyad private retreats, where a wealth of images of all sorts illustrates, among many other themes, the power of the new princes. In a celebrated fresco in the Jordanian bath at Qusayr Amrah, for example, six kings of the earth are shown greeting or saluting an Arab colleague. Although many comparable later examples have disappeared, literary evidence suggests that the Umayyad examples were not unique.

At the same time, the more common Muslim attitude toward the artistic practices they encountered was to reject the use of images as symbols of the faith and of the state. In part this rejection was based directly on Islamic theology, insofar as the absolute power of God and the sin of idolatry make the utilization of representations untenable. But there are reasons to believe that theological justification followed, rather than preceded, rejection. Social attitudes and political needs may, in fact, have been far more important. The egalitarian moralism of Arab Islam inspired a mistrust of any intermediary between man and God or, for that matter, between man and secular authority. There was no clergy, and at least initially and in theory caliphs were chosen by the whole community. From a political point of view there were obvious risks involved in adopting the ways of the predominant Christian system. Imitation would have cost the new culture its integrity as a new and better way, an exemplary path for others to follow.

Muslim iconoclasm, therefore, may be properly regarded as the result of concrete historical circumstances and not as a theological doctrine, as in the Old Testament. Its survival for so many centuries and its predominant importance in the Arab world, rather than in either Iran or Turkey, are no doubt attributable to a deeply established sentiment in the mentality of the Arab world. It is not a reflection of any traditional Semitic attitude. Although the matter still requires much investigation, this continuous iconoclastic tendency may be the product of a constant interplay between traditionally image-free nomadic worlds and urban, bourgeois morality.

Be this as it may, representations of living forms played a much more limited role in Arab-Islamic art than in most other artistic traditions. Three exceptions occur, however.

Detail of a cylindrical ivory casket
made by Andalusian Umayyads.

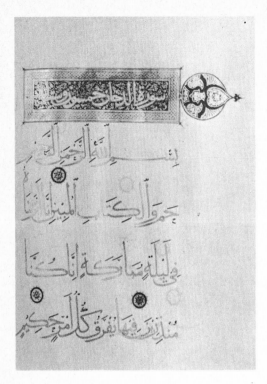

The widespread rejection of representational imagery within the religious art of Islam fostered the perfection of calligraphy and illumination as a visual art form.

In the art of princes, a much more international taste dominated, and foreign influences were more constant. As a result, lifelike representations were employed—for example, in Spanish ivories with beautiful carvings of a princely life, in the woodwork in Egypt, and in numerous fragments of wall paintings in the palaces of Samarra. Unfortunately, little remains of this great art of princes, so admired by foreign visitors. Its characteristics are more easily detected through its impact elsewhere—for example, in the sculptures of the Armenian church at Akhtamar. A central feature of this princely art of images is its emphasis on royal pastime as the main expression of power. Hunting, feasting, listening to music, and watching dancers or acrobats are the most common themes of the princely tradition. Presumably, representations of this world of pleasure and fun served to remind the viewer of the difference between the ruler and the ruled.

The second exception is more difficult to explain. In the twelfth and thirteenth centuries, almost all techniques suddenly become animated with images. Ceramics, glassware, and metalwork, produced for very broad segments of society, are covered with all sorts of images, ranging from astronomy to a princely cycle applicable to the urban bourgeoisie as well. Even animated sculpture appears in a number of official architectural monuments, such as the citadel of Aleppo, a caravanserai in Sinjar in Iraq, and a gate in Baghdad. But the most remarkable example of this explosion of images occurs in the creation of an Arab art of book illustra-

96

tion. Scientific manuals, such as the herbals of Dioscorides and of pseudo-Galen, and literary works, such as the *Kitab al-Aghani*, the ancient stories of *Kalila and Dimna*, and *Maqamat* by al-Hariri, the best example of the newer genre of picaresque adventures—all these books are illustrated with miniatures. Almost always directly connected with some textual reference, these illustrations display a striking wealth of practical observations on the life of the times. Then, in the fourteenth century, almost as abruptly as it began, this fascination with representations disappears. Why did it develop? And why at this particular time? The most plausible explanation, although not entirely satisfactory, is that the twelfth and thirteenth centuries were periods of unusually broad contacts between all parts of Europe and Asia. Everywhere, from England to China, exciting innovations appeared simultaneously at all levels of society and in all realms. It was a time of new conquests for Islam, in Anatolia and in India. The victory over the Crusaders was a major achievement. And many Arab Christians converted to Islam. In ways that are still quite unclear, the growth of images in the twelfth and thirteenth centuries seems to have been one of several ways in which the Arab world expressed the excitement and vitality of the times, a vitality soon to be sapped by the Mongol invasions.

The third exception, which occurred in folk art and folk traditions, is of lesser importance. Like any other rich culture, the Arab-Islamic world possessed a substratum of popular cults and beliefs imbued with ancient magic or pseudomagic images. Some of these appear occasionally on ceramics and may have affected certain stylistic tendencies in Egypt and Iraq.

Interesting though they are, these exceptions should not mask the fact that images are absent in most Arab-Islamic art and that representations are never used in any art form related to the Faith. This does not mean, however, that the Arab-Islamic world did not develop means to express itself visually. Its major contribution to world art lies precisely in its success in finding other ways to express its ideas.

The most important is writing. At the simplest level is calligraphy, the art of beautiful writing, with all sorts of temporal and regional differentiation in style. Calligraphic art is best known and has been best preserved in manuscripts of the Qur'an dating from the eighth or ninth century or later, but almost every Arabic manuscript exhibits a preoccupation with aesthetic values in the writing of script. In addition, a wide variety of illumination techniques were introduced to enhance the beauty of a book. The names of great calligraphers have been preserved, even though their actual works have not often been identified. Calligraphers did not always give as much care to writing on objects as they gave to writing in books. On objects they often replaced meaningful phrases with imitations of letters. Yet their writing on objects shows more personality than their writing in books. On objects the calligraphy functions almost like a signature.

The artistic function of writing was not limited to the aesthetic qualities of the script, however. Especially on objects and in architecture, the choice of texts served an iconographic function as well. Specific passages were selected in order to communicate the kind of information that images and representations provide in other artistic traditions. Thus, on many ceramics and bronzes proverbs or expressions of good wishes indicate the social purpose of the objects involved. In other instances, mostly in architecture, the choice of passages from the

During the twelfth century, the ancient art of inlaying brass or bronze with silver, copper, and gold was revived in the Arab world. Finely wrought objects of Arab design brought into Europe by merchants and veteran Crusaders were greatly admired and imitated.

Qur'an has a precise purpose, and in still other examples signatures and dates have led to any number of social and economic observations.

Beyond its iconographic and literal significance, calligraphy serves a third, more aesthetic purpose in Arab-Islamic art. When the decorators of the Alhambra covered its walls with endless repetitions of formulas such as "There is no victor but God" and when artisans inscribed objects with the simple phrase "Blessing from God" (often reduced to "Blessing" alone), it was not mere ritualistic redundancy. Their objective was to evoke the key Muslim idea that all creations and all acts occur only by the will of God. The means by which this evocation occurs is the Word, whose presence must be the constant accompaniment of man's life.

The other means whereby Arab-Islamic art was able to express ideas visually without resorting to representations is a stylistic tendency that, for lack of a better term, we may call "the arabesque." The arabesque consists of two main and interdependent features. One is the dematerialization of the natural world. Few designs in Islamic art ever strive for accurate reproductions of visible elements, even when their ultimate sources are in nature. Persons or animals are rarely depicted with the volume and spatial qualities that are theirs in reality or in the classical tradition. In general, the artist chooses a few characteristic details and reproduces them in flat, two-dimensional designs, often coloring them arbitrarily. Plants may be endowed with animal features, and human heads can appear in the midst of almost any pattern. The second consistent feature of the arabesque is that almost all arabesque designs can be analyzed and described more easily in abstract terms—dark or light, full or void, symmetrical or repetitive—than in terms of their concrete details.

By dematerializing the visible world and by substituting artificial principles of composition for natural forms, Muslim art succeeded in achieving something remarkably contemporary. It demonstrated that everything can be made beautiful and exciting and that an almost infinite number of transformations can be attached to any one motif. This development has frequently been interpreted as another example of a Muslim proclamation of God as the only creator. Whether this is correct or not, the result has been a striking freedom for Muslim artists to create an especially rich world of forms. And it is probably correct to seek meanings in these forms beyond their purely decorative value. As late as the fifteenth century, Arabic texts constantly refer to the *lifelike* quality achieved in successful artistic creativity. If this judgment is mystifying to non-Muslims, if it seems contradicted by their own experience as they look at Muslim works of art, it is perhaps because these monuments and objects reflect a reality beyond the obvious.

ART OF THE OBJECT

At the time of the European Middle Ages, Islamic objects were prized throughout the world and especially in the West. Bodies of Christian saints were wrapped in Near Eastern textiles, and several schools of ceramicists, ivory makers, and metalworkers in Europe tried for centuries to imitate Islamic techniques.

It is indeed true that Islamic objects display great technical variety and inventiveness. Ceramicists developed luster, glazes, and a host of other techniques to extend the possibilities of design and color. They sought ways to imitate the qualities of expensive gold and silver objects in cheaper clay. As a result, artisans and patrons did not feel constricted by technical limitations. Although it is a subject of much debate, the first examples of these new techniques probably appeared in Iraq in the second half of the eighth century. More or less the same pattern of development occurred in metalwork, glass, and textiles, although each medium obviously exhibits its own peculiarities.

Why did the Muslim world value the art of the object so highly? What is the meaning of the whole phenomenon? The key point is that, much earlier than any other society in the Middle Ages, Islamic culture combined egalitarian ideals and urban values. This synthesis led to the extensive development of beautiful objects that could serve formal purposes in the relationships between men as well as the needs of daily life. These objects were produced inexpensively enough to permit as many levels of society as possible to enjoy them. There is indeed a deeply democratic aspect to the creativity of Islamic art.

The most obvious kind of object used in social and personal relations—textiles—has not been well preserved or studied. We do know that the state strictly controlled the manufacture of textiles through a complicated system of private and public enterprises. Robes and cloth were given as gifts, and they indicated or symbolized honors, ranks, and achievements. They were carefully stored in private houses, and royal treasuries contained thousands of them. Although masses of textile fragments exist today, scholars are not yet able to relate them to the precise ceremonies and uses documented in literary sources. Because textiles were easily transported, they were major carriers of Arab-Islamic taste, and quite frequently the movement of textiles explains the appearance of Arab-Islamic styles and motifs in remote areas.

Gold and silver objects were also obvious gifts and symbols of importance, and a surviving description of the Fatimid treasure in Cairo provides us with a tantalizing list of magnificent works, none of which exists today. It is only through their occasional impact on later, humbler works of art and through a small number of royal ivories from Spain that we can begin to imagine what these luxurious objects might have been like.

If we are not on very secure ground in defining the official and royal objects used by rulers and presented as princely gifts, we do have a somewhat better understanding of the utilitarian art available at the lower social level of the urban world. Exquisite pottery and elaborately decorated bronzes demonstrate a considerable variety of characteristics within a single technique and indicate a wide breadth of taste in traditional Islamic culture. The mass production of artistically fine utensils transformed daily life and daily activities—eating, drinking, serving water or food, washing—into pleasing and attractive events. The introduction of sensuous pleasure into routine settings and the practice of conspicuous consumption reflect the strikingly modern attitude toward the functions of art that was so characteristic of the traditional Muslim world.

The growth of an art devoted to the creation of individualized, personal objects, as opposed to huge paintings and sculptures, indicates the emphasis the Muslim culture placed on the private world. As in any culture, there was, of course, a tendency toward sameness of taste and design at any one time. Yet no matter how repetitive any technique became, unique objects frequently were produced in the Muslim world. These original creations are the great works of art of the culture, but they came into being only because of the consistently high level of technical accomplishment within the culture as a whole. The superb "Baptistère de St. Louis" in the Louvre (actually a bronze basin inlaid with silver made for a Mamluk prince) and the *Maqamat* manuscript illustrated by al-Wasiti in 1237 are among the crowning achievements of a tradition that had existed for centuries. They were made for personal, private enjoyment. It is perhaps the greatest distinction of Islamic art that, almost from its inception, it found aesthetically brilliant ways to satisfy individual needs and desires.

Bronze lion, Cairo,
Fatimid period.

101

Alhambra, Court of the Lions

The Alhambra is one of the best known and most studied monuments of Islamic architecture. Yet, curiously, much about it is still not clearly understood. Even the purpose for which it was constructed may be less obvious than is suggested by contemporary guidebooks or by the exciting, romanticized stories of such writers as Washington Irving.

The historical background of the Alhambra is fairly clear. Although the city of Granada dates from pre-Islamic times, the superbly defensible spur of land overlooking it from the northeast was hardly used at all until the eleventh century, when minor local rulers began to develop it as a fortress and when one of the court viziers may have planned a palace there. Little is known of these early activities beyond the pale reflections preserved in chronicles and poetry. In the thirteenth century the Nasrid dynasty, the last Muslim dynasty of Andalusia, made Granada its capital and turned the hill of the Alhambra (Arabic *al-Hamra'*, the Red Palace) into a royal city. The outer walls were completed, water was brought by aqueduct from the mountain above, and a citadel was established on the westernmost part of the ridge. A mosque, baths, and houses were built for the private retinue of the princes, splendid gardens were designed and planted inside the walled area and on the slope of the mountains above it, and a royal burial place was marked off. Not much remains of most of these constructions, however, except the outer walls and the citadel, and it is virtually impossible to reconstruct the character of the Alhambra in full flower—a citadel-city-within-a-city, so typical of late medieval Islam. A few existing texts, especially the horticultural poem of Ibn Luyun, suggest the loving care that was lavished on the gardens, but their actual appearance can only be imagined.

What does remain today, reasonably well preserved, are two large architectural units, set at a right angle to each other. Each has a central open court with a "waterpiece" in the middle — a long pool in the Court of Myrtles and a fountain in the Court of the Lions. A series of rooms and halls open onto the courts, either directly or through arcades. There is a bath between the two units, and a number of smaller rooms and courts are located between the two formal units and the citadel proper. In all likelihood, living quarters were located below the Court of the Lions in an area that was rebuilt after the Christian conquest.

In accordance with traditions that date back to the Renaissance, modern custom has assigned names and functions to most of the rooms and courts. But none of the names is original, and few of the functions ascribed are likely. In reality, the Alhambra, as redesigned in the second half of the fourteenth century (probably shortly after 1369) by Muhammad V, was not intended for any specific ceremonial or practical purposes. In part, it was built as a monument to celebrate the victory of the prince over the enemies within his realm and over the Christians at Algeciras, the last significant Muslim victory in Spain. The poem inscribed on the Fountain of the Lions refers to the warriors of the holy war, and many inscriptions throughout the palace recall the prince's military prowess. But, in another and much more profound way, the Alhambra was designed as an abstract setting for whatever activity the prince chose to perform, and this chimerical quality is evident in its composition.

The striking feature of the Court of the Lions is the infinite subtlety of its forms. Real, tangible architectural structures are arranged in a way that creates fleeting, ever-changing impressions. Sturdy marble is combined with cheap stucco. The design of the court seems almost perfectly symmetrical, but in fact it is modified by axes of composition that do not correspond to the obvious features of the plan, as can be seen, for example, in the manner in which single and double columns have been ordered.

Throughout the Alhambra—especially in the Court of the Myrtles, where the effects are particularly striking—open and covered spaces are combined and contrasted according to a system whereby interiors are always in the presence of exterior spaces, with pavilions projecting into open areas. This elusive, illusory quality is found in the decoration, also. Every fragment of so-called *muqarnas* (stalactite) design is a three-dimensional shape outlining a void, forming a complex line, and having an independent design of its own on its surface. By daylight or at night, the same features appear in opposite ways, dominant or recessive. Columns that are brilliantly lighted at night recede during the day to become dark frames around sunlight.

It is possible to suggest that these extraordinary and carefully contrived contrasts have specific, yet somewhat contradictory, meanings. One interpretation projects a paradisiac setting, inasmuch as the poems inscribed under one of the domes to the side of the Court of the Lions imply that it was metaphorically the rotating dome of heaven. The other interpretation suggests an embodiment of the idea that nothing made or seen by man is real, since "there is no victor but God," as inscriptions throughout the building repeat again and again. This mystical Islamic interpretation may be the official one; but, in a deeper sense, the true meaning of the Alhambra is in the eye, the mind, and the soul of the beholder.

OLEG GRABAR

The Kairouan Mosque

The Great Mosque of Kairouan is the ancestor of all the mosques in western Islamic lands. According to tradition, the site of its *mihrab* was revealed to 'Uqbah bin Nafi', the conqueror of North Africa, who built a simple mosque there. The mosque was redone in 695 and enlarged between 724 and 743. Major renovations were carried out in 836, 862, and 875, so that Kairouan may be regarded essentially as a ninth-century monument on earlier foundations.

Whether seen from the outside or inside, it is the best preserved and in many ways the most typical of the early Islamic mosques. The exterior is simple and clear; a massive square minaret had stood there to call the Faithful to prayer and to symbolize the conquering presence of Islam. Behind the blank walls a few doors—not formal gates—lead to a courtyard, in the back of which is the huge hypostyle hall punctuated on its axis by two cupolas. The almost luminous clarity of the composition is a striking illustration of the ideals and way of life of early Islam. There is no exterior decoration; in the interior only the domical area over the *mihrab* has some ornamentation in the form of luster tiles imported from the imperial capital in Iraq. The wooden *minbar* (pulpit) is the oldest preserved in the whole of the Islamic world, and even parts of the prince's *maqsurah* or secluded praying area remain.

Early Islamic puritanism, inherent in the view of the Orthodox caliphs that nothing should divert attention from the act of prayer, is symbolized by the purity and simplicity of its architectural forms. Furthermore, the shape and size of the monument emphasize the unity of the community of the Faithful. All are equal in the single large space at Kairouan, and all may belong in it. The slight exception made to the place of the foremost was justified, not because the prince was more important than others, but because his safety required it. Several early caliphs had been attacked or assassinated in the mosque.

This open space is located inside the city, a large common area in the midst of tiny houses and lanes, a civic center in which all social activities can take place. In such mosques taxes were announced, men were drafted into the army, teaching was expounded, and political matters were settled. Even though the Mosque of Kairouan has a number of features (for example, its minaret and domes) that eventually became typical of western Islamic architecture, its basic features could be found anywhere in the Islamic world, from the steppes of Central Asia to Morocco, and at all periods. It was one of the Arabs' unique cultural contributions—effective architectural planning, responsive to social needs.

OLEG GRABAR

Great Mosque of Cordoba

The Great Mosque of Cordoba, preserved fortunately because Christian conquerors used it as a cathedral instead of destroying it, is one of the finest examples left of an early hypostyle mosque. It was begun in 785 and enlarged in 848, 961, and 987 as the city of Cordoba grew and developed. Its plan, a plethora of columns supporting arcades and covered with a flat roof, is simple and flexible. It illustrates the characteristic desire of early Muslims for a space large enough to contain the multitude of the Faithful yet suitable for teaching, private meetings, or whatever other needs the community may have felt.

The focus of the mosque was its *mihrab*. A *mihrab* is normally a semicircular niche that serves to indicate the direction of Makkah and to symbolize the place where the Prophet stood as leader of prayers. The *mihrab* of Cordoba is unique, however, in that it is a small windowless room. The effect is quite striking from afar. At a distance it becomes less a niche than an opening, dark and even mysterious, a source of divine Presence or at least a door to it. It is the first *mihrab* in Islamic architecture to which it is possible to attribute a mystical significance.

The *mihrab* was also meant to be an exquisite work of art. The Caliph al-Hakam who had it built in 961 is reported to have "ordered" the Byzantine emperor to send him a mosaicist who could decorate the *mihrab* in the same way that al-Walid I had decorated the Mosque of Damascus. The Byzantine emperor reportedly complied, sending not only a mosaicist but also three hundred and twenty bags of mosaic cubes (*tesserae*). The mosaicist, it is said, trained local workers so well that they surpassed him in ability, while from all over Andalusia people came to help decorate the monument. Whether this account is true or not, the point is that al-Hakam wanted to create a unique monument in imitation of the Great Mosque in Damascus, the first major mosque in the Muslim world.

He transformed three bays in front of the *mihrab* into a separate enclave within the mosque—a *maqsurah* or enclosure reserved for the prince. An elaborate arcade of polylobed arches was put around these bays, and each bay was covered with a fancy cupola. The principal one, which is illustrated here, has two particularly noteworthy features.

One is its system of construction. It preserved the traditional passage from square to dome through an octagonal zone of transition. But a set of eight intersecting arches were then added above the octagon. These arches may have been intended originally to function as structural ribs to distribute the thrusts from the dome to a large number of points on the square. The use of such ribs (which, centuries later, became so typical of Gothic architecture) was rare at this time, and the Muslim experiment is one of the earliest found anywhere, certainly the earliest to be found in the western Mediterranean.

But, even if the purpose of the design initially was structural, the ribs of Cordoba did not serve this one function only; eventually their masonry formed a single mass with the rest of the dome. Their more specific purpose was to break down the normal spherical space of the dome into many planes set at different angles from each other. This multiplication of planes gave a comparatively small dome a monumental character and created an illusion of great height. But, beyond these architectonic achievements, the dome illustrates a very profoundly Islamic concern: to modify the appearance of obvious or traditional shapes. In the dome, as in the polylobed arches below, the illusion was achieved by breaking forms down into smaller and smaller units, in a manner similar to the way in which contemporary poets at times reduce words to syllables or even letters.

The second noteworthy feature of this dome is its surface decoration of mosaic. This is one of the last major examples of wall mosaics in the Muslim world. Unlike the Damascus mosaics they purport to imitate, the Cordoba mosaics are limited in subject matter to writing, abstract vegetation, and simple lines. It can be argued, however, that these designs have an iconographic meaning, as do the architectural landscapes of Damascus. The vegetal motifs and the rich texture of the decoration may indeed be an intimation of a paradisiac setting in the sense that they are both stimulating to the eye and totally removed from any known reality.

It is, therefore, the divine world that is suggested by the dome in front of Cordoba's *mihrab*, as envisioned by the universal Islamic consciousness.

OLEG GRABAR

Sultan Hasan Madrasah

This most celebrated masterpiece of Cairene architecture was built between 1356 and 1363. Its purpose is clear enough: it was a *madrasah*, an institution endowed by a wealthy patron to train spiritual and legal leaders within the Muslim community. The tomb of its founder was attached to it.

The precise origin of the institution known as the *madrasah* and the time when it acquired a monumental character are still unclear. Monumental *madrasahs* were common by the twelfth century, however. From then onward, especially in Syria, Egypt, and Anatolia, they were among the most consistently endowed institutions of most Islamic cities. Since they were generally endowed privately, many of them had the patron's mausoleum attached to them. In spite of a purist Muslim interdict on the external expression of man's glory after death, these mausoleums did serve to "immortalize" their inhabitants.

The Sultan Hasan monument is not, then, typologically different in any way from a tradition that was at least two centuries old at the time of its foundation—except for two important peculiarities:

Firstly, it belongs to a rather small group of *madrasahs* that were, so to speak, ecumenical; each one of the four rites (*madhhabs*) of Sunni Islam are represented in its functional design. Around a courtyard there are four large vaulted halls (*iwans*), each of which is restricted to one rite. Each one of these four corners had, on several floors, dwellings for students and professors, and it is the windows of these rooms that are visible on the exterior of the monument.

Secondly, the founder's tomb is located in an unusual and somewhat improper site. Rather than being placed near the entrance or in some secluded corner of the building as was customary, the inordinately large tomb is situated not only on the building's main axis, but even in the direction of the *qiblah*, which indicates the direction for prayer.

It is, however, not these technical peculiarities that make the *madrasah* of Sultan Hasan such a remarkable and interesting monument. One curious feature, for example, is the name it bears. The Sultan Hasan who is buried there was a singularly unimpressive personality who was made sultan at the age of 11, deposed at 16, re-installed at 23, and killed at 26 in the year 1357. Although apparently a fairly pious young man, he does not appear to have been a significant figure in Egyptian history, and he cannot be compared to Baybars, Nasir, Qala'un, Barsbay, or Qaytbay, all rulers of these centuries who built major monuments all over Cairo. How then did a weak ruler, murdered in his youth, find the time or the support to commission the most magnificent *madrasah* in Cairo and one of the few great ones remaining in the Muslim world? Precise documents are lacking, and it is only by reflecting on the atmosphere of the times and certain characteristic aspects of Muslim piety that an explanation can be proposed. The mid-fourteenth century was the time of the Black Death as well as a period when Egypt's prosperity in terms of East-West trade was being threatened by considerable political instability. The Mamluk rulers, slave princes of Turkic or Caucasian origin, were in shaky control, while the urban bourgeoisie, who were well represented in the intellectual establishment, had considerable bureaucratic and financial power within the state. The *madrasah* of Sultan Hasan can be regarded as a monument of popular piety, built deliberately to reassemble the unraveling strands of Egyptian society. It was built in honor of a Mamluk prince, but a weak one. It emphasizes traditional Muslim learning, but it also gives a uniquely unorthodox importance to the cult of the dead. Even today folk piety has woven legends around the saintly Sultan Hasan, and women used to gather in the monument to hear stories about him. It is a monument to the complexities of the Muslim faith in the later Middle Ages. Its very magnitude and monumentality attest to the growing strength of the folk tradition in relation to that of the aristocracy.

Another striking aspect of the *madrasah* of Sultan Hasan is its physical character. It is a rare example of an urban monument that is visible from all sides. It is huge, with a gateway 26 meters high and one minaret at least 82 meters high. But its most curious distinction is its design of vertical lines, recessed windows, and walls bare except for a subdued cornice that runs all around the building. All these features are strikingly contemporary and may have inspired the American architect Louis Sullivan in his designs of urban commercial buildings in nineteenth-century America. For, regardless of the specificity of their concerns, the architects of the *madrasah* of Sultan Hasan developed architectural forms that are universally valid for the functions of a city.

OLEG GRABAR

Tulunid Wood Carving

This partially broken wooden plaque comes from Egypt, where it had probably been designed as a panel to adorn some object, possibly as architectural decoration. The beveled cutting technique employed by the artist identifies it as belonging to the second half of the ninth century. This beveling technique, which is utilized in wood, stucco, and sculpture, involves setting the two sides of any cut at different angles to the plane of the wood, thereby giving greater relief and more complex light and shade effects. It is found in nomadic art of Central Asia as early as the fourth century B.C., and it became famous in the Muslim world through its frequent use in the Abbasid capital of Samarra in Iraq, from whence it spread to all parts of the empire. The technique's appearance in Egypt is generally associated with the first semi-independent Muslim dynasty, the Tulunids, much of whose taste was inspired by Iraq.

The subject of this panel—a sitting bird, possibly a duck—is obvious enough, but the rendition is fascinatingly elusive. There is a head, a neck, and then a shape that can be interpreted as a body only because the neck and head are present. But there is more than an apparent confusion or ambiguity in the character of the bird. For the various lines and planes that identify the subject are, themselves, ambiguous. For example, in its beak the duck holds a leaf—a very ancient motif of Near Eastern art. But it is impossible to determine where the leaf begins and the beak ends. Similar, greatly simplified leaf motifs occur on the animal's body in place of feathers or wings. There is a curious unreality or impossibility in the relationship between the ingredients of the design and the creature they are supposed to depict.

This ambiguity and unreality are among the most original features of Islamic decoration, at least during the first centuries of Muslim rule. Their formal and aesthetic characteristics are quite contemporary, and it is possible that Picasso, among others, was occasionally inspired by similar designs on Iraqi pottery. But how should one explain them? Are these designs the results of a deliberate decision to represent subjects from nature in a particularly original way? Or are they pure ornament—forms that are only secondarily related to an external reality?

A possible answer is provided by an Islamic *Tradition* that supplies the following answer to a painter who asks whether he would be permitted to practice his profession when he became a Muslim: "Yes," answers the religious leader Ibn 'Abbas, "but you must decapitate animals so that they do not seem to be alive and try to make them look like flowers." In other words, represented beings should appear to be impossible in nature, for God alone is a Creator. It has further been argued that this type of representation illustrates an aspect of the medieval belief in atomism: anything visible is only accidentally bound to its apparent form, and any recomposition of its parts is possible. Whatever explanation we choose, the implication is clear. Artists of early Islam made a rational, conscious attempt to find stylistic devices that would somehow illustrate or at least suggest a uniquely Muslim view of the universe—a universe in which divine creation alone is permanent and real. At the same time, on a purely formal level, the wooden duck and other similar designs are also fascinating exercises in technical dexterity, an aesthetic act described by a great scholar of a previous generation as a "meditation"—a concentration on pure forms in which recognition of individual subjects becomes secondary to a purely sensual appreciation of a work of art.

OLEG GRABAR

Rock Crystal Ewer

Vessels made of rock crystal always figured among the most highly prized objects at Muslim courts. But only very small objects or fragments have been found in most excavations and very few complete vessels have been preserved. One of these is a ewer in the San Marco Treasury in Venice. The "San Marco" ewer has a pear-shaped body with a narrow neck and a wider spout. A single handle is surmounted by the sculpture of a horned deer, and two handsome cheetahs adorn its body, one on each side of a formal vegetal composition. The inscription says simply, "Blessings from God to the imam al-'Aziz Billah," referring to the Fatimid caliph who ruled between 975 and 996. In all likelihood it was made for the prince himself, for one other crystal of the same type has an inscription indicating that the object was made "personally" for a major dignitary of the court.

The connoisseur must admire the technical virtuosity that was involved in carving the details of flowers and animals and the delicate pattern of the handle out of such hard material. The historian can find much to fascinate him in the background of the various motifs: the cheetah of royal hunts and the royal gardens called paradises; the floral arrangement, which dates back to ancient Iranian art; the antelope peacefully at rest on the handle, which is related to a long past of Near Eastern and Central Asian art.

It is indeed an object of luxury designed for a setting of pleasure. And if its history were fully known, it would very likely illustrate a major point about Islamic art. For centuries prior to the European Renaissance, Islamic art objects were the most highly prized accoutrements sought by those who valued gracious living. And the courts of Cairo and Baghdad had developed a sumptuary art of the object that made the products of their workshops and studios the secular art par excellence throughout the Mediterranean.

Like many other objects in the San Marco Treasury, the ewer was probably taken by Venetians when they looted Constantinople in 1204. The ewer could have reached Constantinople in either of two ways. It may at one time or another have been given to the Byzantine emperor by his Fatimid counterpart, for we know that the princes of the Middle Ages regularly exchanged gifts, often of most unusual kinds. (Textiles were the most common items passed from one court to another. But one account tells of the Fatimids somehow obtaining from Byzantium a saddle that allegedly belonged to Alexander the Great. It is not reported whether either emperor actually believed the tale, which sounds like something invented by an antique dealer of yore. The point is that exchanges between princes involved not only elaborate objects but also very tall stories.)

Alternatively, the crystal ewer could have been part of the Fatimid treasure that was looted by rebelling soldiers in the middle of the eleventh century. Fortunately, the list of the looted objects has been preserved. It included ceremonial tents, Chinese ceramics, weapons, and complete miniature gardens with trees, animals, rivers and boats of gold, silver, and other precious materials. Some of these objects were probably melted down or destroyed, but others were sold, and thus all over the Mediterranean objects from Egypt became common. It would have been easy for Byzantine merchants or agents to have acquired a crystal ewer from the booty at a fairly reasonable price.

OLEG GRABAR

Frontispiece of the *Pseudo-Galen* Book of Antidotes

There are many very peculiar features about this celebrated miniature. It is found at the beginning of a manuscript that deals with snake bites and how to cure them, but it certainly has nothing to do with the subject. In the center a prince in a military fur cap is shown feasting. He holds a drink in his hand, and another military type is preparing what may be the earliest representation of shish kebab. To the side one can distinguish court attendants, one with a polo stick, another with a falcon, a third with a cup. These are all typical offices at a thirteenth-century court, and it is simple enough to conclude that this is a representation of a formal princely meal. One can even see the architectural setting of the feast, a large hall in a palace built of fancy brick and stucco. The presence of several hunters, most of them with falcons, in the upper part of the miniature further confirms this interpretation, as the hunt was a typical royal pastime.

However, two parts of this image present a problem. The lower register contains a scene that is more difficult to interpret. To the left four men on horseback seem to be arguing about something. Although one of them is holding what looks like a polo stick, they wear curiously silly white hats, not at all typical of a military aristocracy. Then to the right there is a group of veiled women and a child on camelback. All details are precise enough to imply that the artist was familiar with such practicalities of daily life, but what does this informal scene have to do with the main subject? Even more puzzling are the four men, also wearing strange headgear, working on the balcony atop the main building. They look as though they might be shoveling snow.

In other words, it is a confusing picture in which formal, official subjects are combined with scenes of everyday life. This mélange could be explained as a reference to some unique past event or set of circumstances, and it could be argued that the picture might have made very specific sense in its own time. But, since there is no way to verify this hypothesis, it may be simpler to suggest that the picture illustrates a very characteristic aspect of thirteenth-century Arab life, especially in Iraq or Syria. At that time, very different social activities intermingled much more than in previous or later centuries, when rulers tended to isolate themselves in their own world of palace and citadel. In this picture the artist has simply packed as much contemporary life as he could onto one page.

Why put such a picture at the beginning of a book on antidotes to snake bites? Because the picture was not intended to illustrate the book. The first page of a book of this period functioned more like the jacket of a modern book: it attracted a potential buyer's attention. In some cases, it was simply a personalized reference to the book's patron, like the "ex libris" of a bibliophile.

Such frontispieces were common in the twelfth and thirteenth centuries. They are part of the rather sudden rediscovery by Arab artists of human events as a major subject for illustration. Often Christian themes and ideas were included, as, for example, the use of golden haloes. But these haloes were employed as decorative devices only and were not intended to signify saintliness. All of the people in this frontispiece — and two of the birds — have them.

OLEG GRABAR

114

The "Blacas" Ewer

The "Blacas" ewer is particularly celebrated because it was one of the first pieces of Islamic metalwork to have been studied, while it was still in the collection of the Duke of Blacas. Well known as it is, however, it has never before been published and discussed in its entirety, though it exhibits many very puzzling features.

It is a rather squat, multifaceted brass object, completely covered by silver inlays. The decoration is artfully ordered in alternate rows of bands and medallions, composed in such a way that neither system overwhelms the other and each is in perfect balance with the other. An inscription on the neck provides the following information: "Engraved by Shuja' bin Man'ah al-Mawsili, in the blessed month of *rajab* of the year 629 [May, 1232] in Mosul." The ewer is thus one of the finest products of a school of metalworkers that flourished in that Iraqi city during the thirteenth century.

The technique of inlaying brass or bronze with silver (and occasionally gold or copper) was not originated within the Arab empire. Earlier examples are found in China and in the ancient Near East. But in the middle of the twelfth century this ancient technique suddenly became the most popular means of decorating metal objects. As far as we know now, the revival began in northeastern Iran and moved westward from there; throughout the thirteenth century it was a typical feature of objects from all over the Arab world. Although the technique continued to be used in Egypt and in Iran after the end of the century, it soon lost much of its effectiveness. For a variety of reasons that are not entirely clear, it was craftsmen from Mosul who specialized in the elaboration of this technique, to the extent that even objects made in Syria were actually either made by Mosul craftsmen or attributed to them.

The most captivating aspect of these objects is the richness of their decoration. On the "Blacas" ewer, for example, the main medallions contain typical scenes of what is known as "the princely cycle": courtly audiences, hunting, feasting, dancing, and music. The smaller medallions repeat the same motifs. On the neck are representa-tions of planets and of the signs of the zodiac. Two of the bands contain inscriptions expressing good wishes. The lower one is fairly straightforward, even though the writing is stylized. But the middle one boasts an extraordinary feature: the letters are almost entirely transfigured by representations of complete animals, parts of animals, and human beings engaged in a wild assortment of activities. It is a striking example of the animated writing that also developed during these most creative centuries of artistic endeavor in the Muslim world.

Although qualitatively superior to many bronzes of the time, this ewer is not unique in technique, subjects of decoration, or style. What was the point of this elaborate decoration on metal objects? Were they fancy royal objects, or can some other meaning be attached to them? There are still no definitive answers to these questions, but a few observations may be made. First of all, all the inlaid metalwork was on objects that were obviously used for daily functions, such as washing, drinking, providing light, and writing. While it is unlikely that they were used every day by everyone, few, if any, of them are suitable for ceremonial or official functions. Furthermore, many of the objects were commissioned by the urban bourgeoisie of Muslim cities; very few are specifically dedicated to ruling princes, and some even have Christian subjects combined with princely cycles and signs of the zodiac. It is not likely that all these subjects were meant to make direct and immediate reference to the topics they portray. Scenes of princely life or astrological symbols are employed in most of them as metaphors of good wishes for the user of the object, intimations of the enjoyment he would experience were he to engage in these activities. Beyond its aesthetic merits, therefore, the decoration on the "Blacas" ewer and many similar objects illustrates a deeply felt Islamic concern during these centuries with transforming human activities, even those of the most prosaic kind, into pleasurable and sensuous pastimes. Such objects, acquired or plundered by Crusaders or sold by Italian merchants, may have helped to humanize the life of the Western "barbarians."

OLEG GRABAR

Music

Ali Jihad Racy is a Professor of Ethnomusicology at the University of California at Los Angeles. He has written and lectured widely on music of the Near East and North Africa. A virtuoso performer of the *nay* and the *buzuq*, he plays a variety of Arab folk and urban music. His composition, *Ancient Egypt,* has been recorded for phonograph and he performs traditional Arab music on the phonograph record, *Taqasim: Improvisation on Arab Music.*

Music
Ali Jihad Racy

Arab music is a broad concept. It encompasses music history, treatises, genres, and instruments, as well as musically-related philosophies, attitudes, and social contexts within the Arab world. Arab music covers a vast geographical area ranging from the Atlas Mountains and parts of the Sahara in Africa to the Arabian Gulf region and the banks of the Euphrates. It displays strong aspects of unity and diversity, and it attracts the interest and attention of both the scholar and the performing artist.

Unity stems from the sharing of old musical legacies and from the presence of common elements in the various Arab musical traditions. Whether from Morocco, Egypt, or Iraq, Arabs are able to identify today with a multi-faceted musical heritage that originated in antiquity, but that gained sophistication and momentum during the height of the Islamic Empire between the eighth and the thirteenth centuries.

Since the spread of Islam from the Arabian Peninsula towards the middle of the seventh century until the present century, Arab music has been shaped by five principal processes, some purely intellectual and cultural, others political.

CONTACT WITH ASSIMILATED CULTURES

The first process took place during the early centuries of Islam, with the growth of cosmopolitan cultural centers in Syria under the Umayyads (661–750) and in Iraq under the Abbasids (750–909). The ethnic blending that occurred during these centuries brought the music of Arabia into close contact with the musical traditions of Syria, Mesopotamia, Byzantium, and Persia. This contact resulted in the cultivation of new Arab music. While retaining strong local elements, such as the singing of poetical lyrics in Arabic—the language of the Qur'an and the *lingua franca* of the Islamic Empire—this music featured new performance techniques, new aspects of intonation, and new musical instruments. Proponents of the new trend included Persians and others from non-Arabian backgrounds.

Court affluence and acquaintance with the worldly splendor of conquered empires stimulated humanistic interests and artistic and intellectual tolerance on the part of the Arab rulers. In a short time court patronage of poets and musicians became common practice, in contrast to the antipathy of some early Muslims towards music and musicians. The Abbasid caliphs al-Mahdi (reigned 775–85) and al-Ammin (reigned 809–13) are particularly known for their fondness for music. In contrast to the *qaynat*, or female slave singers, who were prevalent during the early decades, the emerging court artists were often well-educated and from distinguished backgrounds. Among such artists were the singers and scholars Prince Ibrahim al-Mahdi (779–839) and Ishaq al-Mawsili (767–850), and the *'ud* (lute) virtuoso, Zalzal (died 791), who was Ishaq's uncle.

CONTACT WITH THE CLASSICAL PAST

The second process was marked by the introduction of scholars of the Islamic world to ancient Greek treatises, many of which had probably been influenced previously by the legacies of ancient Egypt and Mesopotamia. This contact was initiated during the ninth century under the Abbasid Caliph al-Ma'mun (reigned 813–33). This ruler established *Bayt al-Hikmah*, literally "the House of Wisdom," a scholarly institution responsible for translating into Arabic a vast number of Greek classics, including musical treatises by major Pythagorean scholars and works by Plato, Aristotle, and Plotinus.

The outcome of this exposure to the classical past was profound and enduring. The Arabic language was enriched and expanded by a wealth of treatises and commentaries on music written by prominent philosophers, scientists, and physicians. Music, or *al-musiqa*, a term that came from the Greek, emerged as a speculative discipline and as one of *al-'ulum al-riyadiyyah,* or "the mathematical sciences," which paralleled the Quadrivium (arithmetic, music, geometry, and astronomy) in the Latin West. In addition, Greek treatises provided an extensive musical nomenclature, most of which was translated into Arabic and retained in theoretical usages until the present day. This nomenclature covered such concepts as intervals of various sizes, tetrachords, pentachords, octave species, consonants, and dissonants. Greek literature on music also provided new impetus for the old Semitic notion of musical influence, or the efficacy of sound. The doctrine of *ethos*, discussed in Plato's *Republic* and in other Greek sources, and the Pythagorean doctrine of the harmony of the spheres and the numerical principle governing the universe all had a strong impact upon medieval Arabic writings. They contributed to cosmological speculation linking music to such concepts as the zodiacs, the elements, the seasons, and the bodily humors.

Theoretical treatises written in Arabic between the ninth and the thirteenth centuries established an enduring trend in Near Eastern musical scholarship and inspired subsequent generations of scholars. An early contributor was Ibn al-Munajjim (died 912) who left us a description of an established system of eight melodic modes. Each mode had its own diatonic scale, namely an octave span of Pythagorean half and whole steps. Used during the eighth and ninth centuries, these modes were frequently alluded to in conjunction with the song texts included in the monumental *Kitab al-Aghani*, or *Book of Songs*, by Abu al-Faraj al-Isfahani (died 967). In this system, each mode was indicated by the names of the fingers and the frets employed when playing the *'ud*.

Lute players are among the most common themes of early Abbasid art, as in this Iraqi lusterware bowl of the tenth century.

Another major contribution was made by the philosopher al-Kindi (died about 873), who in his treatises discussed the phenomenon of sound, intervals, and compositions. Al-Kindi presented an elaboration on the diatonic 'ud-fretting known at his time and proposed adding a fifth string to the four-stringed 'ud in order to expand the theoretical pitch range into two octaves. Al-Kindi is also known for the cosmological links he made between the four strings of the 'ud and the seasons, the elements, the humors, and various celestial entities. Comparable emphasis on cosmology and numerology was presented by the Ikhwan as-Safa', "Brethren of sincerity," in their tenth century epistle on music.

One of the most prolific contributors was Abu Nasr al-Farabi (died 950), whose *Kitab al-Musiqa al-Kabir, The Grand Treatise on Music,* is an encompassing work. It discusses such major topics as the science of sound, intervals, tetrachords, octave species, musical instruments, compositions, and the influence of music. Al-Farabi provided a lute fretting that combined the basic diatonic arrangement of Pythagorean intervals with additional frets suited for playing two newly introduced neutral, or microtonal, intervals. Al-Farabi also described two types of *tunbur*, or long-necked fretted lute, each with a different system of frets: an old Arabian type whose frets produced quarter-tone intervals, and another type attributed to Khorasan with intervals based on the *limma* and *comma* subdivisions of the Pythagorean whole-tone. Discussions on the phenomenon of sound, the dissonants and the consonants, lute fretting, and references to melodic modes by specific names are also found in the writings of the famous philosopher and physician Ibn Sina, or Avicenna, (died 1037).

Another influential theorist who contributed to the knowledge and systematization of the melodic modes was Safi ad-Din al-Urmawi (died 1291). In two authoritative treatises, Safi ad-Din discussed various aspects of musical knowledge including rhythm and meter. He also expounded on the subject of melodic modes, describing the intervals of each mode in accordance with a detailed theoretical scale similar to the one found in the Khorasani *tunbur* described by al-Farabi. Accordingly, each Pythagorean whole step in the seven-tone scale was divided into two *limmas* (90-cent intervals) and a small remainder or *comma* (a 24-cent interval). Thus, it was possible to accommodate the neutral intervals found in certain modes. Safi ad-Din's contribution to modal theory had a profound influence upon later scholars and particularly upon the musical systems of contemporary Iran and Turkey. Although there is no evidence that musical notation was employed in actual performance, al-Kindi and Safi ad-Din left us fragments of songs recorded in a system of notation based on alphabetical symbols.

CONTACT WITH THE MEDIEVAL WEST

The third major process affecting Arab music was the contact between the Islamic Near East and Europe at the time of the Crusades in the eleventh, twelfth, and thirteenth centuries and during the Islamic occupation of Spain (713–1492). This contact had a widespread impact on both Islamic and European traditions. The westward movement of scientific scholarship into the Muslim universities of Spain is known to have influenced the Christian West and to have promoted the translation of Arabic works, including commentaries on Greek sources, into

Ivory plaque of the Fatimid period in Egypt.

اقرع بناص من شعر فقال لذ رياض لله حسبيب من غرزو بحر
صف مع امكان الوصل وجود السبيل فقال بياض اهل الوفا قليل
لن السمرة يا بياض أنت شاعر مفلو وأله يب أرب وبغين بعول ما

*The 'ud, known as the "amir al-tarab" or "the prince of enchantment" was a favorite
instrument among composers and amateur performers. Here, from* The Story of Bayad
and Riyad, *the courtier Bayad sings to Riyad and her handmaidens.*

Latin. Although it is difficult to assess precisely the nature and extent of the Near Eastern musical impact upon medieval Europe, such scholars as Julian Ribera, Alois R. Nykl, and Henry George Farmer have argued that substantial influence existed in areas ranging from rhythm and song forms to music theory, nomenclature, and musical instruments.

Influence in the case of instruments is indicated by name derivations: for example, the lute from *al-'ud*; the nakers, or kettledrums, from *naqqarat*; the rebec from *rabab*; and the anafil, or natural trumpet, from *al-nafir*. Added evidence comes from manuscript illustrations of instruments that have obvious Near Eastern origins. One such document is the thirteenth-century collection of songs entitled *Cantigas de Santa Maria*, prepared for the Spanish King Alfonso X, who was known as *el Sabio* (the Wise). This work was decorated with miniature illustrations in color, showing musicians, including Moors, performing on a wide variety of instruments such as the lute, the psaltery, and the double-reed shawm.

The contributions of Moorish Spain to Arab music were profound and far-reaching. The Easterners' adaptation to a new physical environment and the introduction of Eastern science and literature into settings of wealth and splendor, as represented in the courts of Seville, Granada, and Cordoba, were inspirational to the new artistic life of al-Andalus. Zaryab (died about 850) was a freed slave who moved from Baghdad to Cordoba, where he became a highly respected singer, *'ud* player, and music teacher. Zaryab is credited with compiling a repertoire of twenty-four *nawbat*, (singular *nawbah* or *nubah*), each of which was a composite of vocal and instrumental pieces in a certain melodic mode. The *nawbat* were reportedly associated with the different hours of the day. The *nawbah* tradition was largely transported to North Africa by the Muslims who were expelled from the Iberian Peninsula in the late fifteenth century.

Moorish Spain also witnessed the development of a literary-musical form that utilized romantic subject matter and featured strophic texts with refrains, in contrast to the classical Arabic *qasidah*, which followed a continuous flow of lines or of couplets using a single poetical meter and a single rhyme ending. The *muwashshah* form, which was utilized by major poets, also emerged as a musical form and survived as such in North African cities and in the Levant,

127

Tenth Century Abbasid Coin

Falling water activates the drummers on the water clock described and illustrated in
The Book of Knowledge of Ingenious Mechanical Devices by al-Jazari.

an area covering what is known historically as greater Syria and Palestine. In this area, the *muwashshah* genre became particularly popular in Aleppo, Syria.

The fourth major process influencing Arab music was the hegemony of the Ottoman Turks over Syria, Palestine, Iraq, the coasts of Arabia, and much of North Africa (1517–1917). During this four-centuries span, the center of power in the Sunni Muslim world shifted to the Ottoman court in Turkey, while Iran was gradually emerging as a separate political, cultural, and religious entity, eventually instituting Shiism as the state religion. Musically, the Ottoman period was characterized by gradual assimilation and exchange. Arab music interacted with Turkish music, which had already absorbed musical elements from Central Asia, Anatolia, Persia, and medieval Islamic Syria and Iraq. This interaction was most obvious in larger cities, particularly Aleppo, Damascus, Baghdad, and Cairo. In the rural communities—for example, among the Syrian Bedouins and North African Berbers—musical traditions apparently maintained a fair degree of continuity and stability.

During this period in Arab history, certain aspects of musical life may have resulted from broader cultural and political contacts. In the Ottoman world, musicians, like members of other professions, belonged to specialized professional guilds (tawa'if). In Egypt, such musicians included the alatiyyah, literally, "male instrumentalists," and the 'awalim, literally "learned females." According to M. Villoteau, whose extensive description of Egyptian music is part of the accounts prepared by the Napoleonic mission to Egypt, the former groups entertained male audiences, while the latter specialized in performing for female audiences. Instruments associated with professional musicians of the cities, included the 'ud, the qanun (zither) and the nay (flute) and were commonly used in Turkey and in the Arab world.

The sama'i (or Turkish saz semai) and the bashraf (or Turkish pesrev), both instrumental genres used in Turkish court and religious Sufi music, were introduced into the Arab world before the late nineteenth century. Instrumental and possibly vocal and dance forms were transmitted partly through the Mevlevis, a mystical order established in Konya, Turkey, in the thirteenth century. Known for cultivating music and including famous composers and theorists, this order spread into parts of Syria, Iraq, and North Africa. Military bands, similar to the type connected with the Janissary army, existed in various political centers of the Ottoman world. (An example found in Cairo was described by Villoteau.) With respect to theory and nomenclature, Arab and Turkish musical systems overlapped considerably. Melodic and metric modes in Turkey and in the Arab world, particularly Syria, have exhibited and still exhibit strong similarities.

CONTACT WITH THE MODERN WEST

The fifth and most recent process is the contact between Arab music and the modern West following the Napoleonic conquest of Egypt (1798–1801) and the subsequent cultural and political interaction during the nineteenth and twentieth centuries. One of the earliest manifestations of Westernization in the Arab world was Muhammad 'Ali's importation of the European military-band concept into Egypt in the early nineteenth century and the establishment of military schools in which Western instruments and musical notation were employed.

Later in the century, on the occasion of the opening of the Suez Canal, Khedive Isma'il (reigned 1863–1876) built the Cairo Opera House, which became an historical landmark and a symbol of Westernization in the Near Eastern Muslim world. The Opera House was inaugurated with the performance of Rigoletto by Verdi, in November 1869, followed by Aida in December, 1871. Isma'il, who sought to Europeanize Egypt, patronized and promoted the fame and social status of Egyptian artists, such as the female singer Almaz (1860–1896) and the male singer 'Abduh al-Hamuli (1843–1901).

Westernization was further promoted by nineteenth-century American and European Protestant missionaries in the Levant. The Protestant hymnal introduced was based on contra *facta*, or the setting of newly written religious poems to various well-known tunes, mostly European. These tunes appeared in standard Western musical notation.

The twentieth century is marked by an increase in the role of Western theory, notation, instruments, and overall musical attitudes. In his *Kitab al-Musiqa al-Sharqi*, written around 1904, the Egyptian theorist and composer Kamil al-Khula'i mentioned that the piano, the accordion, and the mouth organ were becoming common household instruments in Egypt. The twentieth century also marked the continuation and growth of a medium that had begun in the nineteenth century and flourished in Egypt: the musical theater. Dramas mainly by European authors were Arabized and presented as combinations of acting, singing, and sometimes dancing. Among the theatrical artists were the Syrian-born Abu Khalil al-Qabbani (1841–1902), who also performed at the Columbian World Fair in Chicago in 1893, and the Egyptian Shaykh Salamah Hijazi (1852–1917), a Sufi-trained singer and stage actor whose theatrical songs were heard on early recordings throughout the entire Arab world.

Between World War I and the late 1920s, Cairo witnessed the rise of a new theatrical form, a type of musical play that typically combined comedy and vaudeville and was comparable to the European operetta. Among the prime contributors to this form was the celebrated composer Shaykh Sayyid Darwish (died 1923), who is now considered the father of modern Egyptian music. By the early 1930s, the impact of Westernization on Egyptian music was considerable, as testified to in the reports issued by the Congress of Arab Music held in Cairo in 1932.

With the emergence of independent Arab states following European domination, many Arab governments accepted Western music as a fine art and as a component in formal music education. In many Arab capitals today, traditional Arab music and Western music are taught in government institutions organized in the Western conservatory tradition.

UNIFYING TRAITS OF ARAB MUSIC

Today, traits contributing to unity in Arab music are numerous. These traits may not be universally applicable, however, and their orientation and detailed features may differ from one community to another. Furthermore, because of common historical backgrounds and geographical and cultural proximity, many non-Arabs—particularly Turks and Persians— share many of these traits, a fact that enables scholars to study the Near East as one broad musical area.

One aspect of unity in Arab music is the intimate connection between the music and the Arabic language. This is demonstrated by the emphasis placed upon the vocal idiom and by the often central role played by the poet-singer. Examples are the *sha'ir*, literally "poet," in Upper Egypt and among the Syrian-Desert Bedouins, and the *qawwal*, literally "one who says," in the Lebanese tradition of *zajal*, or sung folk-poetry. This link is also exemplified in the common practice of setting to music various literary forms, including the *qasidah* and the *muwashshah*.

Another salient trait is the principal position of melody in Arab music and the absence of complex polyphony, a phenomenon distinguishing music of this part of the world, and a good portion of Asia, from the music of Europe and certain areas in Sub-Saharan Africa. Instead,

Arab music exhibits refinement and complexity in the melody marked by subtle and intricate ornaments and nuances. Melody in Arab music also incorporates microtonality, namely intervals that do not conform to the half-step and whole-step divisions of traditional Western art music.

The concept of melody is commonly connected with modality, a conceptual organizational framework widely known under the name *maqam* (plural *maqamat*). Each of the *maqamat* is based on a theoretical scale, specific notes of emphasis, and a typical pattern of melodic movement, in many instances beginning around the tonic note of the scale, gradually ascending, and finally descending to the tonic. Although it is the basis for various musical compositions, the *maqam* scheme may be best illustrated through such nonmetric improvisatory genres as the instrumental solo known in Egypt and the Levant as *taqasim*, vocal forms such as the *layali* and the *mawwal*, and religious genres such as Qur'anic chanting and the Sufi *qasidah*.

In Egypt and the Levant, theorists divide the octave scale into small microtones comparable to those discussed earlier by al-Farabi and Safi ad-Din. Several types of micro-intervals have been advocated, including the *comma* division (roughly one-ninth of a whole step), which is found in some Syrian theories. Yet, it is generally conceived that the *maqamat* are based on a referential octave scale consisting of twenty-four equal quarter-tones. Despite the essentially aural nature of Arab music, Western notation has become fully established, and extra symbols are widely used. In addition to the regular flat and sharp signs, the symbol ♭ lowers a note by approximately a quarter tone while the symbol ♯ raises a note by roughly a quarter tone.

Following is a list of the scales of *maqamat* most often used in Egypt and the Levant:

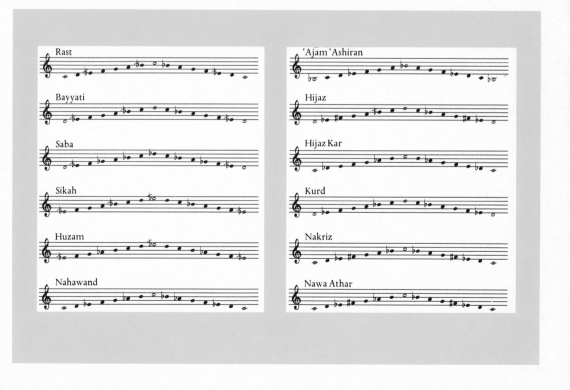

The modal conception and organization of melody is paralleled by a modal treatment of rhythm. In Arab music, metric modes are employed in various metric compositions and are widely known by the name *iqa'at* (singular *iqa'*). Influencing the nature of phrasing and the patterns of accentuation of a musical composition, these modes are rendered on percussion instruments within the ensemble, including the *tablah* (a vase-shaped hand-drum) and the *riqq* (a small tambourine). Each *iqa'* has a specific name and a pattern of beats ranging in number from two to twenty-four or more.

As presented in contemporary music theory, an *iqa'* consists primarily of rests and beats distinguished by timbre. In the Egyptian tradition, the *dumm* (represented by a note with a downward stem) indicates a deep sound produced by hitting closer to the central position of the drum or tambourine head. The *takk* (represented by a note with an upward stem) is a high pitched crisp sound produced by beating or tapping near the rim of the instrument. Although the theoretical representation of a metric mode is essentially simple, the interpretation can be highly complex and varied. While maintaining the essential features of organization and emphasis within the pattern, percussion players usually improvise further rhythmic sub-divisions and create numerous variants using a vast vocabulary of timbral effects.

Following is a list of the beat patterns of *iqa'at* most commonly heard in the contemporary music of Egypt and the Levant:

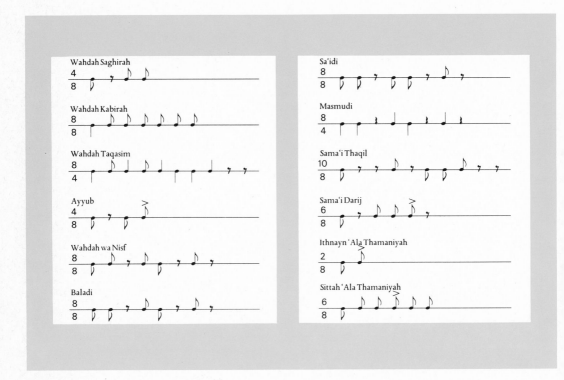

An eleventh-century ivory casket from Cordoba.

In Arab music, and in Near Eastern music in general, compound forms predominate. Such forms are based on the assembling together of instrumental and vocal pieces that share the same melodic mode. Within a compound form, the individual pieces may vary in style, improvised or precomposed, featuring a solo singer or chorus, metric or nonmetric. A compound form is usually known by its local generic name and by the name of the melodic mode it belongs to. Examples include an established Iraqi repertoire typical of the cities and known generically by the name *maqam*. Other examples are the Syrian *fasil* and the North African *nawbah*.

In Egypt, the late nineteenth early twentieth-century *waslah*, customarily incorporated a precomposed ensemble prelude, either a *dulab* or the more elaborate *sama'i*; a number of solo instrumental improvisations; a *muwashshah* sung by a small chorus; and vocal improvisations, namely the *layali*, which is a vocalization using the syllables *ya layl*, and the *mawwal*, which uses a poetical text in colloquial Arabic. The Egyptian *waslah* culminated in the *dawr*, which although basically precomposed allowed considerable freedom of interpretation by the *mutrib*, or main male vocalist, especially in passages based on call and response between him and the accompanying chorus.

Another feature of musical unity in the contemporary Arab world lies in the area of musical instruments. Instruments such as the *qanun*, *'ud*, *nay* and the Western violin are found in most urban Arab orchestras. Furthermore, certain types of instruments are frequently associated with specific social functions. Bowed instruments often accompany the solo voice. In this case, the singer and the accompanist are typically the same person. The Bedouin *sha'ir* uses the *rababah* to accompany the love song genre known as the *'ataba* and the heroic poems known as *shruqi* or *qasid*. Similarly, the Egyptian *sha'ir* uses the *rababah* to accompany his recitation of the medieval Arab epic known after its hero, Abu Zayd al-Hilali. In folk life, wind instruments are generally played outdoors; for example, the *mizmar* of Egypt and the *tabl baladi* (a large double-sided drum) are used at weddings and similarly festive events, mostly for the accompaniment of dance. At Lebanese, Syrian, and Palestinian weddings, the *mijwiz* is an adjunct to the *dabkah* or line dance.

Aspects of unity are also found in the traditional musical content of Arab social and religious life. Since Islam is the prevalent religion of the Arab world, Qur'anic chanting is the quintessential religious expression, transcending ethnic and national boundaries. This form is nonmetric, solo-performed, and based upon the established rules of *tajwid*, the Islamic principles of recitation. Of comparable prevalence is the *adhan*, or Islamic call to prayer, which is heard from the minaret at the times of prayer throughout the Arab and Muslim world. Sufi performances of music and dance have been held in private and in public for centuries throughout North Africa and the Levant. Exhibiting considerable unity in song genres and in style of performance, Sufi music has been influenced by, and in turn influenced, the various secular vocal traditions.

Finally, a more recent contributor to musical unity has been the modern electronic media. The rise of wide-scale commercial recording around 1904, the appearance of the musical film in Egypt in 1932, and the establishment of public radio stations in later years promoted the creation of a large pan-Arab audience. Today the word *ughniyyah* generally refers to a prevalent song category featuring a solo singer and an elaborate orchestra equipped with both Western and traditional Arab instruments. Presented by such celebrities as Egypt's Muhammad 'Abd al-Wahhab and the late female singer Um Kulthum, these songs are now enjoyed by a huge audience extending from Morocco to Iraq.

Despite such unity, the Arab world is also a land of musical contrasts. In a sense, Arab music is the summation of musical traditions, each of which has its own cultural and aesthetic substance and integrity. From a broader perspective, diversity exists among larger geographical areas. For example, the music of North Africa, primarily Morocco and Algeria, differs from the music of Egypt and the Levant in matters of intonation, modality, preference for certain musical instruments, and degree of exposure and retention of Andalusian musical influence. Similarly, the music of Egypt differs in matters of rhythm and intonation from the overall musical traditions of the Arabian Peninsula and Iraq.

From a closer perspective, individuality can be seen in various smaller areas and repertoires. The *Ginnawa* ethnic group of Morocco has a musical style that is closely associated with West Africa; similarities include the use of syncopated rhythm and emphasis on percussion. In Nubia and Sudan, the music employs pentatonicism, the use of five-tone scales. In Kuwait and Bahrain, pearl fishermen's songs utilize a high pitched male voice accompanied by distinct low-pitched drones, complex polyrhythmic clapping, and percussion instruments including a clay pot comparable in construction and playing technique to the *ghatam* of South India. In the Baghdadi *chalghi* ensemble accompanying *maqam* singing, the instruments usually include the *santur*, a type of hammer dulcimer, and the *jawzah*, a spike-fiddle, both having close counterparts in the musical traditions of Persia and Central Asia. Similarly, individual musical features can be found in the liturgies of various non-Muslim religious groups of the Arab world, including the Maronites of the Levant and the Copts of Egypt.

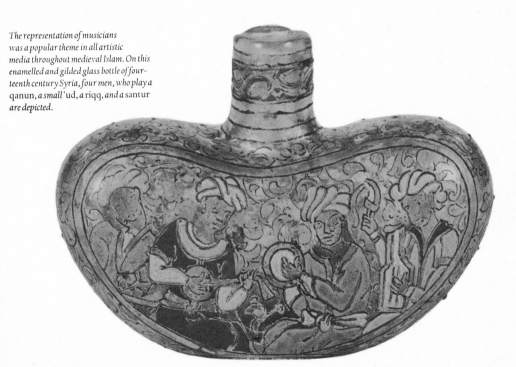

The representation of musicians was a popular theme in all artistic media throughout medieval Islam. On this enamelled and gilded glass bottle of fourteenth century Syria, four men, who play a qanun, *a small* 'ud, *a* riqq, *and a* santur *are depicted.*

'Ud

Maqrunah

Qas'ah

Musical instruments of the Arab world reflect the unity and diversity within the music itself. Certain types of instruments, including end-blown reed flutes, double-reeds, single-reeds, fiddles, plucked lutes and frame drums predominate. Yet, in each area, there may be a preference for particular instruments or instrument types. Moreover, details of construction and playing techniques are affected by local intonation and sound ideals, availability of construction materials, external musical influences, and the functions assigned to each instrument.

In the Arab world today, instruments include an important category whose domain is mostly the urban communities and whose popularity tends to transcend national and geographical barriers. In Egypt, before World War I, these instruments constituted a traditional ensemble known by the name *takht*, literally "platform." As described by Edward Lane and others, these instruments were the *'ud*, the *qanun*, the *nay*, the *riqq*, and the *kamanjah*, a spike fiddle, which during the late nineteenth century was replaced with the Western violin, but which also remained as a folk instrument under the name *rababah*. After World War I, the *takht* was gradually expanded into an orchestra that combined these Arab instruments and other instruments borrowed from the West, especially members of the violin family.

The *'ud*, typical of Egypt and the Levant, is a pear-shaped, short-necked, fretless instrument. It has five double courses of nylon or gut and metal-wound silk strings. Occasionally, a sixth single course is added. Plucked with an eagle's feather or a piece of plastic, the five courses are tuned to G', A', D, G, c. The first course may also be tuned to F'. Like its counterparts within the ensemble, the *'ud* is suitable for both solo and ensemble playing. Having a warm timbre, low tessatura, and microtonal flexibility, the *'ud* is known as *amir al-tarab*, or "the prince of enchantment." It is the favourite instrument among theorists, composers as well as amateur performers. Intricate visual ornamentation is typical of the *'ud*, especially in the rosette design and the wood inlay.

The *qanun* is a flat zither-type instrument, trapezoidal in shape. Its twenty-six triple courses of strings are made from nylon or gut and metal-wound silk. The performer plucks the strings with short horn-plectra placed between the tip of each index finger and a small metal ring. The bridge of the *qanun* rests on segments of fish skin covering small square spaces on the wood top. The strings are tuned to the basic notes of a given scale. The pitch of each course is lowered or raised by a whole step, half step, or quarter step by lowering or raising fixed metal levers that stop the strings at specific distances.

The *nay* is an open-ended, obliquely blown flute made from reed, not bamboo. Exhibiting a breathy tone, it has a wide range of almost two and a half octaves. It is also extremely expressive and capable of producing dynamic and tonal inflections. The development and use of the *nay* has been attributed to shepherds, but it is, in fact, an urban instrument. The *nay* also appears in some Sufi musical performances.

The western violin, *kaman* or *kamanjah*, has been fully adapted to the Arab musical ideal in matters of tuning and playing technique. Almost indispensable to the modern Arab ensemble, the violin in Arab music is customarily tuned to G, d, g, d'.

In the urban ensemble, two percussion instruments are essential and may appear side by side. The *riqq*, also called *daff*, is a small tambourine; the *tablah*, also called *darbukkah*, is a vase-shaped hand-drum.

In the urban music of Iraq, all of the above instruments are used. In addition, two other instruments are locally important. One is the *santur*, a hammer dulcimer with metal strings, and the *jawzah*, a four-string spike-fiddle whose sound box is part of a coconut shell covered with skin. These instruments are members of the traditional ensemble that accompanies Iraqi *maqam* singing.

In the urban traditions of North Africa, other instruments are essential. Among them is the Andalusian *'ud* of Tunisia. Having a fretted neck, this *'ud* type has four double-courses of strings. Also included is the Moroccan Moorish *rabab*, a small boat-shaped fiddle whose appearance is somewhat similar to that of the medieval European *rebec*.

In the area extending through the Levant and Iraq, folk musical instruments tend to exhibit common features and performance characteristics. The melody instruments generally demonstrate an affinity for accentuated motifs, elaborate and intricate ornamentation, and sound continuity. These instruments are most often played solo or with percussion instruments and accompany singing and dancing.

Probably the most important instrument employed throughout

Rabababh

Minjayrah

Tabl

137

Rababah

Mizmar

Darbukkah

this region is the Bedouin *rababah*. Played with a horsehair bow, this instrument has a quadrilateral sound box covered with skin and a single string made from horsehair. Capable of a wide range of dynamic accents and ornaments, this instrument is the essential melody instrument of the nomadic Bedouins. It is customarily played by the *sha'ir*, or poet-singer, to accompany heroic and love songs.

Another Bedouin instrument is the *mihbaj*, a wood coffee-grinder consisting of approximately a foot-tall base and a two-foot pestle. The *mihbaj* serves the double purpose of being a household item and, when an expert artist uses it, a percussion instrument as well. It is also a symbol of affluence, social status, and the much-cherished Arab virtue, hospitality.

In Levantine and Iraqi villages, certain wind instruments are inseparable from wedding songs and dances. One is the open-ended, end-blown reed flute that is known as *minjayrah* among the Lebanese and as *shabbabah* among the Palestinians. This flute type has a limited melodic range, but produces a distinctly ornate and breathy tone, often combined with the performer's intermittent humming. Unlike the urban *nay*, this flute is often played by shepherds.

Another essential wind instrument is the double-clarinet type, the *mitbiq* in Iraq and the *mijwiz*, literally "doubled," in Lebanon and its vicinity. This instrument consists of two identical reed-tubes, each having five or six holes. Fitted into each tube is a smaller tube, slit in a manner enabling it to vibrate and produce a sound. Unlike flute types, the *mijwiz* and other double clarinet types are played by a process known as "circular breathing," which allows the performer to produce a continuous non-interrupted sound. Comparable in blowing technique and construction is the Palestinian *yarghul*, which has, instead of two melody tubes, one melody tube and a longer tube without holes, used for producing a sustained accompanying sound or drone.

In the Levant and Iraq, double-reeds or oboe-type instruments are also played characteristically with a *tabl*, a large double-sided drum. The *zamr*, or the *zurna*, usually accompanies folk dances and is typically used at outdoor festivities.

One instrument played in both folk and urban contexts in this same region is a long-necked fretted lute with metal strings commonly called *buzuq*. Generally associated with itinerant Gypsies, the *buzuq* has a carved sound-box and resembles the Turkish *saz* from which it appears to have been derived. Modern versions with mechanical pegs also exist.

In this area, percussion instruments include the *darbukkah*, a conically shaped hand-drum of pottery or metal, and the *daff*, a small tambourine used typically by the Lebanese performers of *zajal*, or sung folk-poetry.

In Egyptian folk music, particularly in villages along the Nile, a wide variety of instruments exist. Instrumental music plays a prominent role, and larger ensembles of melody and percussion instruments are typical. Doubling, or using more than one of the same instrument in the same ensemble, is fairly common. The instrumentalists are usually professionals who perform under the direction of a *rayyis*, a leading instrumentalist.

Mizwid

Among Egypt's folk instruments is the *salamiyyah*, an open-ended reed-flute, characteristically breathy in tone and commonly seen in folk-oriented Sufi performances. The *zummarah* is comparable to the Lebanese *mijwiz*, while the *arghul* resembles the Palestinian *yarghul*. The double-reed *mizmar* appears characteristically with a large double-sided drum called *tabl baladi*. Typically, three *mizmars* play together. The *rababah*, a two-string spike fiddle whose sound box is made from a coconut shell, is characteristically used by the *sha'ir* to accompany folk epics.

The percussion instruments of Egypt are numerous and play an essential role in the music. They include the *riqq*, the *tablah*, the *tabl baladi*, the *tar*, a large frame drum, and the *mazhar*, a large tambourine, with sets of cymbals. Small brass finger-cymbals, or *sajat*, are used by the dancers.

Sajat

The Arabian Gulf region presents a wide variety of instrument types and playing techniques. Percussion plays a central part. In terms of sonority and construction, the instruments seem to reflect the area's exposure to the Levant, Africa, and perhaps South Asia. Pearl fishermen's songs, or *fijri*, of Kuwait, Qatar, and Bahrain employ percussive sound in the form of complicated group hand-clapping. In these songs, a small double-sided hand-drum, known as the *mirwas*, is used. Large, slightly elongated, double-sided drums, comparable in features to both Indian and African drum-forms, are also used. Another member of the pearl fishermen's song ensemble is the *jahlah*, a clay pot played with both hands. In addition, the Gulf region features a variety of wind instruments including both double and single-reeds, in addition to the nomads' single-string *rababah*.

Mihbaj

North Africa has numerous folk instruments, both melodic and percussive. These instruments accompany various genres of dance and song, both secular and sacred. The instruments also represent the

Buzuq

Nay

Riqq

large ethnic variety found within this vast geographical area. In matters of construction and playing technique, they also demonstrate the influence of both the Asiatic Near East and Africa proper.

North African folk instruments include the *qasabah*, an end-blown reed flute which produces a breathy sound enriched with overtones. Used mostly to accompany songs, this instrument is common in Southern Algeria and the Oasis area of Tunisia.

A North African single-reed instrument comparable to the Levantine *mijwiz*, but equipped with two horn bells, is the *maqrunah*, which is commonly played in Libya and Tunisia. In these countries, and in Algeria, this instrument also appears with a bag and is played in the bagpipe style. In this form it is known by the name *mizwid*, literally "bag," or "food pouch."

Double-reed instruments are also prevalent. The *zukrah* of Tunisia and the *ghaytah* of Morocco play an extensive role in public festivities. In Morocco, ensembles usually combine several of these instruments with percussion. A long natural trumpet called *nafir* is occasionally used in Morocco as a signalling instrument.

Fretless, long-necked lutes, whose sound boxes are covered with skin, appear to be a speciality of western North Africa and certain parts of the African Sahara. The Moroccan *ginbri*, whose neck is cylindrical in shape, is common among members of the *Ginnawa* brotherhood, whose religious rites are apparently rooted in sub-Saharan Africa. Another common instrument, whose function is comparable to that of the *rababah* in Egypt and among the eastern Bedouins, is the Moroccan folk *rabab*, a long-necked fiddle with a round skin-covered sound box and a single string made of horsehair positioned to the side rather than in front of the neck. It is typically used for voice accompaniment by the *rwayyis*, a professional group of entertainers and praise singers.

In North Africa, percussion instruments include the *tabl*, a cylindrical double-sided drum; the *qas'ah*, a large, shallow, kettledrum found in southern Tunisia; the double *naqqarah*, pottery kettledrums of Morocco; and various forms of vase-shaped hand-drums and tambourines. In Moroccan Berber music of the Atlas Mountains, a number of snare frame-drums, or *bandirs*, may be played simultaneously. This group of instruments also includes the *qaraqib*, metal clackers that roughly resemble double-castanets and are held two in each hand. These are commonly used by *Ginnawa* performers, particularly during weddings and other festive events.

Finally, instruments of the Arab world have been influenced by urbanization and Westernization. Folk instruments are becoming popular in the cities and are frequently modified to suit urban musical styles. Concurrently, urban instruments are being introduced into folk musical traditions. In the Arab world, Western instruments are prevalent and in some cases are connected with new musical repertoire. Keyboard instruments are usually adjusted to produce some of the neutral intervals of Arab music. Viewed in their great variety, Arab musical instruments are a living testimony to Arab history, musical and visual aesthetics, and the social and cultural facets of a rich and complex society.

Naqqarah

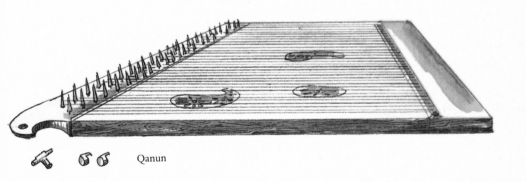

Qanun

The Golden Age of Arab Music

The first century of the Abbasid period (750–850) has often been called the "Golden Age" of Arab culture because of the outstanding intellectual achievements of that period and the magnificence of the caliphal court at Baghdad. This period was equally a "Golden Age" for music and for the musicians who enjoyed the patronage of the caliphs and their subordinates. Not only did court musicians receive a monthly salary, but also they were lavishly rewarded by the caliph and his courtiers for outstanding accomplishments and performances. Many musicians amassed sizeable fortunes and aroused the envy of the less favored.

Although the singing of poetry was the most favored musical performance, the court at Baghdad supported both vocal and instrumental virtuoso performers. Often a single performer combined a wide range of musical skills – singing, playing musical instruments, composing, and expounding on the theory of music. Twelve or more such virtuosi might be attached to the court at a single time. In addition, large numbers of instrumentalists (*alati*) and singing girls (*qaynat*), sometimes numbering up to one hundred or more, were maintained to accompany the soloists or perform in ensembles.

During performances, the musicians were separated from the caliph and other members of the audience by a curtain. In conformance with the social demands of the period the privacy of the caliph and his companions was protected and personal contact with musicians, who were generally considered to be of lowly social status, was limited. This custom, however, was often disregarded, since some performers were actually members of the caliphal family, while others were close companions of the rulers and courtiers. Individual performers sometimes competed with each other as they took their "turn" (*nawbah*) in the alternating succession of performances. *Nawbah* may also have referred to one of the "times" of day designated for performances. Later the same term was used for the performance itself or for a performance group.

Many famous musicians are known to have been teachers as well as performers and composers. Pupils were trained individually or in schools established for that purpose. Training could take place anywhere, even in the palace itself. Each musician's training included not only lessons in singing, playing of instruments, composition, and theory, but also a wide range of literary, religious, linguistic, and cultural studies. Consequently, the musicians were often among the most cultivated people of their time.

Most of the famous musicians of the Golden Age were Arabs, as is revealed in the biographical information to be found in al-Isfahani's *Kitab al Aghani* and Ibn 'Abd Rabbihi's *Al 'Iqd al Farid*. They and the ubiquitous presence of Qur'anic chant were important Arabizing influences. In addition, the religious importance of Makkah and Medina, and the annual pilgrimage to the holy sites ensured continued contact with the music of the peninsula. There was, therefore, a strong Arab core in the music of the period. Contacts with new regions falling under Arab rule did have an effect on musical style and performance practice, however, and these innovations caused the musicians of the time to take sides – either in defense of a strict, classical Arabian tradition or in favor of a new style influenced by foreign, particularly Persian, music. The classicists were led by the noted singer, instrumentalist, composer, and theorist, Ishaq al-Mawsili. Their opponents followed Ibrahim bin al-Mahdi, a member of the caliphal family and a highly trained and talented musician. Despite the contention, which often was fierce, performers from both factions were avidly supported by the music lovers at the court of Baghdad, and the differences between them did not negate an underlying unity.

As Arab culture moved with Islam to increasingly distant parts of the globe, the interaction between the Qur'an-based/Arab musical ideals and the numerous regional traditions continued. It survives even today as Arab music seeks new balances between its basic elements of style and aesthetics, and the richness of regional varieties and alien forms.

The Golden Age provided a germinal model of Arab music on which future developments, both in the Arab world and in many other parts of Asia and Africa, were to be based. It was in that time that the unifying factors of vocal prominence, melodic and rhythmic modal systems, ornamented monophony, compound forms, and typical instrumental types – which can be found today in such performances as the Iraqi *maqam*, the Turkish *taqsim*, the Iranian *avaz*, and the Moroccan *nawbah* – crystallized to form the Arab musical tradition.

LOIS IBSEN AL-FARUQI

Musicians within arabesques. A brass inkwell in-laid with silver of the late Seljuq style, probably made by a Persian artist working in Syria or Iraq in the early thirteenth century. The complex provenance of this object demonstrates the close ties that existed between the various regions of the Islamic world.

The Andalusian Tradition

In the southern districts of Spain, where the Arabs held sway for nearly eight centuries (711–1492), a musical tradition that has profoundly affected that of North Africa and Western Europe as well as the Iberian Peninsula was born.

We mark the beginning of the Andalusian musical tradition from the arrival of the famous musician, Zaryab, in Spain in 821. This talented singer, lutenist, and composer had been forced to flee Baghdad because of the jealousy of Ishaq al-Mawsili, his rival and mentor at the court of Harun ar-Rashid. It was Zaryab who brought the Arab music traditions of the "Eastern" or *Mashriqi* regions of West Asia and initiated its development in the "Western" or *Maghribi* lands of Spain and North Africa.

On hearing of Zaryab's availability, al-Hakam, the Umawi sultan of Cordoba, invited him to join the court as chief musician. Though the sultan died before Zaryab actually reached the capital, al-Hakam's son and successor, 'Abd ar-Rahman, received the musician with great respect and provided him with assistance and a generous salary. Zaryab was an intelligent and talented musician, who is supposed to have memorized over one-thousand songs, as well as mastered the arts of singing, lute performance, composition, and music theory. In addition he was a person of wide cultural interests and knowledge, and particularly well versed in astronomy and geography. With the help and encouragement of the Umawi ruler, Zaryab imported large numbers of musicians from the East. He was also responsible for founding the first music conservatory in Spain. Zaryab introduced many practical and novel teaching methods for improving vocal production and *'ud* performance. Other innovations with which he is credited are the establishment of the multi-movement *nawbah* or suite and a number of improvements of the *'ud* – for example, a heavier-built body, stronger and more sonorous strings, a plectrum made from an eagle talon rather than wood, and an additional, fifth string.

Other important Andalusian contributions to Arab music were the *muwashshah*, a strophic poem performed with music, which was invented at the beginning of the tenth century, and the *zajal*, a similar but more folkish version that used the vernacular language. The *muwashshah* and the *zajal*, comprising repeated rondo-like returns to a musical refrain, are two of the most important vocal genres of the Arabs of both Maghreb and Mashreq. The former is represented mainly in art music; the latter, primarily in the folk repertoire.

After centuries of growth and development, the Muslim Arabs and other non-Christians of Andalusia fell on less favorable circumstances as the soldiers of the *Reconquista* sought to regain the Iberian Peninsula. District after district fell to the advancing armies. Finally, in 1492, Granada, the last important Arab stronghold was taken by the soldiers of King Ferdinand and Queen Isabella, and they were expelled from Andalusia. Most of the Andalusian Arabs migrated to North Africa, carrying their musical and cultural traditions with them. To this day the classical music of Morocco, Algeria, Tunisia, and Libya is regarded as a transplanted Andalusian tradition.

The contemporary Andalusian tradition in the Maghreb is embodied in the *nawbah*. Each of the suite's five standard movements (named for the rhythmic modes or *iqa'at* on which they are based) contain a core of choral *muwashshahat* to which other vocal and instrumental preludes or interludes are added. Although the *iqa'at* used and the number and names of additional pieces may vary slightly from country to country, the *nawbat* of various regions of the Maghreb reveal many features to confirm their common Andalusian ancestry. Each *nawbah*, for example, is dominated by a single melodic mode; each evidences an acceleration from one movement to the next; and every movement includes a final section of acceleration (*musarraf*) that prepares for the faster segment to follow. The *nawbah's* conformance to the general characteristics of Arab music are no less obvious. Although the instruments of the Maghribi ensemble may differ in structure or size from the Mashriqi counterparts, and although names and constituent elements of the *maqamat* and *iqa'at* may vary, the contemporary Andalusian music of the Maghreb retains unmistakable links to the music of other parts of the Arab world.

The musical tradition of Moorish Spain not only had an effect on North African music; it also significantly influenced music in medieval Europe, although the details of that influence are less precisely documented. Numerous instru-

The Alhambra dominates the city of Granada, where the Nasrids, the last dynasty of Andalusia, established their capital in the thirteenth century.

ments, whose names and construction indicate their Arab origin, found their way into European usage. In the twelfth and thirteenth centuries, the Andalusian city of Seville was already a center for the manufacture of musical instruments, and Spanish manuals on the subject were available in the thirteenth century.

Another important Moorish influence on European music was the interaction that took place between the minstrels of Arab Spain and their European counterparts, the troubadours. There are indications that song texts, poetic/musical structures, performance styles, vocal production, performance contexts, as well as costumes and makeup of the European minstrels were all affected by the Andalusian tradition. Even the "Morris" dancers of the distant British Isles are thought to have derived from "Moorish" models.

Many features of the Andalusian musical tradition have also lived on in the music of Spain itself. Particularly prominant influences from that heritage are found today in the flamenco music of the Spanish gypsies. The ornamental melodic style, the improvisatory rhythmic freedom, the sometimes "strange" (to Western ears) intervals, the segmental structure, and the repeated excursions and returns to a tonal center are some of the features that indicate Arab influences on *cante flamenco*. Many terms associated with that tradition are derived from Arab roots. Songs often begin with a vocalise on the syllables *Ay* or *Lelí*, so commonly used in Arab vocal improvizations; and the exclamation *Olé*, used by flamenco aficionados, expresses appreciation and encouragement to performers in the same way that Arabs still use its parent term, *Allah*.

Lois Ibsen al-Faruqi

The Exact Sciences

Abdelhamid I. Sabra is Professor of the History of Arabic Science at Harvard University (Cambridge, Mass.). Previously he has taught at the University of Alexandria in Egypt and at the University of London and has been Reader in the History of the Classical Tradition at the Warburg Institute. He is associate editor of the *Dictionary of Scientific Biography*, published under the auspices of the American Council of Learned Societies and author of *Theories of Light from Descartes to Newton*. He is currently preparing an edition and English translation of Ibn al-Haytham's *Optics* (*Kitab al-Manaẓir*).

The Exact Sciences

Abdelhamid I. Sabra

The phrase "Arabic science" refers to a vast and complex enterprise that was effectively launched by the early Abbasid caliphs at Baghdad shortly after 750. For at least six hundred years thereafter it maintained a vigorous, if somewhat checkered, existence, gradually spreading over a geographical area that extended from Andalusia to the lands beyond the Oxus River (now the Amu Darya) in Central Asia.

This immense and long-lasting enterprise has been called "Arabic," firstly, because it owed its inception to Arab initiative and Arab patronage and, secondly and more importantly, because the Arabic language was the medium in which it developed. The individuals who took part in its growth represented many ethnic groups and, at least in the beginning, professed different faiths. For example, among the first translators, physicians, and astronomer-astrologers who were attached to the Abbasid court were many Syrian Christians and Persians. Some, like Thabit bin Qurrah, were Sabians from pagan Harran; others, like Masha'allah, were Jews. In the later history of Arabic science some of the most important figures hailed from such non-Arab lands as Khwarizm, Farghana, Khurasan, Sijistan, and Fars. The Arabic language was the unifying thread—a fact of specific significance for the general history of science and culture, as well as for the history of science in Islam.

To some extent Arabic science may be regarded as the continuation of a Greek tradition that had been preserved by the Hellenized peoples who came under Arab rule. But, as historians have noted, it was more than that. Baghdad was in fact heir not only to Alexandria but also to Persia and India, and the scientific texts available for translation into Arabic included works in Sanskrit, Syriac, and Pahlavi, as well as in Greek. This wide-ranging process of translation into Arabic led to an accumulation of scientific learning that surpassed anything previously known.

Even more surprising, the Arabic language rapidly became an international language of science in a stronger sense than had been true of any other language. Until the translation movement began, Arabic had been the language of poetry, of the Qur'an, and of the recently developed disciplines concerned with Islamic religion and with the Arabic language itself. By the eleventh century the great Persian scientist al-Biruni was describing the Arabic language as the language most suited for scientific expression. But he was speaking after the event. The ninth-century decision to turn Arabic into the vehicle of scientific traditions that hitherto had been foreign to it was an act of great originality and imagination.

In medieval Arabic scientific writings, we do not find a distinction between "exact" and "inexact" sciences. Rather, following Aristotle, those who wrote scientific works in Arabic distinguished between the "mathematical" and the "physical" sciences. The former group were concerned with quantity, whether discrete (number) or continuous (geometrical magnitude), whereas the latter dealt with things that possess a principle of motion, such as the elements, whose inherent properties of lightness and heaviness are responsible for their natural motion upward or downward. The distinction was not clear-cut, however. Aristotle himself classified astronomy, optics, and music among what he called "the more physical" of the mathematical sciences, thereby recognizing the existence of sciences of a mixed character. Even with regard to arithmetic and geometry, the Greeks admitted both a purely theoretical study of the properties of numbers and a not-so-pure art of calculation, and they debated whether geometrical theorems were not ultimately based on mechanical operations. All these concepts survive in Arabic science, and they should be borne in mind when reflecting on the character of Arabic achievements in the field of the exact or mathematical sciences.

MATHEMATICS

Arithmetic, which usually heads the list of mathematical disciplines, is a logical starting point in an account of Arabic mathematics. The Arabs derived most of their early information about the theory of numbers (*'ilm al-a'dad*) from two sources: Books VII through IX of Euclid's *Elements* and the *Introduction to the Science of Numbers* by Nicomachus of Gerasa. The latter work was translated into Arabic by Thabit bin Qurrah (died 901), who also revised a translation of the *Elements* by Ishaq bin Hunayn (died about 910). Nicomachus' *Introduction*, an exposition of Pythagorean arithmetic, had enjoyed a certain vogue in late antiquity, and it strongly influenced the anonymous tenth-century authors of the *Epistles of the Brethren of Sincerity*. But, despite the fact that some treatises, such as those of Thabit and Kamal ad-Din al-Farisi (died 1320) on amicable numbers, dealt with number properties, Arabic works devoted to number theory were remarkably few. Worthy of particular mention, however, are Thabit's remarks on infinite collections. Arguing against widely accepted views derived from Aristotle, Thabit asserted that it was simply a fact that an infinite collection could be a part of another infinite collection. (For example, the class of even numbers is half that of all natural numbers, and both classes are infinite.) It did not occur to Thabit to try to develop a theory of transfinite numbers, but his remarks typify the critical and explorative attitude found in many Arabic writings, even those that purport to be straightforward commentaries on the works of ancient or Islamic authorities.

Of even more consequence in regard to number theory was the gradual emergence in Arabic arithmetic of a concept of irrational numbers. For the ancient Greeks, the irrational (the subject of Book X of Euclid's *Elements*) existed as a geometrical magnitude, not as a number; the diagonal of a square, for example, is demonstrably incommensurable with the side considered as unity. In general, the Arabic commentators on the *Elements* followed Euclid's conception. Some Islamic mathematicians, however, starting from a non-Euclidean concept that expressed ratios in terms of continued fractions were gradually led to regard all ratios, whether of commensurable magnitudes or not, as numbers. Prominent in this development was the work

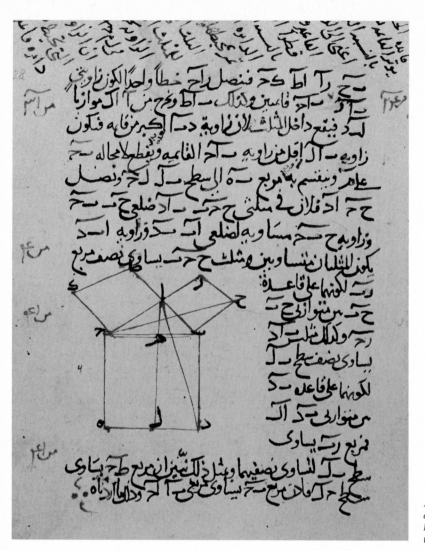

At-Tusi's version, based on earlier Arabic translations, of Euclid's proof of the Pythagorean theorem.

of ʿUmar al-Khayyami (died about 1130) in the eleventh century and Nasir ad-Din at-Tusi (died 1247) in the thirteenth century. Whereas the definition of proportion from which this research started may, itself, have been of Greek origin (though it was not the definition adopted by Euclid), the resulting expansion of the concept of number to include irrationals does not seem to have been anticipated in Greek mathematics.

The Arabic word *hisab*, which refers to the art of reckoning and, generally, to the process of determining unknown from known quantities, was used to cover the fundamental arithmetical operations (addition, subtraction, multiplication, and division), root extraction, and algebraic procedures. As far as arithmetic, as distinguished from algebraic, reckoning is concerned, the Arabs inherited three different systems, which were employed separately for centuries before they were successfully fused in the fifteenth century.

The first of these systems, possibly indigenous to the Middle East, was known as "finger reckoning" (*hisab al-yad, hisab al-'uqud*). In this system, numbers were expressed in words, not symbols, and the fingers of one or both hands were held in certain positions to retain the results of intermediate steps in making a calculation. Because finger reckoning was used by the scribes or secretaries in the various chanceries, it was also known as "the arithmetic of the scribes" (*hisab al-kuttab*).

From India came a superior system of reckoning, which (thanks to the place-value idea on which it was based) was able to express any number, however large, by means of nine figures and a symbol (zero, or *sifr*) indicating an empty place in an array of figures. In medieval Arabic treatises, these figures are called "Indian," and although the exact manner of their transmission and diffusion in the Arab world and in Europe remains unclear, there seems to be no reason to doubt their Indian origin. The figures were expressed in somewhat different forms in the eastern and western parts of the Arab world, and it was the western figures that migrated to Europe, where they became known as "Arabic numerals." The system of Indian reckoning was first transmitted to Europe through a translation, probably made in the twelfth century, of a handbook on the subject written by Muhammad bin Musa al-Khwarizmi (flourished about 825). In fact, al-Khwarizmi's treatise survives today only in Latin versions based on that translation.

The third arithmetical system of reckoning inherited by the Arabs was called "the arithmetic of the astronomers" or "the arithmetic of degrees and minutes." Although it was Babylonian in origin, Arabic mathematicians became familiar with it through translations of Greek astronomical works, and it was always used in astronomical and astrological calculations. It employed sexagesimal fractions (those having base sixty), and it designated numbers by letters of the alphabet.

As early as the tenth century, a Damascene arithmetician, Abu al-Hasan bin Ibrahim al-Uqlidisi, wrote a book in which he applied schemes of Indian reckoning to the other types of calculation, but he did not succeed in unifying the various systems. Although he was apparently the first to introduce the idea of decimal fractions, his work had no influence on his successors and has survived only in a unique manuscript. It was not until al-Kashi wrote his *Key to Arithmetic* at Samarkand in the beginning of the fifteenth century that the place-value decimal system was successfully applied to both integers and fractions. Although al-Kashi's breakthrough came late in the history of Arabic science, it preceded similar developments in Europe by almost two hundred years. His book had a wide circulation in the Islamic world, and there is evidence to show that its ideas were known in Constantinople in the second half of the fifteenth century.

Al-Khwarizmi, who wrote the first handbook in Arabic on Indian reckoning, was also the first author in the field of Arabic algebra. The word "algebra" transliterates the term *al-jabr*, which designates one of the two basic operations that al-Khwarizmi used in solving quadratic equations. He may have used Indian or Greek sources, or both, and his geometrical method of proving the canonical equations to which he reduced his problems is unquestionably Euclidean. Nevertheless, his book as a whole does not seem to have had a prototype in another language.

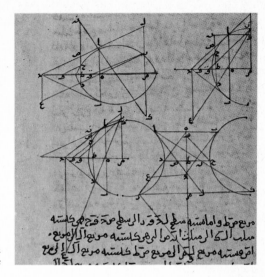

Illustration from a copy in
Ibn al-Haytham's hand of Appollonius' Conics

Europe first became acquainted with Arabic algebra through the translation of the first part of al-Khwarizmi's *Kitab al-Jabr wa al-Muqabalah* in the latter half of the twelfth century. By this time, however, much more important work in this field had been done in Arabic — for example, by al-Karaji (flourished about 1000), 'Umar al-Khayyami (died 1130), as-Samaw'al (died about 1175), and Ibn al-Haytham (died about 1040). Much of this work was aimed at the solution of geometrical problems suggested by Greek mathematicians.

Arabic geometry absorbed not only the contents and methods of Euclid's *Elements* but also the higher techniques of Apollonius and Archimedes. The three sons of Musa bin Shakir, who lived in Baghdad in the ninth century and were attached to the Abbasid court, dealt with Archimedean problems. Their most important work in this field, *On the Measurement of Plane and Spherical Figures*, became known to the West through the twelfth-century Latin translation by Gerard of Cremona. Mathematicians who were able to tackle problems in higher mathematics included Muhammad bin 'Isa al-Mahani (died about 880), Abu Ja'far al-Khazin (died 971), 'Umar al-Khayyami, and Ibn al-Haytham. Ibn al-Haytham formulated a problem that came to be known as "Alhazen's problem," the name given to it by seventeenth-century Europeans: For any two points opposite a reflecting surface—which may be spherical, cylindrical, or conical, whether convex or concave—to find the point or points on the surface at which the light from one of the two points will be reflected to the other. In his attempt to solve this general problem Ibn al-Haytham proceeded by considering separately the particular cases involved. For spherical surfaces (both convex and concave), he solved the problem by the intersection of a circle and a hyperbola—an achievement equivalent to solving an equation of the fourth degree. Ibn al-Haytham's remarkable treatment of this problem is contained in his *Optics* (*Kitab al-Manazir*), which became known to European mathematicians through a medieval Latin translation.

Another classic problem to which Arab mathematicians devoted special attention dealt

153

with the theory of parallels. This theory comprises the group of theorems (including, for example, the theorem stating that the angles of a triangle are equal to two right angles) whose proof depends on the following Euclidean postulate (the so-called "parallels postulate"): If two straight lines in the same plane are cut by a third in such a way as to make the interior angles on one side of the cutting line together less than two right angles, then the two lines will meet if extended on that side. No one in the Middle Ages doubted the truth of the postulate or the truth of any of the propositions derived by means of it. But many mathematicians felt that the postulate could not be accepted without proof. Such dissatisfaction had been explicitly and strongly expressed in antiquity. It is to the credit of medieval Arabic geometricians that, having recognized the problem they inherited from their Greek predecessors, they persistently pursued its solution for at least five hundred years. By contrast, although the same problem was transmitted to Europe in the twelfth century, through Latin translations of Arabic translations of Greek works, it does not seem to have provoked any widespread interest until the seventeenth century, when European mathematicians became acquainted with Arabic research on the subject.

The mathematicians of medieval Islam who worked on the parallels problem included al-'Abbas bin Sa'id al-Jawhari (flourished about 830), Thabit bin Qurrah, al-Mahani, 'Umar al-Khayyami, Ibn al-Haytham, Nasir ad-Din at-Tusi, Muhyi ad-Din al-Maghribi (flourished about 1260), and Athir ad-Din al-Abhari (died 1265). Their different lines of approach illustrate the ancient methodological controversies alluded to earlier in this chapter. Thabit, for example, made essential use of the idea of motion in offering an alternative to Euclid's parallels postulate. In justification of his procedure, he argued that motion is in fact at the base of the whole of geometry. Ibn al-Haytham, in the eleventh century, adopted a similar approach. On the other hand, al-Khayyami, supported by Aristotelian ideas, objected to introducing the concept of motion into geometry. Like many other Islamic mathematicians, however, he adopted a definition of parallel lines as equidistant lines, whereas Euclid had defined parallels as non-secant lines. Finally, at-Tusi's "proof" of the Euclidean postulate, contained in his recension of Euclid's *Elements*, returns to the Euclidean definition without introducing motion.

In the course of attempting to prove Euclid's postulate, Arabic geometricians were led to formulate and prove some non-Euclidean theorems, but they did not envisage the possibility of a non-Euclidean system of geometry. The Arabic text of a "proof" incorrectly attributed to at-Tusi was published in Rome in 1594. This was translated into Latin by Edward Pocock for the English mathematician John Wallis, and the translation was published in 1613. Through this publication the Italian Jesuit mathematician Gerolamo Saccheri became acquainted with the "proof," which he discussed in his important work *Euclides ab omni naevo vindicatus* (1733). Arabic research thus forms part of the history of the problem whose investigation finally led to the discovery of non-Euclidean systems in the nineteenth century.

ASTRONOMY

Medieval Arabic astronomy was predominantly Greek in character. Although Indian and Persian elements came into it as a result of the early translations from Sanskrit and Pahlavi, it

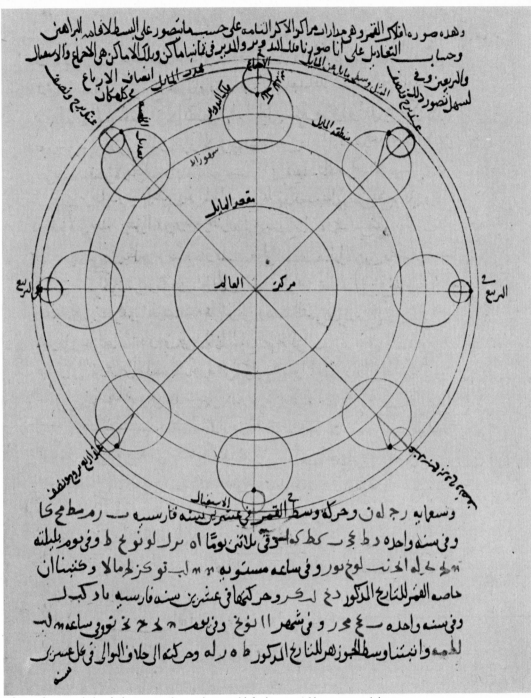

In his most famous work, Ibn ash-Shatir suggested non-Ptolemaic models for the motions of the sun, moon and planets.

was Ptolemy's sophisticated and powerful methods, as expounded in the *Almagest*, that quickly and permanently dominated Arabic research. In the absence of any obviously compelling need to go beyond the Ptolemaic system, Arabic astronomers engaged in the important and difficult task of making it more accurate, more efficient, and more elegant. They made new observations aimed at improving the Ptolemaic parameters—inclination of the ecliptic, mean planetary motions, equinoctial precession, and so forth. They developed ingenious and increasingly efficient computational techniques. And they devised new planetary models designed to make Ptolemaic planetary theory more in harmony with its avowed principles.

Observational activity, which began as early as the eighth century, was quite impressive, though largely divorced from theoretical developments. It was given strong impetus at the time of Caliph 'Abdallah al-Ma'mun (813–833), who ordered the preparation of new astronomical tables (or *zijes*). The result was the influential *Ma'munic zij*, which was based on observational and computational instruments, such as astrolabes, quadrants, and armillaries of various centers of astronomical research in the Islamic world—at Shiraz (by 'Abd ar-Rahman as-Sufi, died 986), Cairo (by Ibn Yunus, died 1009), Ghazna (by al-Biruni, died after 1050), Maragha (by at-Tusi and his collaborators), and Samarkand (by Ulugh Beg, died 1449), to mention only a few of those centers. The results of some of these observations were incorporated in many of the large number of *zijes* produced in medieval Islam. Considerable effort went into the designing and constructing of ever more precise and more sophisticated observational and computational instruments, such as astrolabes, quadrants, and armillaries of various types. The description of an instrument constructed in the thirteenth century at Maragha by the Damascene astronomer al-'Urdi has been compared with a similar one made and used in the sixteenth century by Tycho Brahe.

In their attempt to improve upon the calculus of chords, which they found, for example, in Ptolemy's *Almagest*, Arabic mathematicians gradually developed the trigonometric technique. Some trigonometric functions—for example, the sine—were known to the Indians. Working from this base, the Arabs were able to develop the remaining functions during the ninth century, principally through the efforts of Habash al-Hasib. During the tenth century the use of these functions reached a high level in the work of al-Battani. These mathematical developments, however, occurred within the context of astronomy, and they are to be found in astronomical treatises. It was in the work of Nasir ad-Din at-Tusi that trigonometry achieved the status of an independent branch of pure mathematics. His contribution was to combine the results obtained by earlier investigators and to replace Menelaus' complete quadrilateral by a simple triangle, thus freeing trigonometry from spherical astronomy. Trigonometry as an independent discipline can therefore be considered an invention of Arabic science. Not only the relatively elementary tables of sines devised by al-Khwarizmi, but also the more advanced work of al-Battani, were transmitted to the West in medieval Latin translations.

Planetary theory developed along several distinct lines, influenced both by the example of the different models presented in the translated works and by the methodological discussions concerning those models. The Arabs were acquainted with the Eudoxian model through a description of it in the works of Aristotle and his Greek commentators. This was a homocentric

One of the most important instruments used by early astronomers was the planispheric astrolabe. This brass instrument is signed by Ibn al-Husayn bin Ahmad, an astrolabist from Baghdad.

model in which each planet was associated with a nest of spheres that rotated about the center of the world (that is, the center of the earth). The speeds of the spheres in each nest and the situation of their respective poles were so chosen as to produce the apparent motion of the planet, which was supposedly embedded in the innermost sphere. Aristotle adopted this system and incorporated it into a rigid cosmological theory based on the idea of natural place. Not only did he insist that celestial bodies must rotate in perfect circles with constant speed, a concept later accepted by Ptolemy, but, having assumed that the spheres were transparent though physical bodies, he further urged, in the name of demonstrable physical science, that there should be only one center for all heavenly motions.

Despite the tremendous prestige of Aristotelian teaching, most professional astronomers in medieval Islam simply ignored his system. It was only in twelfth-century Spain that philosophers like Ibn Tufayl, Ibn Rushd, and Maimonides revolted against the entire Ptolemaic system and demanded a return to a theory that was more in agreement with Aristotelian cosmology. However interesting their attitude may be from a historical point of view, it would be wrong to consider it as representative of Arabic science as a whole or even as a significant trend. It should be noted, however, that by the end of the twelfth century the Spanish astronomer Abu Ishaq al-Bitruji actually produced a system purporting to satisfy the demands of his older contemporary and teacher Ibn Tufayl. From the astronomical point of view the new theory was not a success, but the Latin translation of al-Bitruji's book was widely appreciated.

Ptolemaic planetary theory subscribed to the principle of uniform circular motion for celestial bodies but admitted eccentric and epicyclic motions. The sun, for example, moved in a circle eccentric to the center of the world. The other planets moved in little circles, called "epicycles," which were themselves carried around large circles called "deferents." Arabic astronomers tended to accept or reject this theory depending on their position in an ancient debate about the relation, or lack of relation, between physics and mathematical astronomy. In the *Almagest* Ptolemy presented his planetary models as a mathematical theory formulated in the language of arithmetic and geometry. He was not, however, entirely consistent. Some "physical" proofs crept into his presentation. Al-Biruni, who favored the exclusively mathematical approach, censured Ptolemy for having introduced merely "persuasive" arguments into a science that admitted only demonstrations. But in this respect al-Biruni was in a definitely small minority. Most astronomers in Islam believed that astronomy was based on physical, as well as mathematical, premises. This meant that for the most part they accepted the principles of the Ptolemaic mathematical theory, including the concepts of eccentrics and epicycles, but insisted that the theory must have an acceptable physical interpretation. Their attitude was influenced by Aristotle, but more directly by Ptolemy himself, whose book *Planetary Hypotheses* included an unsuccessful attempt to represent the motions of the planets in terms of physical spherical shells rotating inside one another.

The difficulty of converting the geometrical language of the *Almagest* into physical language was not the only problem Arabic astronomers had with Ptolemy. In a book composed expressly as a criticism of the views advanced both in the *Almagest* and in *Planetary Hypotheses*, Ibn al-Haytham focused his attack on Ptolemy's concept of the "equant." Ptolemy had stipu-

158

The constellation, Draco, as depicted in as-Sufi's Treatise on the Fixed Stars.

صورة التنين على ما نرى في السماء

lated that the planet's epicycle moved uniformly with respect to a point (later called the "equant point") other than the eccentric-center. But, Ibn al-Haytham objected, this would mean that the eccentric sphere carrying the epicycle was itself moving with nonuniform velocity—in violation of the principle of uniformity accepted by Ptolemy and all other astronomers. The observation underlying this criticism may not have been original, but Ibn al-Haytham was perhaps the first to conclude that Ptolemy's models in the *Almagest* were false and must be replaced by new models that would preserve the uniformity principle. Although Ibn al-Haytham did not, himself, propose a new planetary theory, his incisive objections directly or indirectly inspired the important reform of planetary astronomy that was initiated two centuries later by Nasir ad-Din at-Tusi and his colleagues at Maragha and continued in the following century by Ibn ash-Shatir at Damascus. These astronomers successfully produced planetary models that could be translated into physical language without violating the accepted astronomical principles; that is, the models represented the apparent motion of a planet as the resultant of a combination of motions, each of which was uniform with respect to its own center.

This was the culminating achievement of Arabic research in planetary theory. Recently historians have noted a strong similarity between the models produced at Maragha and Damascus and those of Copernicus, but whether or not Copernicus was influenced by these Arabic prototypes remains a matter of conjecture.

OPTICS

For the most part, Islamic achievements in optics, a field in which the Arabs made substantial progress, were also solidly based on the foundation laid by the ancient Greeks. Ptolemy's treatise on optics, the most mature work on the subject produced in antiquity, was translated early into Arabic, and a Latin version was made from the Arabic in Sicily in the twelfth century. The treatise now survives only in the Latin version, both the Greek original and the Arabic translation having been lost. Greek optics was primarily a theory of vision, and it was a subject of interest not only to mathematicians like Euclid and Ptolemy but also to philosophers like Aristotle and to medical writers like Galen. The Arabs' own investigations were inspired by the rich and varied discussions initiated by all these writers. Thus, al-Kindi followed in the footsteps of Euclid, Hunayn bin Ishaq elaborated the ideas of Galen, and Ibn Sina, as a peripatetic philosopher, remained close to Aristotle. It was in Ibn Sina's lifetime, however, that Ibn al-Haytham formulated a theory of vision quite distinct from any other that existed then or had existed earlier. The new theory was thought out and presented in terms of the debate, referred to earlier, regarding the relation between physics and mathematics. Ibn al-Haytham was a mathematician, not a natural philosopher, but he typically combined physical doctrines with mathematical methods.

From natural philosophers Ibn al-Haytham derived the idea that vision occurs when a "form" emanating from the object enters the eye. As a mathematician, he was impressed by the geometrical approach taken in the works of Euclid and Ptolemy. His own contribution can be

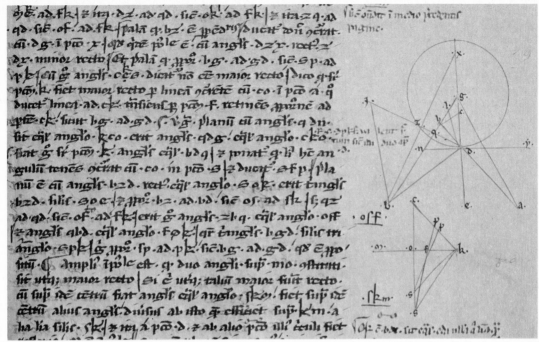

Diagram illustrating Ibn al-Haytham's solution of what has come to be known since the seventeenth century as "Alhazen's problem": given points a and b (as eye and object), to find (in this particular case) the point d on the spherical convex mirror at which the light from one of the two given points will be reflected to the other. Ibn al-Haytham solved the problem by means of the intersection of a circle and a hyperbola.

characterized as an attempt to apply the geometrical method to the physical doctrine of forms. That is to say, he tried to show how a form capable of representing the visible features of an object, whether large or small, can enter through the pupil and make its way to the brain, where the process of vision is completed. This was not mere eclecticism. To achieve the desired synthesis, Ibn al-Haytham was led to alter important, sometimes essential, components of the earlier theories, and he was able to formulate questions that had not been conceived before. He also realized that a theory of vision based on an impression produced in the eye or brain is incomplete without an explanation of how the impression comes to be perceived as an object located at a certain distance, having a certain size and shape, and so forth. This in turn led him to construct a highly original theory of the psychology of visual perception. But what is most remarkable about *The Book of Optics* (*Kitab al-Manzir*), in which Ibn al-Haytham expressed the results of his investigations, is the structure of its arguments, which are consistently experimental or mathematical. Even when he relies on the authority of others—as in his description of the structure of the eye, which is derived from contemporary anatomical works—one can easily see how he reshapes the borrowed material to suit his own purpose.

Ibn al-Haytham's *Optics* is a large and comprehensive work that includes, not only a new theory of vision, but also important discussions of the rectilinear propagation, reflection, and refraction of light and color. Its superiority to the treatises of Euclid, Ptolemy, al-Kindi, and Ibn Sina, all of which were translated into Latin, soon became clear to Latin medieval writers. In the thirteenth century, Roger Bacon referred to Ibn al-Haytham frequently as "the author on optics." Witelo's comprehensive book on optics made liberal use of Ibn al-Haytham's text, and John Pecham's summary of Ibn al-Haytham's work was widely read. With the exception of Witelo, however, none of these writers was in a position to appreciate fully the mathematical character of the *Optics*, and it was not until the Renaissance and the seventeenth century that this aspect of the book was understood and exploited.

For reasons that are not quite clear, the *Optics* of Ibn al-Haytham appears to have been virtually unknown in the Islamic world until the end of the thirteenth century. It was only then that the Arabic text received the attention it deserved, in the form of a critical commentary written in Arabic by the Persian Kamal ad-Din al-Farisi. The commentary came too late to be transmitted to the medieval West, but it marked one of the highest points of experimental research in Islam.

Starting from problems suggested or implied in Ibn al-Haytham's work, Kamal ad-Din was able to make at least one important breakthrough: his successful explanation of the rainbow phenomenon, which had resisted the efforts of all his predecessors since antiquity. Aristotle, in his *Meteorology*, tried to explain the phenomenon in terms of reflection from rain droplets acting like little mirrors. His particular treatment of the problem, combining observation and geometry, influenced all future research. Ibn Sina, in the part of his *ash-Shifa'* corresponding to Aristotle's treatise, reported some observations of his own, but refused to accept the Aristotelian explanation. He mentioned the analogy between a raindrop and a glass sphere. This inspired Kamal ad-Din, who had also been studying Ibn al-Haytham's goemetrical investigations of burning spheres. As a result of a series of experimental inquiries into the behavior of light as it passes through a glass vial filled with water, Kamal ad-Din was able to give a satisfactory account of both the primary and the secondary bow: The light from the sun enters the drop (to which the vial corresponds) before it is reflected at its far side to the observer; the primary rainbow is produced by one such reflection, whereas the secondary bow is produced by two internal reflections. The reversal of the order of the colors in the two bows is thus explained. As for the production of the colors as such, no satisfactory explanation was forthcoming until Isaac Newton published his famous discovery in 1672.

Almost equally impressive was Kamal ad-Din's investigation of the *camera obscura* phenomena. Here, too, he was continuing research begun by Ibn al-Haytham, who had succeeded in formulating some of the principles on which the working of the *camera* depends. The problem was to explain the formation of inverted images of shining objects, such as the eclipsed sun or moon, inside a dark chamber that allows the light to go through a small hole in one of its walls. Astronomers since antiquity had been puzzled, for example, by the fact that, whereas a crescent moon casts a round image through a circular aperture, a partially eclipsed sun casts a crescent-shaped image. Neither Ibn al-Haytham nor Kamal ad-Din succeeded in solving the general problem of the *camera*, though some of their conclusions formed part of the solution. What is remarkable, however, is the truly scientific manner in which they investigated the phenomena by applying mathematics to a difficult experimental situation.

SUMMARY

The preceding examples give some idea of the range, vigor, and sophistication of medieval Arabic research in the field of the exact sciences, but they do not exhaust the results achieved in the disciplines discussed, let alone in the whole field. The Arabs not only assimilated Greek science but also made themselves masters of its methods and techniques. Their role did not consist merely of handing over to Europe what they had earlier acquired from the ancients; rather, having digested what they learned from their predecessors, they were able to enrich it by new observations, new results, and new techniques. Not all of these accomplishments were transmitted to the West by the wave of translation from the Arabic into Latin in the twelfth and thirteenth centuries. Some of the great works of Arabic science—for example, those of al-Biruni—did not become known to the West until they were made available by modern scholarship. But many of the studies that were transmitted to Europe in the Middle Ages were specifically Arabic products.

The importance of the Arabic contribution to the history of science is not in doubt, but much of its content and many of its details are still unknown. The extant manuscripts in this field are stored in libraries scattered all over the world—in Europe, in America, in Asia, and in the Middle East—and the vast majority of them have been neither published nor examined. To unfold their contents will require the hard work and devotion of many scholars over many future generations.

A spherical astrolabe, the only one known to exist today.

The Sons of Musa bin Shakir (Banu Musa)

(Ninth century)

According to intriguing accounts in medieval sources, Musa bin Shakir—the father of Muhammad, Ahmad, and al-Hasan—was in his youth a highwayman, active on the Khurasan road. Courageous and skillful in his profession, he dressed as a soldier, tied rags around the legs of his horse to hide its distinctive white markings, and was careful to appear at the mosque before and after every raid. In later life he reformed, becoming well enough known as an astrologer to join the court of the Caliph al-Ma'mun (813–833). At his death he left his three young sons in the custody of the caliph, who entrusted them to Ishaq bin Ibrahim al-Mus'abi, a one-time governor of Baghdad, who in turn placed them under the tutelage of Yahya bin Abu Mansur, an astrologer at Bayt al-Hikmah, the famous library and translation center patronized by al-Ma'mun. The caliph seems to have maintained a special interest in the welfare and intellectual development of the sons of Musa (the *Banu Musa*). He inquired about them so often while on his military expeditions that Ishaq used to grumble, "Al-Ma'mun has appointed me a nurse to the sons of Musa bin Shakir."

The three sons were obviously gifted. Muhammad, the eldest, was learned in geometry and astronomy. Ahmad excelled in mechanics. Al-Hasan was deeply interested in geometry, for which he had a natural ability. Having completed Books I–VI of Euclid's *Elements*, he was able to work out the propositions of the remaining seven books on his own. It is an indication of al-Ma'mun's pious attitude toward ancient learning that he once upbraided al-Hasan for not having read the whole of such a basic and revered text as the *Elements*, even though he did not need to.

Although poor at first, the *Banu Musa* were able to command sizable incomes in later life. A medieval source puts the annual incomes of Muhammad and Ahmad at 400,000 and 70,000 dinars respectively. This is in keeping with reports that they spent lavishly on the acquisition and translation of ancient manuscripts. Both Hunayn bin Ishaq and Thabit bin Qurrah are said to have worked for them as translators.

By the time al-Mutawakkil acceded to the caliphate in 847, the *Banu Musa* had secured a powerful position at the caliphal court. Reports about the activities of Muhammad and Ahmad during al-Mutawakkil's reign (847–861) if true, indicate something of their influence and character. First we are told about their intrigue against the philosopher Ya'qub bin Ishaq al-Kindi. Not only did they drive a wedge between the caliph and al-Kindi, who had previously enjoyed a favorable position at the court, but they also confiscated the philosopher's library. A story attributed to the tenth-century mathematician Abu Kamil says they were persuaded to return the books to him only because they had gotten into trouble themselves.

According to the story, al-Mutawakkil wanted a canal dug in al-Ja'fariyyah, a city that was being built for him near Samarra. He entrusted the work to Muhammad and Ahmad, who, in turn, subcontracted the job to Ahmad bin Muhammad bin Kathir al-Farghani, the astronomer and engineer who constructed the "new Nilometer" at Fustat (Cairo).

The brothers' choice of al-Farghani was motivated primarily by their selfish desire to exclude a good engineer named Sanad bin 'Ali, whom they had deliberately kept away from the caliphal court. They very nearly became victims of their own intrigues, however. As work progressed it became apparent that al-Farghani had not been a good choice. He had made a serious miscalculation in his design, and the mistake would be obvious to everyone—including the caliph—when the canal was completed. In desperation the *Banu Musa* implored Sanad to intercede on their behalf with the caliph. He agreed, but only on condition that they release al-Kindi's library, which they did. As things turned out, all those involved in the canal project were spared when the Caliph was murdered, as astrologers had predicted.

In the works attributed to the *Banu Musa* it is sometimes difficult to separate individual contributions. For example, the following works are ascribed to the three sons collectively: *On the Qarastun* (beam balance), *On the Measurement of Plane and Spherical Figures*, *On Determining Two Mean Proportionals*, *On the Trisection of the Angle*, and a *Recension of Apollonius' Conics*. To Ahmad is attributed a treatise *On Mechanical Devices* and another in which he sought to demonstrate the nonexistence of a ninth sphere. Muhammad is individually credited with a number of treatises, including *On the First Motion of the Sphere*, *On the Beginning of the World*, and *On the Atom*. Among the works ascribed to al-Hasan are *Questions* exchanged between him and Sanad bin 'Ali, and a treatise *On the Round and Elongated Figure* (ellipse?).

The important treatise *On Mechanical Devices* has recently been published and translated into English. *The Recension of the "Conics*," which is extant, is based on a translation made by Hilal bin Abu Hilal al-Himsi under the guidance of Ahmad (Books I–IV), and by Thabit bin Qurrah (Books V–VII). Historically the most important work of the three sons was the treatise *On the Measurement of Plane and*

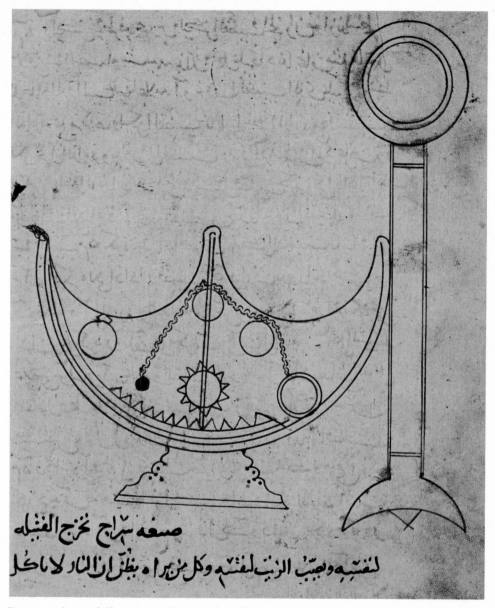

صفه سراج نخرج الفتيله

لفتيله ويجيب الزيت لفتيله وكل من يراه بظن ان النار لا تاكل

Diagrammatic drawing of self-trimming lamp from On Mechanical Devices.

Spherical Figures. It constituted an important development of Archimedes' works *On the Measurement of the Circle* and *On the Sphere and Cylinder.* In it the sons made use of Eudoxus' method of exhaustion and of Archimedes' concept of infinitesimals, and it influenced later scholars both in the Muslim East and in the Latin West. The twelfth-century Latin translation by Gerard of Cremona, known as *Liber trium fratrum de geometria,* or *Verba filiorum Moysi filii Sekir, i.e. Maumeti, Hameti, Hasen,* played an important role in transmitting Archimedean ideas and methods to Europe. It is known to have influenced the work of the thirteenth-century mathematician Leonardo Fibonacci of Pisa.

ABDELHAMID I. SABRA

Abu 'Ali al-Hasan bin al-Hasan bin al-Haytham (Alhazen)

(965?–1040)

The renowned Arab mathematician and scientist Abu 'Ali al-Hasan bin al-Hasan bin al-Haytham was born at Basrah, Iraq, in 965. Some time after he had achieved fame as a scholar he was induced to move to Cairo by the Fatimid Caliph al-Hakim, who died in 1021. Possibly the caliph, who is known to have patronized the great astronomer Ibn Yunus (died 1009), simply wished to add a luminary to his court. According to one report, however, al-Hakim heard that Ibn al-Haytham had a plan for regulating the waters of the Nile and summoned the scholar to Cairo for the specific purpose of putting this plan into effect.

On his way to Aswan at the head of a group of workers, Ibn al-Haytham began to have doubts about his scheme. The ancient Egyptian buildings he observed on the banks of the Nile were so impressive that he realized that his plan, if it were at all feasible, would have been carried out by the capable engineers who had designed and built them. His fears were confirmed when he inspected the place to the south of Aswan called *al-janadil*. Here he had expected to see the water descend from a high ground, and he found that he had been mistaken. He now had to break the bad news to the caliph. His apology was accepted without penalty, and he was even put in charge of a government office.

Ibn al-Haytham, however, did not feel safe in his new position, being so close to the eccentric and unpredictable al-Hakim. To be relieved from his duties without appearing to be disloyal, he feigned madness until al-Hakim's death. He then left the house to which he had been confined and moved to the Azhar Mosque, where he resumed his activities as an author and teacher of mathematics. According to one story, he earned his living by copying a number of basic mathematical works (including Euclid's *Elements* and Ptolemy's *Almagest*) once a year. He died in Cairo about 1040.

The preceding account, derived from a thirteenth-century source, suggests that Ibn al-Haytham spent much of his later life in loneliness, either as a pretended madman or as a recluse leading an ascetic life in a *qubbah* (a small domed structure) at the gate of the Azhar Mosque. This impression is counterbalanced, however, by other scattered bits of information that indicate that he traveled a great deal and had contact with other well-known scholars of his time. He tutored the young prince al-Mubushshir bin Fatik (died about 1060) in mathematics and astronomy and exchanged "questions on the Milky Way and on place" with the Egyptian physician Ibn Ridwan (died 1061).

Two lists of Ibn al-Haytham's works that were compiled by the author himself have been preserved by Ibn Abi Usaybi'ah (died 1270). The first list, written when Ibn al-Haytham was sixty-three, contains twenty-five titles on mathematics and forty-five titles on physical and metaphysical questions. These works include discussions of Euclid, Apollonius, and Archimedes, as well as commentaries on the philosophical works of Aristotle and on the medical works of Galen. Some are devoted to questions of Islamic theology. The second list, written seventeen months after the first, contains twenty-one titles covering roughly the same range of subjects as the first. More than sixty works of Ibn al-Haytham are now known to be extant, and most of them are included in a third list, which also was preserved by Ibn Abi Usaybi'ah.

Ibn al-Haytham's most important contributions were in the fields of optics, astronomy, and mathematics. His most important single work is the comprehensive *Kitab al-Manazir* (On Optics). Until the revival of optical research in Persia toward the end of the thirteenth century, Ibn al-Haytham was mainly known to the Islamic world as a mathematician and as an astronomer, but his best-known and most influential work in Europe was the *Optics*. It was largely on the basis of this book that George Sarton described Ibn al-Haytham as "the greatest Muslim physicist and one of the greatest students of optics of all times." The only text in print is of the medieval Latin translation, but there is a first-rate analytical study of it in Arabic by Mustafa Nazif.

Other extant works by Ibn al-Haytham on optical subjects include *On the Light of the Moon*, which argues that the moon shines like a self-luminous object though its light is borrowed from the sun; *On the Halo and the Rainbow*; *On Spherical Burning Mirrors*; *On Paraboloidal Burning Mirrors*; *On the Burning Sphere*; and *On the Shape of the Eclipse*, which examines the *camera obscura* phenomena.

Although Ibn al-Haytham's achievements in astronomy do not equal those of the best astronomers in Islam, his extant works show that he had mastered the techniques of Ptolemaic astronomy. Some of these works also reveal his ability to deal in a more than ordinary way with the standard problems that received attention from Arabic astronomers (such as the problem of determining the *qiblah*, the direction

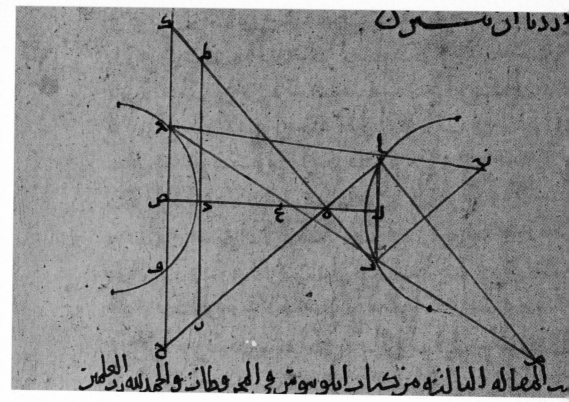

Ibn al-Haytham is said to have earned his living in Cairo by copying mathematical classics for sale. The attached diagram is from a copy he made of an Arabic version of Apollonius' Conics.

to be faced in prayer). A critique of Ptolemaic planetary models as presented in Ptolemy's *Almagest* and *Planetary Hypotheses* appears to have inspired research that led to their replacement by non-Ptolemaic arrangements in the thirteenth-century Maragha and fourteenth-century Damascus. The only one of his astronomical treatises known to the medieval West was *On the Configuration of the World*, in which the Ptolemaic planetary theory is described in terms of transparent physical bodies whose combined motions produce the apparent motions of the planets. The treatise was translated several times into Hebrew and Latin and has been shown to have influenced Renaissance astronomers.

Ibn al-Haytham secured a notable place in the history of mathematics by his treatment of the problem now bearing his Latinized name, Alhazen. This problem is discussed in the mathematical sections of his *Optics*. More than twenty other mathematical treatises of his have also survived. Some of these deal with Euclidean problems—for example, *Solution of the Difficulties in Euclid's Elements* and *Commentary*

on the *Premises of Euclid's Elements*. Others deal with quadrature problems—for example, *On the Quadrature of the Circle* and *On Lunes* (figures contained between the arcs of two circles). Still others are on properties of conic sections. There is also a long treatise on the methods of analysis and synthesis, with illustrative applications to geometry, astronomy, and music.

In a short and not very informative autobiographical note appended to his first bibliography, Ibn al-Haytham wrote that at an early age he was perplexed by the plurality of sects and beliefs. Convinced that the truth was one, he doubted them all. Later on, when he was more capable of rational thought, he made it his aim to seek the "essence of truth." After much study he came to the conclusion that "truth could only be reached through opinions whose matter was sensible and whose form was rational." Though this does not tell us a great deal, it is in keeping with what we know of Ibn al-Haytham's strikingly empirical approach, and it is consistent with his abiding interest in the mathematical sciences.

ABDELHAMID I. SABRA

167

Abu al-Hasan Thabit bin Qurrah as-Sabi' al-Harrani
(Died 901)

Abu al-Hasan Thabit bin Qurrah as-Sabi' al-Harrani was, as his name tells us, one of the Sabians of Harran in Mesopotamia. These were the descendants of an ancient Semitic pagan community who, after the conquests of Alexander the Great, adopted Greek culture and language. Their strong attachment to Hellenistic culture earned their city, Harran, the name of Hellenopolis. They were deeply influenced by Neoplatonism and Hermeticism, among other trends in Hellenistic thought. As adherents of a religion that assigned important roles to the stars, they cultivated astrology, which required knowledge of astronomy and mathematics as well. At the time of al-Ma'mun (813–833), they were advised to adopt the name "Sabians" (after the sect mentioned in the Qur'an) to avoid conversion to Islam. As a group bearing that name they survived for a long time after the Arab conquest. Given the Sabians' knowledge of Syriac and Greek, in addition to their interest in the Greek sciences, it is not surprising that some of the important translators of Greek scientific works into Arabic should have come from among them. Undoubtedly Thabit bin Qurrah was the most prominent of these translators.

The story of how Thabit moved to Baghdad was first told by the tenth-century bibliographer Ibn an-Nadim in his *Fihrist*. In fact, he gave two alternative accounts. The first is that Thabit had earned his living as a money-changer at Harran until he was discovered by the well-known mathematician Muhammad bin Musa bin Shakir, who was on his way back to Baghdad from what had possibly been a manuscript-hunting trip to Byzantium. Impressed by Thabit's linguistic skills, Ibn Musa took him to Baghdad, where such talents were in demand. The other account is that Thabit went to Baghdad on his own to study with Muhammad bin Musa. In any case we are told that, as a translator, Thabit was patronized by the three sons of Musa bin Shakir—Muhammad, Ahmad, and al-Hasan—who are known to have been active in acquiring Greek scientific manuscripts and having them translated into Arabic.

It was Muhammad again, according to the same source, who introduced Thabit to the Caliph al-Mu'tadid and recommended his appointment as a court astrologer—an influential position that brought benefits to the Sabian community at large. Although an employee of the caliphal court and an intimate companion of al-Mu'tadid, Thabit never converted to Islam.

Thabit wrote both in Syriac, his native language, and in Arabic. His Syriac writings included tracts on Sabian doctrines, rituals, and prayers; a large work on music, which was not translated into Arabic; and a medical treatise, in which he criticized the philosopher al-Kindi (his patrons, the sons of Musa, were enemies of al-Kindi). This last work, later translated into Arabic by one of Thabit's Christian students, 'Isa bin Usayd, was much praised by Ishaq bin Hunayn (died about 910).

Thabit was responsible for some of the most important Arabic translations of Greek works—for example, Archimedes' *Sphere and Cylinder* and *Measurement of the Circle* and Apollonius' *Conics* (Books V to VII). He revised Ishaq bin Hunayn's translations of Euclid's *Elements* and Ptolemy's *Almagest* (both revisions are extant) and also, it is reported, made independent translations of these two works. Medieval Europe first came into immediate contact with Archimedes' work when Thabit's translation of *Measurement of the Circle* was rendered into Latin in the twelfth century. There were, in fact, two Latin versions, the second by Gerard of Cremona. Thabit's revision of Ishaq's Arabic version of Euclid's *Elements* was translated into Latin in the same century.

Thabit was not only a translator but also a prolific author. The list of his works, as preserved by the thirteenth-century biographer Ibn al-Qifti in his *Ta'rikh al-Hukama'*, contains more than seventy titles. They range over many fields—mathematics, physics, astronomy, astrology, philosophy, ethics, scientific instruments, music, mechanics, and medicine. In addition, Thabit wrote commentaries on Aristotle's *Physics*, Euclid's *Elements* (Books XIV and XV), and Ptolemy's *Almagest* (Books I and II). He also composed epitomes of works by Galen and Hippocrates, Nicomachus' *Arithmetic*, Ptolemy's *Quadripartitium*, Aristotle's *De interpretatione* and *Analytica Priora* and Ptolemy's *Almagest*. Some of his astronomical works became available to the medieval West in Latin translations, and many of them survived in the original Arabic.

Several of Thabit's descendants were also illustrious figures in Arabic science. His son Sinan (died 943) was one of the most esteemed physicians of his time and was put in charge of some of the hospitals established at Baghdad during the reign of al-Muqtadir (908–932). He served as personal physician not only to al-Muqtadir but also to his successors, al-Qahir (932–934) and ar-Radi (934–940). A

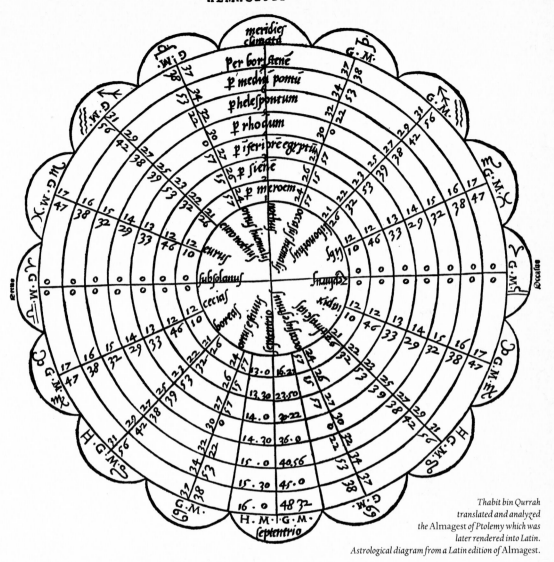

*Thabit bin Qurrah
translated and analyzed
the Almagest of Ptolemy which was
later rendered into Latin.
Astrological diagram from a Latin edition of Almagest.*

Sabian most of his life, he finally converted to Islam under pressure from al-Qahir. An extant list of his works shows that he wrote on history, politics, and religion, as well as on astronomy and mathematics. Thabit's grandson Ibrahim bin Sinan (died 946), a mathematician, did important work in geometry and astronomy and also made significant contributions in the field of scientific instruments—notably, a treatise on shadow instruments, which he began when he was seventeen and which was much appreciated by later scholars, and a comprehensive work on sundials. Another grandson, Thabit bin Sinan (died 976), was a distinguished

physician and hospital director like his father. A "well-known" work of general history is attributed to him, and a sequel was written by his nephew, the scribe and belletrist Hilal bin al-Muhassin bin Ibrahim as-Sabi'.

Certainly the Ibn Qurrah family occupies a unique position in the history of Arabic culture. It can safely be said that Islamic science would not have been the same without the astounding efforts of the Sabian Thabit in transmitting influential Hellenistic modes of thought to the Arabs. If his gifted heirs were lesser luminaries, they nonetheless sustained a family tradition of remarkable distinction.

ABDELHAMID I. SABRA

The Life Sciences

Sami K. Hamarneh was Curator-Historian of Pharmacy and Health at
the Smithsonian Institution's National Museum of History and
Technology from 1959 until his retirement in 1977. He has taught at
George Washington University and at the University of Pennsylvania
and has been a Visiting Professor at the University of Aleppo. He
currently is a Professor at King Fahd Medical Research Center at
King Abdulaziz University. Dr. Hamarneh is the author of a series of
three volumes on *Indexes of Arabic Manuscripts on Medicine and
Pharmacy* (The National Library of Cairo, 1967; the Zahiriyal Library
of Damascus, 1969; and the British Library of London, 1975);
Temples of the Muses and a History of Pharmacy Museums, 1972;
Origins of Pharmacy and Therapy in the Near East, 1973; *The Physician,
Therapist and Surgeon Ibn al-Quff*, 1974; *Islamic Bicentennial Exhibition*,
Washington, D.C., 1976; and *Directory of Historians of Arabic-Islamic
Science*, 1980.

The Life Sciences

Sami K. Hamarneh

"Life sciences" is a modern term. It designates those highly structured disciplines that focus on the study of living organisms and conveniently distinguishes them both from the physical sciences, which deal with inanimate matter, and from the arts and humanities. In a sense, therefore, it is misleading to apply this term to the medieval Islamic world, which was not characterized by the formal specialization of the present day. The "life scientists" of the time were not simply zoologists or entomologists, pediatricians or veterinarians. The physician, for example, might also be a mathematician, a poet, an astronomer, a musician, a linguist, a chemist, a philosopher, or a theologian. Even in the practice of medicine he might be, not only an internist, an oculist, and a surgeon, but also a hospital administrator, a psychologist, and a designer of medical facilities and equipment. Moreover, he might apply his knowledge of music, astrology, alchemy, or mathematics in an effort to increase his ability to choose and compound his cures. The great scientists of the period in the East were masters of many disciplines and typified "the Renaissance man" in the Occident.

In retrospect, however, we recognize that a process of academic and occupational differentiation was going on in medieval Islam in all fields of human endeavor, including the sciences. The Islamic empire raised the sciences to a level of formal sophistication never achieved before and provided a foundation on which the modern sciences have grown.

The full flowering of the arts and sciences, and of medical science and natural history in particular, during the period of the Islamic empire is at least partially explained by the reverential and acquisitive attitudes characteristic of the Arab people from earliest days. In a monumental work on the classification of nations, *Tabaqat al-Umam*, the Toledan judge and historian Abu al-Qasim Sa'id al-Andalusi (died 1070) describes the cultural attitudes that prevailed in Arabia before and shortly after the birth of Islam:

> The Arabs prided themselves on advancing their philological skill and on perfecting lexicology and etymology. They excelled in poetry and in oratory. In their contacts with and travels to neighboring countries they developed knowledge of peoples and lands. Possessing a natural tendency for eloquent speech, they were noted for their ability to memorize poetry, narrate stories, and retell chronologies.

173

From repeated observations rather than scientific reasoning and experimentation, they acquired some knowledge in astronomy, astrology, and meteorology, areas related to their modes of living. In early Islam, they focused on philologic sciences and Muslim jurisprudence. The only other science that was held in a high esteem among them was the healing art, a profession acquired by very few, yet, because of the need for its services, appreciated by the majority.

After their military conquests and the spread of the new faith, the Arabs assimilated the cultures of their more advanced subjects, incorporating, adapting, and making good use of every talent, skill, and cultural advantage that was not hostile to their religion and spirit. In time, through contact, education, and vigorous translation activities, great advances were made in many fields—not least among them the life sciences.

As rulers of a vast territory, encompassing many cultures, the Arabs were able to draw on diverse sources to advance their knowledge and practice of the healing arts. They utilized indigenous folk medicine as well as written treatises from the Syriac, Persian, Sanskrit, and Greek legacies, the latter being the most important. Examples of the cross-cultural interchanges that took place between the Arabs and their subject peoples are numerous. The Arab physician 'Isa (Masih) bin Hakam of Damascus, in compiling his medical dissertation al-Haruni-yah (named after Caliph Harun ar-Rashid, who died in 809), relied on Greek sources. A junior contemporary, 'Ali bin Sahl Rabban at-Tabari, devoted a large section of his *Paradise of Wisdom* (completed in 850) to a description of Indian medicine, which he had extracted from Sanskrit sources. The physicians of the Bakhtishu' and Masawayh families, who served the caliphs for over a century, contributed to the maturing of Arabic medicine by consulting Syriac treatises and writing books on Syriac medicine.

INTERNAL AND CLINICAL MEDICINE

Almost all branches of the healing arts in Islam were indebted more to the 'indefatigable efforts of Hunayn bin Ishaq al-'Ibadi (809–873) and his team of translators than to any other ninth-century author or educator. Together with his students and associates, Hunayn made the most important medical writings of the Greeks available in Arabic, either by direct translations from the Greek or through Syriac versions, and established a solid foundation for the development of Arabic medicine by devising a distinctive methodology, which was followed, modified, and perfected during the following century.

Before Hunayn's death, the extant works of Hippocrates, Dioscorides, Galen, and Galen's commentators, including the last of the Byzantine physicians of the seventh century, became available to students and practitioners throughout the Islamic domain. Digests, compendiums, and synopses based on the Greek classics were abundant in all areas of the life sciences. Hunayn himself wrote an introduction to the healing arts, *al-Masa'il fi at-Tibb*, known in Latin as the *Vade Mecum* of Johannitius, which presented synopses of Greek precepts on the health sciences. It influenced medical teaching and practice not only in Islam but in Christendom as well.

By the close of the ninth century, a new star began to shine in Arabic medicopharmaceutical circles, the physician Abu Bakr Muhammad bin Zakariya ar-Razi (865–925). Ar-Razi

A frontispiece honoring nine Greek physicians, from an Arabic copy of Book of Antidotes.

بسم الله الرحمن الرحيم

وما توفيقي إلا بالله

جوامع المقالة الأولى من كتاب جالينوس في المجربات وهي التي يذكر فيها منافع

خاصة بنفسه يحيى النحوي الإسكندراني على حسب الجوامع أخرجه لأنه اسقط ما لا يحتاج إليه من الكتاب

الجوامع لابني حجاج إليها قصيرها اساسا وبني عليها كتابه ذكر اسما الاطبا الذين الفوا الترياق واحد بعد واحد

وزياده كل واحد منهم على صاحبه ممن تقدمه ونقصانه عنه وهو تسعه

became the greatest clinician, pathologist, medical educator, and philosopher of his time. His writings advanced the contemporary understanding of internal medicine substantially, and many of his ideas and original concepts regarding psychiatrics, the doctor-patient relationship, the diagnosis of diseases, chemotherapy, and methods of treatment remain valid today. His discourse on smallpox and measles, for example, gained him worldwide recognition. In fourteen chapters, ar-Razi dealt with the causes of smallpox, its diagnosis and treatment (even in its most virulent forms), its universal occurrences, precautions that should be taken against its spread, and the characteristics that distinguish it from measles. A skin rash occurs in both diseases, but ar-Razi identified the specific symptoms of smallpox as fever, headache, nose and skin itching, redness of the eyes and cheeks, and restlessness. He listed the more evident symptoms of measles, in addition to the appearance of spots, as perturbation, distress, and faintness — concepts accepted in present-day pathology. In his treatise on colic, ar-Razi differentiated its symptoms from those caused by kidney stones or the pains of ileus.

A ten-part treatise on clinical and internal medicine, *al-Kitab al-Mansuri*, dedicated by ar-Razi to his patron, Mansur bin Ishaq bin Ahmad bin Asad, and known in Latin as *Liber ad Almansorem* became a basic reference work. In it he discusses such varied subjects as general medical theories and definitions, diets and drugs and their effects on the human body, a regimen for preserving health, mother and child care, skin diseases, mouth hygiene, climatology and the effect of environment on health, and epidemiology and toxicology. In his comprehensive medical encyclopedia, *al-Hawi*, and his treatise on psychic therapy, *at-Tibb ar-Ruhani*, ar-Razi provided considerable insight into the methods, applications, and scope of internal, clinical, and psychiatric medicine, as well as the interpretation of general health precepts. Recognizing the relationship between psyche and soma, he attempted to treat diseases of both mind and body.

Ar-Razi's worthy successor 'Ali bin 'Abbas al-Majusi (died 994), in his *Liber regius* (*al-Maliki*), contributed important original observations on medical theories and diagnosis, including new concepts regarding the impact of environment on health, the nutritional value of diets, and the action of drugs on human beings. His system of codifying, classifying, and theorizing details captured the admiration of later practitioners in both East and West. His work was surpassed only by the elaborate *Canon of Medicine* by Ibn Sina, or Avicenna, the celebrated physician-philosopher (980–1037).

Another physician-philosopher and a reformer in matters related to public health and clean environment was al-Mukhtar bin 'Abdun bin Butlan (died 1068) of Baghdad. Ibn Butlan's *Taqwim as-Sihhah*, on the preservation and restoration of good health, won him great prestige in medical circles during the Middle Ages. It was translated into Latin and was published repeatedly. Ibn Butlan elaborated on the six "non-natural principles" that had been identified earlier by Hunayn: clean air, moderate diet and drink, rest and work, wakefulness and slumber, evacuation of superfluities, and emotional reactions and involvement. If these six principles are kept in equilibrium, he maintained, health results; if abused or imbalanced, sickness occurs. Ibn Butlan also recommended the utilization of fine music to lift the morale of patients and help speed their recovery.

A 1231 copy of Ibn Butlan's Maintaining Good Health, *an eleventh-century hygienic manual.*

After a short period in which the development of medical science seemed to level off in the east, new and vigorous medical activities took place in the central and western regions of the Islamic world. Ibn al-Jazzar (died about 984) was a successful medical practitioner, therapist, and author in Kairouan in modern Tunisia. One of his most interesting publications was a book on the management and care of children from the moment of conception to adolescence. It includes numerous health tips to mothers and midwives. Ibn al-Jazzar also wrote on therapeutics, dietetic, and internal medicine, works that made him famous in Andalusia as elsewhere in Islam. They were translated into Latin and received much attention in European medical circles.

Ibn al-Jazzar's text on child care was surpassed only by a book on gynecology, embryology, and pediatrics by 'Arib bin Sa'id of Cordoba. Ibn Sa'id's book was the most significant work written on this subject in any language up to the tenth century. He dedicated it to his patron, al-Hakam al-Mustansir (reigned 961–976), a generous caliph who did much to promote science and the arts throughout his domain. Two of Ibn Sa'id's junior contemporaries and countrymen, Ibn Juljul and az-Zahrawi, also made major contributions to the advancement of Arabic medicine—in pharmacy and medical botany, in internal and clinical medicine, and in surgery.

The development of Arabic clinical medicine and therapeutics reached its peak in Andalusia, in the works of the physician-statesman Ibn Wafid (died 1068) and in the medical writing, teaching, and practice of Ibn Zuhr (died 1162), who was known in Latin as Avenzoar. In *at-Taysir*, his famous book on the diagnosis and treatment of diseases, Ibn Zuhr described, possibly for the first time in medical history, mediastinal abscesses as well as wet and dry pericarditis. He also emphasized medical experimentation, bedside clinical observation and treat-

177

ment, and pathology. He even criticized Ibn Sina's *al-Qanun* for its almost total emphasis on theoretical concepts and philosophical reasoning at the expense of clinical, practical medicine. Ibn Zuhr's younger contemporary and close friend Ibn Rushd (1125–1198), who was known in the West as Averroes, was more of a philosopher and theologian than a physician. Nevertheless, he wrote two important medical books: *al-Kulliyat*, a text on general medical theories and precepts, which was translated into Latin in 1255 and printed independently in Venice in 1482; and a commentary on Ibn Sina's famous medical poem, *Canticum de medicina*.

Andalusia was the birthplace of another famous physician-philosopher, Rabbi Musa bin Maymun (1134–1204), who wrote extensively on internal medicine, therapeutics, materia medica, and health and environment. His greatest popularity, however, was not in Andalusia, where he grew up, but in Syria and Egypt under the Ayyubid dynasty. In a period of great intellectual productivity, especially in the life sciences, Ibn Maymun helped to keep the torch of learning and scholarship shining brightly. His many publications, including extant manuscripts in the original Arabic as well as Hebrew versions of them, were recently edited and evaluated. It is recorded that Maymun's fame spread to Iraq, where it induced the physician-naturalist 'Abd al-Latif al-Baghdadi (1162–1231) to visit Egypt to hear Ibn Maymun lecture. The fact that the two foremost physicians of their age were familiar with each other's work despite being separated by thousands of miles shows how extraordinarily well diffused scholarly knowledge was in medieval Islam.

HOSPITALS AND MEDICAL EDUCATION

It was in Islam, under the patronage of the Arab caliphs, that hospitals were first established, and they flourished in the Muslim world throughout the period of empire. The early Arab concept of the hospital became the prototype for the development of the modern hospital—an institution operated by private owners or by government and devoted to the promotion of health, the cure of diseases, and the teaching and expanding of medical knowledge. Within the Islamic domain, from the beginning of the ninth century onward, hospitals were generously endowed from the state treasury and operated under lay administration and management. They served both men and women, in separate wards. In the tenth century, during the reign of al-Muqtadir (908–932), Sinan bin Thabit bin Qurrah extended hospital services to meet the needs of neighboring rural areas, prisons, and the "inner city"—a program that has only recently been adopted in the West.

Sinan's contemporary ar-Razi considered hospitals of primary importance in providing practical training in the health professions and in disseminating health information. Late in the tenth century, the fame of the 'Adudi hospital in Baghdad had spread far and wide. This remarkable institution had twenty-four doctors on its staff and was equipped with lecture halls and a generously supported library. Students from the eastern and western regions of the Islamic domain traveled hundreds and thousands of miles to study at 'Adudi, and its graduate physicians were world-famous. As a result of its influence, new hospitals were constructed and older hospitals were reorganized in larger cities throughout the Muslim world.

In the twelfth and thirteenth centuries, hospitals in Syria and Egypt had achieved such high levels of performance that travelers and historians regarded them as one of the treasures of Muslim civilization. They attracted gifted students and the best medical educators and enjoyed rich endowments and generous patronage. They were elegant, spacious buildings, equipped with comfortable lecture halls, extensive libraries, well-stocked pharmacy shops, and efficient laboratories, where medications could be freshly prepared and dispensed.

Ibn Abi Usaybi'ah, the greatest medical historian of medieval Islam, was educated at two of the most famous hospitals in Islam: the Nuri in Damascus and the Nasiri in Cairo. In his writings he eloquently described hospital activities that he had been able to observe and compare firsthand. His favorite student, Ibn al-Quff (died 1286), who later became a famous physician-surgeon, also trained in the hospitals of Damascus.

OPHTHALMOLOGY AND EYE DISEASES

In the hot and dusty plains of the Middle East, endemic diseases of the eye, such as trachoma and ophthalmia, were unusually prevalent. This accounts for the extraordinary progress made by Muslim physicians in the field of ophthalmology. Through daily practice and gradually improved techniques and performances, Arab physicians and oculists attained a level of proficiency in ophthalmic science never reached by the ancient and classical sages. Their literary contributions were admired and copied throughout Europe and were not surpassed anywhere in the world until the seventeenth century.

Among Arabic authors, Hunayn bin Ishaq was perhaps the first to write a systematic manual on ophthalmology, complete with diagrams. His work was elaborated upon by later authors and has survived up to the present time. In ten treatises, written between 840 and 860 and completed by his student and nephew, Hubaysh, Hunayn discussed the anatomy of the eye, brain, and optical nerves and the physiology, diseases, and treatment of the eye. Although he copied extensively from Greek works, he added many new, personal observations. Writing early in the tenth century, ar-Razi was possibly the first to describe pupillary reflexes.

Arabic progress in ophthalmology reached a peak about the year 1000 in the work of 'Ali bin 'Isa, an oculist of Baghdad. His book, *Dhakhirat al-Kahhalin* (*A Thesaurus for Ophthalmologists*), was a comprehensive summary of all the achievements of the past. His contemporary 'Ammar bin 'Ali al-Mawsili was the first to introduce the technique of suction removal of the cataract in order to avoid the "aqueous calamity." He devised and used a hollow needle for the purpose, a technique revived in 1846 by a French doctor, Blanchet. This high level of performance was continued in the work of Ibn al-Haytham (Alhazen) who died in 1039, and a century later in *al-Murshid*, a guide to the oculist written by Muhammad bin Qassum bin Aslam al-Ghafiqi of Andalusia. Interestingly, al-Ghafiqi illustrated his manual with pictures of the surgical instruments he used in performing eye operations, a practice begun by the surgeon az-Zahrawi.

The medical revival that occurred during the Ayyubid dynasty continued under the Mamluks. This is evident in the work of Khalifah bin Abu al-Mahasin of Aleppo—whose writings, completed in 1256, include a useful introduction to eye surgery and descriptions of eye operations, as well as diagrams and drawings of surgical instruments—and in the book *Nur al-'Uyun* (*Light of the Eyes*), completed in 1296 by the oculist Salah ad-Din bin Yusuf of Hamah. Ibn Abu al-Mahasin and Ibn Yusuf were both Syrians. The last great ophthalmologist of the Arabic period was Ibn al-Akfani ash-Shadhili of Egypt, who died of the Black Death in 1348. His work *Kasuf ar-Rayn fi Ahwal al-'Ayn* was a summary clarification of all existing knowledge about the eye.

SURGERY, ANATOMY, AND PHYSIOLOGY

The Arab physician-philosopher Ibn Rushd prudently stated that "whosoever becomes fully familiar with human anatomy and physiology, his faith in God will increase." This statement explains why surgery was accepted by the Arabs from the early days of Islam. Moreover, Muslim surgeons were among the first to use narcotic and sedative drugs in operations: Islam teaches that God has provided man with a great variety of natural remedies to cure his ills. It is man's obligation to identify them and to use them with skill and compassion.

During the ninth century, Hunayn translated the works of Galen on anatomy and surgery, and ar-Razi devoted large sections to this art in his larger medical encyclopedias, *al-Mansuri* and *al-Hawi*. But al-Majusi, or Haly Abbas (died 994), is considered the first great theorist on anatomy and physiology in Arabic medicine. His *Liber regius* was the first Islamic work to deal with surgery in detail, and he was the first to use the tourniquet to prevent arterial bleeding.

The greatest achievements in medieval surgery, however, are attributed to az-Zahrawi of Moorish Spain (about 940–1013). An important part of his medical encyclopedia, *at-Tasrif*, deals with obstetrics, pediatrics, and midwifery, as well as with general human anatomy. The last treatise is devoted to surgery—including cautery, the treatment of wounds, the extracting of arrows, oral hygiene, and the setting of bones in simple and compound fractures. He used antiseptics in the treatment of wounds and skin injuries; devised sutures from animal intestines, silk, wool, and other substances; and developed techniques to widen urinary passages and explore body cavities surgically. His surgery contained about two hundred surgical instruments that he himself had designed and had depicted in his writings. Such instruments, with modifications, were later used by many surgeons in Christendom as well as in Islam.

Az-Zahrawi's discussion of mother and child health and of the profession of midwifery is of particular interest in the history of nursing. His text implies the existence of a flourishing profession of nurses and midwives in general practice, a fact that may be explained by the reluctance of many conservative Muslim families to seek the assistance of male doctors in normal childbirth. Skilled physicians and obstetricians, such as az-Zahrawi, instructed and trained midwives so that they could carry on their duties with competence.

The continuation of warfare, especially during the period of the Crusades, and the revival of learning under the Ayyubids resulted in major improvements in surgical practices in Syria and Egypt, and the study of anatomy and physiology was given greater emphasis by such physician-educators as Ibn Maymun and al-Baghdadi. During the reign of the Mamluks in Egypt, Ibn an-Nafis (about 1210–1288) wrote a very important text on anatomy and physiology

Drawings of dental instruments, including a tongue depressor and tooth extractors.
from a surgical treatise by az-Zahrawi,

حيز الفوز قليل الخبر وبما يعرض له بالعزيز: بازكار احمر الفوز واصله غليظها
بلا تعرض له ايضا بالعزيز وثوب نزف بر اثر كده حتى ينضج ينهم
نبهم واما ان يبقى من خازنه ٥ وازكار ابيط الفوز مشتد يزا وزكار اضله رقيقا
بهزالغي ينبغي ان يفصح ٥ والفعل جدا ان تنظر فبل العمل ان زكار فنرسكي
ورمدا اعار سكوننا ناطلا ونفض بعد النفظ بجبنه بالجلس القليل بعزا
الشمير وراسه بجزط وينفتح فيه وناخذخادم ينز يريدا بتبكسرلسازه
الانبقا بالة هي صورتها

تضع مزيضة ان خابرين بكوز رقيعة كالسكيز باذ اكبنت بما البسار ويبنزلطا
الوزم ووفع بضرط عليها بعز مقاره واقرز رها اي الموزله وتجزبطا الخارج ما
اكل من عنزا بجزب معها شيئا من الصفافات ثم تنطعها با لغ هزه صورة
تشبه النعم الا ان بطا منغصعين بدا والهزة منفض جزا الا خرا احاط
جزا تضع من العنز ومن بولاح مشفي

as a commentary on Ibn Sina's *al-Qanun*. In terms of originality, the commentary surpasses the text itself. It contains the first clear and detailed description of the pulmonary circulation of the blood and several original observations on comparative anatomy. Ibn an-Nafis' contemporary Ibn al-Quff (1233–1286), in his manual on the surgical art, gave the most comprehensive description of surgical operations and treatment of bodily injuries ever contained in any Arabic text of its kind. He explained the function of the capillaries—the minute blood passages that connect arteries and veins—and the action of cardial valves in the veins and in the heart chambers, describing how they open in only one direction to keep blood flowing in the same way. We are also indebted to him for making the first appeal for uniformity of standards for weights and measures used in medicine, pharmacy, and surgery.

ZOOLOGY AND VETERINARY MEDICINE

Long before the rise of Islam, the Arab tribes of the Arabian Peninsula developed a way of life that made them extremely reliant on domesticated animals for survival. Harsh environmental conditions in the Arabian heartland, a nomadic and seminomadic mode of existence, and an economy based largely on trade and travel produced an unusually strong interest in the care and feeding of animals for food, by-products, and transportation. The spread of Islam, the

Illustration from Book on Veterinary Medicine, *a manual on the care and handling of horses, copied in Baghdad.*

outward movement of the Arab people, the obligations of conquest, and the formalization of an Arab-Islamic culture raised this basic interest in animal husbandry to the level of a science.

The first comprehensive zoological study of animals in Arabic was *al-Hayawan*, by al-Jahiz (died about 869). Written in an interesting and eloquent literary style, it covers animal life in Iraq and in neighboring countries, describing the kinds of animals, their characteristics and behavior, and their diseases and treatment. Several other works in this field deal with narrower topics, such as sheep, camels, or wild animals. The most comprehensive work in the field, *Hayat al-Hayawan* (*The Life of Animals*), was written by the Egyptian philosopher-theologian Kamal ad-Din ad-Damiri (died 1405). Ad-Damiri arranged and discussed animals in alphabetical order, listing their characteristics, qualities, and habits, as well as the medicinal values of their organs as mentioned in folk medicine. It is worth noting that this work, like a number of other Arabic texts on animals and natural life, contains rudimentary concepts of evolutionary theory, including the doctrine of survival of the fittest.

In the early centuries of Islam, several important manuals on veterinary medicine were published in Arabic for the use of the farrier. During the ninth century, the philologist Ibn Qurayb al-Asma'i and his contemporaries produced several praiseworthy texts on lexicography and natural history that provided a wealth of information of zoological interest. But the first systematic book on horsemanship and the art of the farrier, *al-Furusiyah wa al-Khayl*, was written by Muhammad bin Akhi Hizam around 860. It discusses the behavior and characteristics of horses, as well as diseases and treatment. Several similar texts followed, many of them containing beautiful illustrations of horses and other domestic animals, depicted with meticulous attention to anatomical accuracy.

The greatest medieval work in veterinary medicine is the comprehensive manual *Kamil as-Sina'atayn*, by Abu Bakr al-Baytar of Cairo (died 1340), who was the groom of King an-Nasir Muhammad. This book covers animal husbandry, breeding, variations in wild and domestic animals, horsemanship, and knighthood and contains a section on birds, especially those domesticated in Egypt and Syria. Al-Baytar devoted a major part of his work to a discussion of animal diseases and to the methods and drugs used in treatment. As in many similar texts written in this period, there are also passages dealing with the use of animal organs in therapeutics, a tradition dating back to Aristotle.

PHARMACY AND PHARMACOLOGY

Pharmacy, as a recognized profession, is an Arab-Islamic institution. Under Islam, it became an independent science—separate from, yet cooperating with, medicine—and it was practiced by skilled and trained specialists. It achieved this status about 800, under the patronage of the Abbasid caliphs. The first privately owned and managed pharmacy shops were opened in the early ninth century in Baghdad, the Abbasid capital, where drugs and spices from Asia and Africa were readily available and where the proximity of military installations increased the need for medications. Within a short period of time, pharmacy shops sprang up in other large cities of the Islamic world.

Pharmaceutical preparations were manufactured and distributed commercially in the marketplace and dispensed by physicians and pharmacists in a variety of forms: ointments, electuaries, conserves, troches, pills, elixirs, confections, tinctures, suppositories, and inhalations. Formulas for these skillfully prepared medications were included in Arabic texts, unofficial pharmacopoeias, and pandects. In time they were included in European pharmaceutical texts, thereby influencing herbals and formularies up to modern times.

Sabur bin Sahl (died 869) was the author of the first known formulary in Islam. It contained many recipes and medications in several pharmaceutical forms for a variety of ailments. Many other compendiums followed, among which were a treatise on pharmacy by ar-Razi and Books II and V of Ibn Sina's *al-Qanun*. But the most important text on pharmacy and materia medica by far was *as-Saydalah*, by Abu ar-Rayhan al-Biruni (died 1051). The author gave the most detailed definition of pharmacy and of the function and duties of the pharmacist that had yet been written. He also defined pharmacology and other branches of the healing arts in which professionals work together as a team to achieve the best results.

About a century thereafter, Ibn at-Tilmidh wrote *al-Aqrabadhin*, a pharmaceutical text explaining how to prepare and prescribe a wide variety of medications. This text became the basic reference for practicing pharmacists in private shops as well as in hospital dispensaries. Some of these hospitals owned tracts of land reserved for the cultivation of medicinal plants, similar to the botanical gardens that later became popular in the West. Fresh, naturally grown products from these gardens were compounded in remedies dispensed for the cure of diseases.

Interest in natural products and ecology was a corollary to the Muslim belief that God provides for the creatures He has created. In nature God provides the right medications for man's ailments, when and where they are most needed. Natural medications are tokens of God's generous attitude toward human beings, His way of enriching their lives and providing for their needs. This belief motivated Muslim naturalists, herbalists, pharmacists, and physicians to seek remedies in nature, rather than in scarce synthetic drugs prepared in laboratories.

The contributions of the Arabs in analyzing the effects of drugs on human beings and animals far exceeded the work done by the ancients in this area. The Arabs discovered many new, simple drugs in their crude forms and gave detailed descriptions of their geographical origins, their physical properties, and the methods of application. They also skillfully described the various pharmaceutical forms of the remedies used and the techniques employed in their manufacture. Their advances in pharmacology and pharmacy were matched by substantial achievements in such related fields as botany, zoology, and mineralogy.

Many Muslim practitioners experimented with drugs in order to learn more about their effect on human beings. Several experiments with drugs and diets that were found useful in treating certain ailments were reported in notebook collections of case histories, sometimes known as *al-Mujarrabat*, which were used in medical schools and copied by later authors. Other manuals of the period included charts, diagrams, and tables and dealt with drugs and diseases in special categories, listing the causes and symptoms of diseases, the seasons of the year in which they occur, and the dosages of drugs administered. Others included mathematical calculations concerning the potency of drugs and the recommended dosages according to age, sex, and the severity of the sickness. Several physicians prescribed and compounded their own medications from recipes they formulated. They gave each remedy a specific name, which often indicated the pharmacological action it would produce—a practice usually followed with modern patent medicines in the West. In their experimentation Arabic authors frequently used a single drug in the treatment of each ailment in order to determine its precise effect.

Increasing incidents of accidental and premeditated poisoning gave impetus to the science of toxicology in Islam. Kings, rulers, and men of wealth dreaded the possibility of poisoning by envious enemies. Court physicians and advisors were encouraged to write on the subject and to recommend precautionary measures, as well as supply candid information. Toxicological manuals and treatises swelled with descriptions of potent drugs found in nature and with prescriptions for specific and universal antidotes. They reported cases of poisoning by means of taste, smell, touch, and sight and gave advice on how to guard against them. Tradition has it that the great theriac—the universal antidote—was devised by the ancient Greeks and perfected in the recipe formulated and recommended by Galen. Galen's treatise on the subject was translated into Arabic, first by Yuhanna bin Batriq and almost a half century later by Hunayn. The theriac, as well as other antidotes, was transmitted from these two versions and was adopted, with modifications, in several Arabic formulas; some Arabic recipes contain more than sixty different ingredients. The introduction of Indian toxicology and the proliferation of Arabic herbals and formularies resulted in further modifications up to the thirteenth

An illustration from the Book of Antidotes *of Pseudo-Galen. A physician looks on as a boy, suffering from snakebite, cures himself by killing and eating the reptile along with some berries from the laurel tree.*

century, when Arab theriacs were introduced to the West. Physicians and apothecaries of the period were fascinated by the "miraculous" effects of the theriacs. Because precision in preparation of these drugs was so important, a tradition of formal demonstration developed in the West. Kings, lords, physicians, and dignitaries in major European cities attended public ceremonies in which large batches of these universal antidotes were compounded, prepared, and certified. They were sold with a guarantee of excellence at exorbitant prices up to the eighteenth century. Ironically, just as warfare promoted advances in surgery, fear of assassination by poison enlarged Arabic pharmacopeias, increased toxicological data, and enriched the fund of knowledge in medical botany, mineralogy, ecology, and therapeutics.

An illustration of an autumn crocus from a 1224 Arabic copy of Materia Medica *by Dioscorides.* Materia Medica, *which describes five hundred plants and their pharmaceutical uses, was one of the first books on medical botany to be translated from the Greek into Arabic.*

MEDICAL BOTANY AND THERAPEUTICS

Physicians and pharmacists in Islam devoted much attention to locating *materia medica* in the three natural kingdoms—plants, animals, and minerals. In their studies of *materia medica*, the Arabs developed a system of classification and investigation based primarily on the five books of Dioscorides, which were completed about 65 A.D. They also borrowed from other sources, however. Certain concepts and some descriptions of simple drugs came from such places as Persia, India, and the Far East, which explains why Arabic *materia medica* abounds in terminology adopted from Berber, Persian, Sanskrit, Greek, and other languages.

In the ninth century, Abu Hanifah ad-Dinawari accumulated impressive data on the medicinal plants known in pre-Islamic Arabia as well as on many others that entered the Arabic vocabulary thereafter. More new words and terminology can be found in the works of Ibn Abu al-Ash'ath in the tenth century, Ibn Wafid and al-Biruni in the eleventh, al-Ghafiqi in the twelfth, and Ibn al-Baytar in the thirteenth. All these authors included substantial amounts of original information as well as data borrowed from other cultures.

AGRICULTURAL SCIENCE AND HUSBANDRY

The legacies of the Greeks and the Nabateans, as well as indigenous traditions, were among the most influential factors in developing agricultural science in Islam. The famous Arabic manual *al-Filahah ar-Rumiyah* is a translation of a Greek text on agriculture. About 904, Ibn Wahshiyah wrote his widely circulated book *al-Filahah an-Nabatiyah*, which, according to his introductory remarks, is a translation from an old text on agriculture based on ancient Nabatean (Aramaic) writings. As Islam expanded, agricultural and horticultural activities flourished, and several detailed manuals were written in Arabic, not only in the eastern regions of the Islamic domain, but in Andalusia as well.

One of the most important and widely read books on the subject to be written in Andalusia was completed by Ibn al-Bassal of Toledo in the second half of the eleventh century. It was edited with a Spanish translation and notes under the title *Libro de agricultura* in 1955. An even more widely recognized text was the twelfth-century *Kitab al-Filahah*, by another Andalusian, Ibn al-'Awwam of Seville. It was translated into both Spanish and French in the nineteenth century. Topics covered in detail in these texts include medicinal plants, species of plants, soil, farming techniques, husbandry, methods of cultivation, tillage, irrigation, agronomy, sharecropping, gardening and landscaping, plant sex life, and fertilization.

Similar activity flourished in Syria, Iraq, and Egypt during the same period and continued to the end of the fourteenth century. In southern Arabia, *Bughyat al-Fallahin*, a manual for farmers published during the fourteenth century under the Rasulid dynasty, includes data compiled from earlier works on agriculture and significant additional information on plants, irrigation, and agronomy in Yemen. Some of the agricultural texts also include astrological advice concerning the days, seasons, and locations that would prove most favorable for sowing seeds and harvesting crops.

ALCHEMY AND ASTROLOGY

From the tenth century to the present time, the origins of alchemy, the true authorship of the Latin and Arabic alchemical writings attributed to Jabir bin Hayyan al-Azdi (known in the West as Geber), and even the existence of this man have been matters of controversy. Some historians believe that Jabir was a name assumed by a number of anonymous authors and that there was no such historical figure. Others believe that he was a real person, born in Kufah in Iraq, who became a Sufist Muslim and served at the Abbasid capital, where he was esteemed as a pioneer alchemist, experimenting in the transmutation of lesser metals into silver and gold.

On the basis of available evidence, it seems reasonable to believe that Jabir did exist and that at least some of the writings bearing his name, such as the book of *ar-Rahmah*, are genuine. Whether or not this is so, it is a fact that Arabic alchemy was alive and flourishing by the end of the eighth century and that Arab alchemists made substantial, voluminous, and influential literary contributions up to the fourteenth century.

By the early ninth century Arab alchemists were reportedly organized into a sort of guild, a group quite distinct from pharmacists and physicians. Their connections almost a century later with the fraternity of Ikhwan as-Safa' (The Brethren of Sincerity) and with the type of mysticism and occultism associated with their writings and life style seem highly probable.

Although the occult art of alchemy, which sought ways to transmute base matter into precious metals and to compound the elixir of life, was alluring to a great many sophisticates, it had many opponents throughout the Islamic period. Some of its antagonists thought that the claims of the alchemists were in fundamental contradiction to Muslim beliefs, despite the attempts of some alchemists to justify their pursuits on religious grounds. The naturalist al-Jahiz and the philosopher Abu Yusuf al-Kindi were among its staunchest critics. Ibn Sina was a moderate opponent of the theory that base metals could be changed into gold. 'Abd al-Latif al-Baghdadi believed in alchemy early in life, but as he grew older he came to consider its theories corrupting to its adherents and became critical of its followers.

Alchemical equipment. The alchemist would place herbs and a small amount of liquid in the bottom section of the distillation vessel (left). The vessel would be placed on an oven (center and right) until the mixture boiled. The steam would rise into the retort, return to a liquid state and flow from the spout as a potent or medicine.

Ar-Razi, however, was a strong supporter of alchemy and a defender of its claims. Fortunately, his approach to alchemy was experimental, rational, and scientific, so that his work actually enhanced alchemy's image. His writings established the foundation for empirical Arabic chemistry, experimental chemotherapy, and objective alchemical procedures. He also described the tools and utensils used in alchemical laboratories, in his recently republished book *On the Secret of Secrets*.

Several important alchemists after ar-Razi continued the search for the "philosophers' stone," which would turn base metals to gold, and further enriched alchemical literature with their writings. Among them were Abu al-Qasim al-Majriti of Andalusia (died 1008), Abu al-Hasan bin Arfa' Ra'sahu (died in Fez, Morocco, 1197), Abu al-Qasim Muhammad al-'Iraqi of Baghdad who flourished in the mid-twelfth century, and the prolific author 'Ali bin Aidamur al-Jildaki (died 1342). Being extremely secretive, possibly because of their repeated failures, these alchemists wrote about their work in highly symbolic, mystical terms, employing arcane jargon almost unintelligible to outsiders and filling their books with figurative and ambiguous expressions, flowery poetry, ornate phrases, and mysterious anecdotes.

Yet, in their search for the "cultivation of gold," alchemists made many contributions to the science of chemistry. They invented many laboratory utensils and improved many others, such as the crucible, alembic, and the retort. They also advanced such chemical techniques and operations as distillation, filtration, straining, calcination, crystallization, and the preparation of chemical elements and compounds. In addition, they improved the manufacture of ceramics, glass, soaps, and perfumes. Because of their belief in the continuance of matter, alchemists contributed significantly to the objectivity of experimentation, to the use of weights and balances, and to the concept of proportional unification of metals.

Unfortunately, alchemy was more akin to the art of astrology than it was to the traditional sciences. The practice of astrology actually antedates alchemy in the Near East, and it is very closely related to the science of astronomy, although many today associate it only with horoscopy and the prediction of future events. Because astrology concerns itself so much with the effects of universal forces on the life and welfare of people, it must be treated as a "life science"—at least as it was practiced in the Islamic period.

The ancient idea that planetary bodies can affect health and well-being associated astrology with medicine. Astrology affirmed the belief that physical sympathy makes earthly things dependent on the movements of celestial bodies, that the virtually incorruptible stars rule over corruptible terrestrial things. Astrologers thought that the position of the seven planets within the zodiac at any time affects human beings. The twelve signs of the zodiac were divided into three groups: the four elements (fire, earth, air, and water); the four humors (blood, phlegm, black bile, and yellow bile); and the four qualities of temperature and humidity (cold, hot, moist, and dry). This division was accepted as a primary concept in Greco-Arab medicine.

At the Abbasid capital, al-Kindi predicted the duration of the dynasty from astrological interpretations, and he considered the twelve signs of the zodiac in his therapeutics. His student Abu Ma'shar, known in Latin as Albumasar, wrote extensively about constellations, birth dates, and horoscopy. Abu Bakr Ahmad bin Wahshiyah concerned himself with the secrets of the planets, alchemy, sorcery, and magic and promoted witchcraft. In the eleventh century, Ibn Jazlah and al-Biruni believed in astrological interpretations, and Ibn Butlan diagnosed and treated diseases in accordance with the occurrences of zodiacal signs. During the twelfth century, Ibn at-Tilmidh in Baghdad and Ibn Zuhr in Andalusia insisted that the position of the planets determines the proper time to perform certain surgical operations, even bloodletting. Their writings record anecdotes involving astrological interpretations that influenced their decisions in diagnosing and treating diseases. They also believed in the healing powers of plants that resembled the ailing organs they were intended to cure. With the decline of Arabic civilization during the European Middle Ages, astrology degenerated into sorcery and witchcraft. In modern times, however, it has been revived in the West as a serious "science."

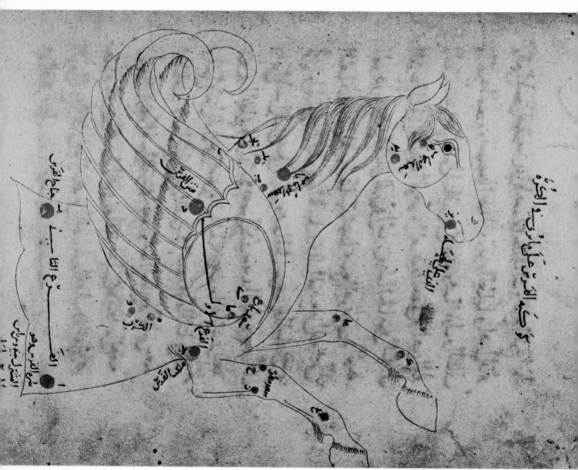

The constellation, Pegasus, from a copy of Treatise on the Fixed Stars *by as-Sufi. In the original manuscript, the figure is drawn vertically with the head at the top of the page.*

SUMMARY

Arabic culture, including its contributions to the life sciences, reached its highest stage of development between the ninth and the eleventh centuries and experienced a number of major revivals during the twelfth and thirteenth centuries. During this period the West was just beginning to awaken from the Dark Ages. From the twelfth century to the Renaissance, via translation and copying activities in Spain, Sicily, and Syria, the bulk of Arabic writings in all fields was made available in Latin. Despite the poor quality of translation and scholarship that prevailed in the West at that time, these Latin versions revived the spirit of learning in Western Europe during the late Middle Ages.

Arabic authors, as a result of the translation of their works into Latin and the vernaculars, became widely known under Latinized names: Rhazes for ar-Razi, Avicenna for Ibn Sina, Averroes for Ibn Rushd, and so on. Their books were widely read and frequently cited and quoted by writers in the West. In the life sciences, Arabic authors not only preserved the classical achievements of the ancients but also added new and original data to the fund of human knowledge, thereby contributing to the well-being of all men everywhere.

A zodiacal disc from an astrological clock designed by the engineer, al-Jazari in The Book of Knowledge of Ingenious Mechanical Devices. *The disc revolves in such a way that the sun and moon are aligned with the appropriate sign of the zodiac throughout the year.*

Abu Zayd Hunayn bin Ishaq al-'Ibadi

(809–873)

During the medieval period, rulers in both the East and the West had a great fear of being poisoned and were therefore extremely cautious in choosing their attendants. They were particularly wary of physicians, whose knowledge of drugs and their effects on human beings could make them highly qualified assassins. During the reign of al-Mutawakkil (846–861), the most famous medical scholar in the capital city of Baghdad was Abu Zayd Hunayn bin Ishaq al-'Ibadi. Hunayn's reputation was excellent, but the caliph still felt it necessary to test his integrity.

Al-Mutawakkil offered to reward Hunayn generously if he would prepare a poison the caliph could secretly use to exterminate an enemy. Hunayn replied, "I have learned only the action of useful drugs, confident that this is all that the Prince of the Faithful would want from me. If, however, he wishes me to prepare poisons, he should kindly allow me time to go and learn of the same." The caliph protested that he wanted the poison right away, but the more the caliph pressed him, the more Hunayn was determined not to violate his conscience. He explained that the physician is sworn never to give injurious or deadly medicine and that professional ethics demand that practitioners do all they can to help their clients, not hurt them. Thrown into prison under threat of execution for his defiance, Hunayn declared, "I am willing to die, but in the end God will vindicate my innocence." Finally al-Mutawakkil released him with the explanation that he had merely been testing Hunayn's honesty and integrity. He then promoted Hunayn and gave him generous rewards.

The renowned French medical historian Lucian Leclerc called Hunayn not only the greatest scholar in ninth-century Arabic medicine but also the one of most gracious characters and most impressive savants of all time. His exemplary life helped establish ethical standards of behavior for his profession.

Hunayn's father, Ishaq, was an apothecary of the 'Ibadi Arab Christian tribe of al-Hirah in Iraq. There Hunayn was born and reared, until his father, recognizing the boy's potential, sent him to the Abbasid capital for advanced education in the healing art. In Baghdad, Hunayn enrolled in the earliest known private medical school in Islam, under the tutorship of the eminent physician Yuhanna bin Masawayhl. But a misunderstanding soon developed between the inquisitive, ambitious, and intelligent student and his teacher, and Hunayn eventually left the school in dismay.

Hunayn's desire for greater access to the ancients' knowledge of the healing art led him to intensify his study of Greek. He rapidly mastered the available medical books in Greek and turned with enthusiasm to the translation of medical writings into Arabic and Syriac, under the auspices of his first patrons, the court physician Jibra'il bin Bakhtishu' and the sons of Ibn Musa bin Shakir. His ability was soon recognized, and about 830 he was appointed by Caliph al-Ma'mun to head Bayt al-Hikmah, a state-supported institution for the translation of classical writings and the promotion of useful knowledge. Continuing to advance in his intellectual pursuits, Hunayn was patronized by caliphs and philanthropists up to the time of al-Mutawakkil.

As a translator, Hunayn was reliable and scholarly. He toured many countries to collect as many of the best manuscripts of the same work as possible, comparing one copy with another in an effort to reconstruct the original text. Once he had an authentic version, he was precise but not overly literal in his translations, and he recommended this approach to his students and associates. In his five decades of active life, Hunayn and his school of translators rendered into Arabic all the most important of the available Greek treatises on life sciences, including the best known of the Hippocratic corpus and the writings of Aristotle, Dioscorides, and Galen, as well as the commentaries and revisions that followed, from the work of Oribasius to that of Paulus of Aeginata.

A prolific author as well as a translator, Hunayn wrote on a variety of medical topics and also prepared a valuable index of the Galenic writings available in Syriac and Arabic translations. The Muslim bibliographer Ibn an-Nadim attributed about twenty-nine titles to Hunayn and placed him foremost among the founders of Arabic life sciences.

Although most of his intellectual contributions were based on Greek thought, Hunayn made significant additions and improved and modified medical theories and teaching procedures. Like his contemporary al-Kindi, he coined numerous medicopharmaceutical and technical words that have since been incorporated into the Arabic language. He systematized and defined the life sciences and devised practical concepts and procedures for study, experimentation, and practice. His *al-Masa'il fi at-Tibb* (*Introduction to the Healing Art*) was the most dependable manual used by the examiners (*muhtasib*) who approved physicians for licensing, and it was commented on, sum-

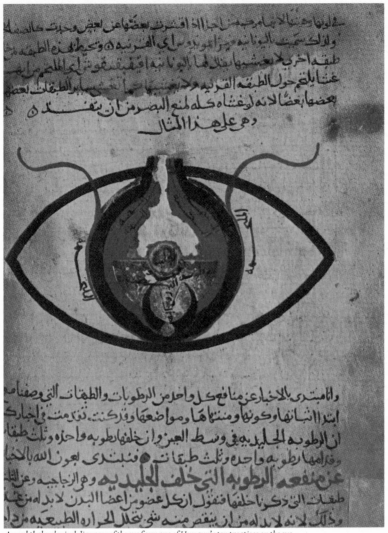

An ophthalmological diagram of the eye from one of Hunayn's ten treatises on the eye.

marized, and interpreted by authors from the tenth to the fourteenth century. After it was translated into Latin, it was widely consulted by physicians in the West, where it appeared in numerous manuscripts as well as in incunabula.

Hunayn's ten treatises on the anatomy, physiology, and treatment of the eye constitute the first systematic and organized text on the subject in Arabic, and the earliest known to include anatomical charts. The influence of these treatises on the development of ophthalmology was profound, not only in Islam, but in Christendom as well.

Oculists quoted and consulted them for several centuries.

Years after Hunayn had proved his trustworthiness to the Caliph al-Mutawakkil, envious competitors brought false accusations against the scholar and turned the caliph against him. Hunayn's books were confiscated, and he was imprisoned and subjected to harsh treatment. Ultimately, we are told, a dream convinced the caliph of Hunayn's innocence, and he once again restored his fortunes, which Hunayn continued to enjoy, without further hardship, until his death in Baghdad in 873.

SAMI K. HAMARNEH

193

Abu Bakr Muhammad bin Zakariya ar-Razi

(865–925)

During the past one thousand years, scholars of East and West have been universal in their admiration of Abu Bakr Muhammad bin Zakariya ar-Razi—"the unchallenged chief physician of the Muslims," "the Arab Galen," "the most brilliant genius of the Middle Ages." The earliest known biographies of this man are two accounts contained in historical records that date back to about 987. Like other, later biographies, however, they are fragmentary. The first was written by Muhammad bin Ishaq an-Nadim of Baghdad, the Abbasid capital, where ar-Razi lived for a few years to gain medical experience at the main government-supported hospital. The second was written by Sulayman bin Juljul of Cordoba, the Umayyad capital in Spain, but his sources of information are no longer known to us.

The two biographies tell how, early in life, ar-Razi was interested in music and played the 'ud, a stringed instrument that is a forerunner of the modern guitar. He also studied philosophy under the tutorship of the Persian Abu Zayd al-Balkhi, before turning to the study of the healing art.

After completing his training in Baghdad, ar-Razi returned to his native ar-Rayy, near modern Teheran, where he assumed directorship of its hospital. He taught the healing arts, and his fame as a practitioner-educator drew many students, beginners and advanced. His contemporaries praised him as a generous, kind, and considerate physician who treated his patients, rich or poor, with friendly concern and with utmost care. He served his Persian rulers as a physician and adviser, but only within the framework of his professional duties, not for monetary gain or increased prestige, as his opponents and critics claimed.

Ar-Razi apparently lived in Baghdad for a few years during the early 890's, where he collected data and wrote his book on hospital experiences (Mujarrabat). He then returned to ar-Rayy to work at its hospital and later became a court physician to its governor, Mansur bin Ishaq bin Ahmad bin Asad, who reigned from 902 to 908. To this patron, ar-Razi dedicated two of his most important medical books, at-Tibb al-Mansuri and at-Tibb ar-Ruhani. The former encompasses the major aspects of the healing art, including human anatomy and physiology, dietetics and the preservation of health, toxicology, pathology, and fevers—which were then considered a separate study. This well-received manual was translated into Latin (Medicinalis Almansoris) and was widely influential in the West throughout the Middle Ages. At-Tibb ar-Ruhani discusses ways to treat the moral and psychological ills of the human spirit.

Ar-Razi was a firm believer in experimental medicine and the beneficial use of previously tested medicinal plants and other drugs. He called for high professional standards for practitioners, and he urged physicians to continue their educations by studying medical treatises, attending lectures, or obtaining training at hospitals. He led the fight against quacks and charlatans in the health field, called for consultation and mutual trust between skilled physicians, and favored a family-doctor practice. He warned patients that changing from one doctor to another would waste their wealth, health, and time. He promoted psychotherapy, pointing out that hopeful comments from doctors encouraged patients, made them feel better, and promoted speedier recovery. He advised his colleagues to allow their patients to eat the kinds of foods they preferred—a practice recommended in modern medicine—but he also stressed the importance of a balanced diet for the preservation or restoration of good health. And he admonished practitioners to avoid extravagance and to dress, eat, and live simply.

Ar-Razi's most comprehensive book was a medical encyclopedia, al-Hawi fi at-Tibb. He spent many years collecting and preparing the data, but he died before he was able to organize the subject matter or put the text into final form. Hurriedly assembled by his students after his death, the encyclopedia lacks the harmony and order characteristic of his other works. In al-Hawi, ar-Razi quotes the medical opinions of various Greek and Arabic authors and compares their interpretations with his own. The encyclopedia is enormous—so huge, in fact, that al-Majusi (died 994) knew of only two complete copies. It was translated into Latin by the Jewish physician Faraj bin Salim in 1279 and, under the title Continens, was one of the first medical books of its size ever to be printed in the West (1486).

Being a free thinker and an independent spirit, ar-Razi did not permit his great admiration of the Greek masters to dull his critical judgment. He attacked Hippocrates' Aphorisms, for example, as disorganized, ambiguous, and unnecessarily brief. To correct these deficiencies, he wrote al-Murshid, which provides a better treatment of the topics on general medicine covered in the Aphorisms. In Doubts on Galen, he described some Galenic writings as verbose and erroneous and attempted to correct their contents.

A prolific author, ar-Razi wrote on philosophy, logic, astronomy, and physical sciences, but he is best remembered for his writings on the life sciences. His profound erudition was matched by an unusual capacity for understanding human nature. His writings summed up all the theoretical and empirical medical knowledge of his time, augmented by his own experiences and observations.

Late in life, ar-Razi was blinded. When an oculist suggested remedial eye surgery, ar-Razi replied, "I have seen enough of this old world, and I do not cherish the idea of suffering the ordeal of an operation for the hope of seeing more of it." Shortly thereafter, ar-Razi died.

SAMI K. HAMARNEH

194

A stained glass window in the Princeton University Chapel commemorates the contribution of ar-Razi to the science of medicine.

Abu 'Ali al-Husayn bin 'Abdallah bin Sina (Avicenna)

(980–1037)

Relating the events of his own life, Abu 'Ali al-Husayn bin 'Abdallah bin Sina was not hindered by false modesty. "People wondered at my attainments!" he tells us, and though he wrote with pride and considerable arrogance, the statement is true. He was "the Master"—philosopher, scientist, mathematician, the most illustrious physician of the tenth and eleventh centuries.

In any age, Ibn Sina would have been a giant among giants. He had memorized the Qur'an by the time he was ten and had mastered the Arab sciences while he was still in his teens. At seventeen he was an established physician. Determined to know all there was to know, he next examined the philosophy of the Greeks and devised his own integrated method of study, utilizing theory, experiment, critique, and research. He first applied this systematic approach—with its extensive process of classification, division, and subdivision and its basic tenet of question and proof—to his early medical career and to his writings, including his famous *Canon of Medicine* (al-Qanun).

In the tenth century, when Ibn Sina was studying the principles of healing, Islamic medicine was a highly developed profession, comparable in many ways with medical practices today. Arab doctors had to comply with licensing regulations in most areas. City hospitals were divided into wards under the supervision of doctors and lay administrators. Traveling physicians brought medical attention to people outside the urban centers. And Arab laboratories evaporated, filtrated, crystallized, and distilled raw drugs, sometimes mixing them with syrups, gums, and fruit rinds to improve their taste.

Ibn Sina was eager for practical knowledge of the illnesses he had studied. Wherever he traveled in Persia, he set up free clinics that would give him opportunities to check his book learning against firsthand information. Here he could observe cases that otherwise would have been inaccessible to him. He carefully recorded his observations and then followed through with a systematic examination of the possible causes and treatments of the maladies under consideration. In the second book of *al-Qanun* he listed 760 drugs sold by the pharmacists of his day, making his own comments on their application and effectiveness. He also wrote a detailed treatise on cordial remedies.

More than a dozen medical works are attributed to Ibn Sina. The *Canon of Medicine* is the greatest of these. It is a million-word manuscript that summarizes the Hippocratic and Galenic traditions, describes Syro-Arabic and Indo-Persian practices, and includes notes on Ibn Sina's own experiments. The Islamic medical world accepted the *Canon* as its major

reference work until the nineteenth century, and Western civilization used the text for more than five hundred years.

The *Canon* points out the importance of dietetics (Arab medicine recommended cure by natural products and methods and healing through dietary regulation in preference to a reliance on drugs), the influence of climate and environment on health, the surgical use of oral anesthetics, the contagious nature of some diseases, and the dangers of spreading disease by soil and water. Ibn Sina recommended the testing of a new drug by experimentation on animals and humans, and he advised surgeons to treat cancer in its earliest stages, making certain to remove all the diseased tissue. He also noted a close relationship between emotions and physical condition. An accomplished musical theorist, he felt that music had a definite physical and psychological effect on patients. Of the many psychological disorders that Ibn Sina described, one is of unusual interest. The symptoms are fever, loss of weight and strength, and various chronic complaints. The disease? Love sickness. The great doctor had a simple remedy: unite the sufferer with the beloved.

It was at the urging of al-Juzjani (his friend, student, confidant, and manager of sorts) that Ibn Sina undertook another important work. Al-Juzjani had suggested that he write a commentary on the works of Aristotle, but the Master was reluctant because he felt that he did not have the time. He finally agreed to a book that would simply set forth the sound philosophies of the ancient Greeks, without argumentation. With this understanding, Ibn Sina began the physics section of the *Kitab ash-Shifa'* (*The Book of Healing*)—the longest of his writings still in existence and perhaps the longest treatise on philosophy ever written by any one man. The complete work has four major sections dealing, respectively, with logic, physics, mathematics, and metaphysics. Ibn Sina abridged the book himself and also translated it into his mother tongue, Persian, giving post-Islamic Persia its first book on philosophy, logic, and the natural sciences. His own thoughts he incorporated in a later work, known as *Oriental Philosophy*.

Because the Muslim world held physicians in rare esteem, they often found themselves the recipients of unique privileges. Some were even made court officials. Ibn Sina served as vizier at the court of the Prince Shams ad-Dawlah at Hamadhan, but the physician's political career lacked the superior qualities of his scientific and philosophic endeavors. His intellectual arrogance often worked against him in the game of court intrigue. More than once he found himself in hiding, where he did much of his writing, or fleeing persecution, his books banned because of violent disagreements with powerful contemporaries. Friends advised him to slow down and to take life in moderation, but that was not in character. "I prefer a short life with width to a narrow one with length," he would reply.

After the death of Prince Shams ad-Dawlah, he was summoned to serve at the court of Prince 'Ala' ad-Dawlah Abu Ja'far in Isfahan. Accompanying a military expedition to Hamadhan in 1037, he was stricken with a severe case of colic that did not respond to treatment. He died at the early age of 57.

Although Ibn Sina was apparently a devout Muslim, his philosophical beliefs strayed considerably from traditional attitudes. He saw God, man, and the universe as independent, though interrelated. God, the only necessary being, causes, but is not caused. Man, a being composed of body and soul, aspires to an intellectual, spiritual happiness. Humanity is divided into several classes, ranging from ruler to commoner. Those fortunate enough to be members of the higher classes have an obligation to help the masses achieve eternal good. Ibn Sina devised an illumination theory that envisioned the soul as a ray of divine light imprisoned in the body but craving release to return to its source. His denial of the resurrection of the body, his acceptance of the eternity of the world, and his belief in free will followed this basic doctrine and met with strong opposition from traditional theologians, who interpreted the Qur'an on a strictly literal basis. Ibn Sina claimed that, though the Qur'an was written to be understood by all men, only the masses were expected to take the holy words at their face value. Men of superior intellect were able to extract allegorical lessons from the simple stories.

Knowing himself superior to the masses, Ibn Sina delighted in shocking the inquisitive public. And frequently he paid the price of imprudent genius. His conceit, unorthodox beliefs, and unconventional conduct embroiled him in controversy, and malicious rumors spread until folk began to treat him as a sorcerer and conjurer of evil spirits. His arguments with fellow scholars verged on violence, and his contempt for mediocrity was scathing.

Posterity treated him more gently and with ever-increasing respect. His writings inspired philosophers, theologians, and physicians in the Muslim world for centuries after his death. In the West, where he was known as Avicenna, he was a primary link with the philosophical thought of ancient Greece and a fundamental contributor to the European reawakening. His *Canon* was the basic medical reference for a longer period than any other book on medicine ever written.

M. A. MARTIN

Excerpt from a Latin translation of Verses on Medicine *by Ibn Sina.*

Abu al-Qasim Khalaf bin 'Abbas az-Zahrawi (Albucasis)

(940?–1013)

The golden age of the Umayyad dynasty in Andalusia reached its peak during the tenth century, both intellectually and politically. Under the aegis of 'Abd ar-Rahman an-Nasir, who reigned from 912 to 961, and his son al-Hakam II, who reigned from 961 to 976, this dynasty established sovereignty over the largest portion of the Iberian Peninsula. Once military and naval superiority had been achieved, education and scholarship were encouraged and patronized. The life sciences, in particular, received generous patronage, and many eminent physicians began to appear on the scene, adding by means of their professional efforts and writings luster and substance to the progress of Arabic medicine and pharmacy. The Andalusian capital, Cordoba, was converted into a great metropolis, where educational and religious institutions, as well as trade and industry, flourished. At the time it was unrivaled in Europe, and in medical achievements it was comparable with Constantinople.

Secure in his political authority, an-Nasir built a new royal city on the slopes of al-'Arus, a mountain six miles northwest of crowded Cordoba, whose population was then estimated at half a million. He named the new capital az-Zahra', after his favorite wife, Zahrah, which means flower. Construction started in 936 and was still going on even after az-Zahra' became the capital in 940. Although az-Zahra' was built mainly for political and military reasons, it became a monument to tenth-century Muslim architecture and ingenuity and quickly won the admiration of the entire world. It contained magnificent royal palaces, residential quarters, a mosque, schools, and gardens. Historians call it "the Versailles of the Ummayads."

It was here, in this royal city, that Abu al-Qasim Khalaf bin 'Abbas az-Zahrawi, known in Latin as Albucasis or Abulcasis, is believed to have been born sometime between 936 and 940. It was certainly here that he lived, studied, and taught and practiced medicine and surgery until shortly before his death in about 1013, two years after the sacking of his beloved city.

Because az-Zahra' was pillaged and destroyed, little is known today of its illustrious son az-Zahrawi. Most extant manuscripts give his father's name as 'Abbas, and some contain his other nickname, al-Ansari, which suggests a linkage with the ancient Arabian tribes called al-Ansar, the supporters of Muhammad at the sacred Muslim city of Medina, or Yathrib as it was known earlier.

Az-Zahrawi was first mentioned by the Andalusian scholar Abu Muhammad bin Hazm (993–1064), who listed him among the great physician-surgeons of Moorish Spain.

The first known biography of him, however, appeared in al-Humaydi's *Jadhwat al-Muqtabis (On Andalusian Savants)*, completed six decades after az-Zahrawi's death. It mentioned his name, his ancestry, his place of residence, the approximate date of his death, and his only literary contribution, *at-Tasrif liman 'Ajiza 'an at-Ta'lif*, which was completed at the end of the tenth century. Al-Hamaydi's account was copied by later biographers, such as Ibn Bushkuwal, Ibn Abi Usaybi'ah, al-Maqqari, and Hajji Khalifah, with no significant additional data, and it remains the only reliable source of information available, apart from az-Zahrawi's own work.

At-Tasrif, a voluminous compendium consisting of thirty treatises, is a compilation of the medical data that az-Zahrawi accumulated during a career that spanned almost fifty years of training, teaching, and practice. He apparently traveled very little, but he had wide experience in treating accident victims and war casualties.

In *at-Tasrif*, az-Zahrawi expressed his concern for the welfare of his students, whom he called "my children," and he took great care to ensure the safety of his patients and win their trust, whether they were poor and lowly or rich and elite. He stressed the importance of good doctor-patient relationships and encouraged understanding and cooperation between his colleagues and their clients. He also emphasized close observation of individual cases in order to secure the most accurate diagnosis and the best possible treatment, whether by drugs or by diet or both. He insisted on compliance with ethical norms and warned against dangerous and dubious practices that some physicians adopted for purposes of material gain. He also cautioned against quacks and impostors who claimed surgical skills they did not possess.

Az-Zahrawi's medical encyclopedia also deals in detail with the anatomy and physiology of the human body and includes notes of importance in surgery. Although he relied heavily on Galen for his information, his discussions contain original observations of historical interest. He elaborated on the causes and symptoms of diseases and their treatment and theorized both on the upbringing of children and youth, with emphasis on their mental and physical health, and on the care of the aged and the convalescent. The encyclopedia also discusses the preparation of pharmaceuticals and therapeutics, covering such important aspects of these specialized areas as emetic and cardiac drugs, laxatives, geriatrics, cosmetology, dietetics, materia medica, weights and measures, and drug substitution.

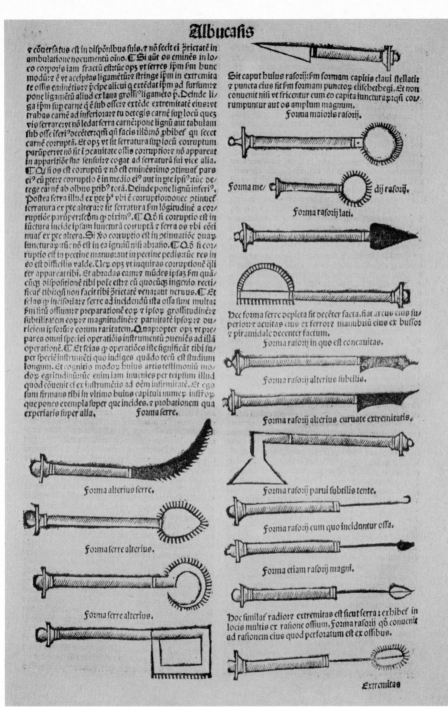

Page from a 1531 Latin translation by Peter Argellata of az-Zahrawi's treatise on surgical and medical instruments. Argellata praises az-Zahrawi as a great surgeon and reproduces his drawings of surgical instruments with only slight modifications.

Two of az-Zahrawi's treatises deserve special attention. One is his twenty-eighth treatise, known in Latin as *Liber servitoris de praeparatione medicinarum simplicium*, which describes chemical preparations, tablet making, extracts filtering, and related pharmaceutical techniques. Its popularity in the West is demonstrated by the fact that it was printed in Venice as early as 1471 by Nicolaus Jensen.

The other treatise of particular importance is the one on surgery. It was the first work in Arabic to treat the subject independently and in detail and to include, for teaching purposes, pictures of instruments recommended for use. These surgical illustrations are the earliest found in the literature of the Middle Ages. There are approximately two hundred drawings, ranging from a tongue depressor and a tooth extractor to a catheter and an elaborate obstetrical device. In this treatise he discussed cauterization, bloodletting, midwifery and obstetrics, and the treatment of wounds and fractured bones. He outlined and recommended the use of caustics in surgery, adequately treated bone dislocation in several parts of the body, and fully described tonsilectomy, tracheotomy, and craniotomy—operations he had performed on a dead fetus. He explained how to use a hook to extract a polypus from the nose, a growth which he dif-ferentiated from cancerous aneurysm; how to use a bulb syringe he had invented for giving enemas to children; and how to use a metallic bladder-syringe he had devised and a speculum to extract bladder stones. Albucasis was the first to describe the so-called "Walcher Position" in obstetrics; the first to depict dental arches, tongue depressors, and lead catheters; and the first to describe clearly the conditions and hereditary circumstances associated with hemophilia. In addition, he described ligaturing of blood vessels long before Ambroise Paré.

After this monumental treatise was translated into Latin by Gerard of Cremona in the twelfth century, Albucasis had a great influence on surgery in the West. His improved techniques and instructions injected new life into a somewhat neglected branch of the health sciences. The French surgeon Guy de Chauliac in his *Great Surgery*, completed about 1363, quoted *at-Tasrif* more than two hundred times. Albucasis was also praised by Pietro Argellata, who died in 1423, as "without doubt the chief of all surgeons." The French surgeon Jacques Delechamps (1513–1588) made extensive use of *at-Tasrif* in his elaborate commentary, confirming the great prestige of Albucasis in medical circles throughout the Middle Ages and up to the Renaissance.

SAMI K. HAMARNEH

Mechanical Technology

Donald R. Hill is a professional engineer, currently employed in a senior capacity in a subsidiary of a major international engineering firm. Holder of a doctoral degree in Arab history, he is the author of the translation of *The Book of Knowledge of Ingenious Mechanical Devices* by al-Jazari, for which he was named co-recipient of the Dexter Prize in 1974 by the American Society for the History of Technology. Dr. Hill is also author of a translation of *The Book of Ingenious Devices* by the Banu Musa, and of *Arabic Water-Clocks*. He is a contributing author to the *Encyclopaedia of Islam*.

Mechanical Technology

Donald R. Hill

Of all the fields in which the Arabs have made significant contributions to the progress of civilization, that of mechanical technology has been the least studied. As a result, historians studying the technologies of Europe and the Far East have been seriously handicapped by an inability to make comparisons with scholarly material on the Middle East. Even more serious, a damaging belief has taken root, both in the West and in the Arab countries, that modern technology is solely a Western achievement and that its products, for better or worse, are alien imports throughout the rest of the world. This false notion has had incalculable social and political effects on the ways in which peoples of these areas view one another.

Culture has never been the sole prerogative of a single people or group of peoples. It has flourished whenever and wherever conditions have been favorable to its growth. Technology in particular, because it is relatively unfettered by ideologies, has always shown a remarkable capacity for diffusion. This diffusion has not been a linear process, with one people taking up where another left off and passing their improvements and developments on to their descendants. More accurately, it has been one of cross-fertilization, an osmotic interpenetration between peoples, regardless of geographical or political separation.

Knowledge in the field of mechanical technology has sometimes been transmitted in writing, and the surviving documents, though all too few, are an important source of information for historians. For various reasons, however, many of the engineers and craftsmen of antiquity did not commit their results to paper. Their achievements must, therefore, have been passed on by word of mouth or by the concrete evidence of the things they had made. For example, the great Italian engineer Juanello Turriano, who worked and wrote in sixteenth-century Toledo, would have been able to inspect the hydraulic works of his Muslim predecessors and to draw upon the long tradition of Hispano-Arab water engineering. We may, therefore, assume an Arab influence on his achievements, although there is no written record to confirm this. We cannot always identify the precise means of diffusion, but so many Arab ideas eventually found their way into the general vocabulary of European engineering that we are justified in believing that most of these were not reinventions, which are rare events in the history of technology, but had been received, directly or indirectly, from the Arabs.

A mechanical boat with moving figurines, designed by al-Jazarī for entertainment at royal parties.

The flourishing of the mechanical arts in the Islamic world between the ninth and thirteenth centuries may be regarded as part of a continuous tradition of mechanical technology that had developed in the Middle and Near East over the course of many centuries. The Egyptians, Greeks, Romans, and Byzantines had all, in various ways, made important advances. Although some significant ideas were certainly derived from Iran, India, and the Far East, both before and after the rise of Islam, the main legacy of the Arabs came from the eastern Mediterranean region, particularly from the Hellenic world.

In Arab mechanical technology two main categories are apparent: firstly, machines designed for everyday use, such as mills, water-raising devices, and war machines; and, secondly, devices designed to cause wonder and aesthetic pleasure within the courtly circles that commissioned their manufacture. For the second category we have adequate written records; for the first we do not. Although this categorical distinction must be made for the sake of convenience, it is an arbitrary one. The inventors of ingenious devices, or "automata" (*hiyal*), such as Ibn ar-Razzaz al-Jazari, also designed useful machines. They were thoroughly familiar with the work of carpenters and millwrights, from whom they derived much of their vocabulary and many of their techniques, tools, and mechanisms. They also learned a great deal from contemporary craftsmen who made objects for decorative and domestic purposes—smiths, metalworkers, jewelers, ceramicists, and painters.

Information about the achievements of the Arab engineers comes mainly from three treatises. About 850, three sons of a certain Musa bin Shakir, who are known as the Banu Musa, composed a work on *hiyal*—trick vessels, fountains, self-trimming lamps, musical automata, and so forth. In 1203, Ridwan bin as-Sa'ati wrote a lengthy treatise dealing with his repair of a monumental water clock built by his father over the Jayrun gate in Damascus. And in 1206, al-Jazari wrote a book describing some of the devices that he had made during the course of his long working life. These include water clocks and candle clocks, trick vessels, measuring vessels, fountains, musical automata, water-raising machines, and a massive door cast in brass and copper. The al-Jazari work is altogether superior to the other two and provides us with most of our information on Arab technology. The author included a much wider range and variety of devices, incorporating all the techniques and components used by his predecessors, as well as many of his own additions and improvements. Even more important, al-Jazari was quite evidently a master craftsman himself, and he described in scrupulous detail how each device was constructed. The other writers described the operation of their machines quite well, but they gave only vague and sketchy information concerning their construction. One is led to suspect that they worked out the designs themselves but left the execution to artisans.

The manufacture of useful machines, apart from war engines, followed an unbroken tradition that had persisted from Greek and Roman times. Interest in a more formal application of mechanics and hydrostatics, however, arose during the period of the great Abbasid caliphs in the ninth century. This interest was stimulated by the translation into Arabic of several Greek treatises, notably the *Pneumatics* of Philo of Byzantium (probably second century B.C.) and the *Mechanics* of Hero of Alexandria (first century A.D.). Also of importance, not least because al-Jazari acknowledged it as a source, was a treatise on the construction of water clocks that has been attributed to Archimedes. (Although this treatise may have incorporated some of the ideas of the great scientist, its origins are still unresolved. The first part was perhaps by Philo, with later sections added by Arab inventors.)

AUTOMATA

Man has always had a strong innate urge to devise mechanistic explanations for the world around him. Throughout history this urge has led to the manufacture of objects and devices that simulate biological and cosmological phenomena. Moreover, the princely patrons of the Arab engineers had international tastes, subject to various influences, and regarded lifelike representations as an acceptable means of artistic expression. It is, therefore, hardly surprising that the Arab engineers directed their talents toward the devising of automata.

Mechanically, automata are the immediate ancestors of the elaborate water clocks of Europe, from which the great astronomical cathedral clocks, complete with jackwork, were derived. They are also comparable to such other complex contrivances of Western culture as mechanical banks, vending machines, and calculating machines. Culturally, they are related to some of the wondrous characters of Western literature, such as the puppet Pinocchio or the robot ballerina Olympia, who dances herself to pieces in one of the *Tales of Hoffmann*. The tradition of aesthetic delight embodied in the fountains of the Banu Musa and al-Jazari passed as a legacy to such men as Tomaso da Siena, who created the water gardens at the Villa d'Este and Bagnaia.

The use of human or animal figures in the construction of automata was handled with great delicacy. In ancient Egypt and in pre-Islamic Arabia, representation had been associated with the worship of idols, and Muslims have, therefore, been justifiably wary of biological representation. In the automata of the Arab engineers, however, there is absolutely no suggestion of iconography, nor is there any tendency to show earthly rulers in an exalted status. Human figures are nearly always menials—servants, stewards, musicians—who are shown performing their normal functions as court attendants. Animals appear, as far as possible, in their natural roles: for example, donkeys operating waterwheels, peacocks displaying their tail feathers, monkeys performing tricks, and snakes attempting to swallow birds. Although these themes and motifs were selected to suit the tastes of the courts, al-Jazari for one was quite aware that some of them were unsuitable for other purposes. He gave instructions, for example, that representations were to be omitted from clocks intended for mosques.

Some historians of technology have expressed discontent because so much of the ingenuity of the Arab engineers was directed to the design and construction of such apparently trivial devices as automata, rather than to the making of useful machines. This view is quite erroneous, however, not only because it neglects the existence of a utilitarian tradition that was not recorded in writing, but also because it fails to consider the contribution made by the makers of *hiyal* to the advance of machine technology. The making of automata in Greece, in Islam, and later in Europe was one of the factors that led men to develop a rationalistic, mechanistic explanation of natural phenomena, an attitude that has been immensely fruitful in the development of modern science. Moreover, much of modern technology has evolved from automata, particularly in the field of delicate mechanisms and scientific instrumentation. For this reason the mechanisms that actuated the automata are of the greatest significance.

The Banu Musa described a wide variety of trick vessels, and al-Jazari also devoted several chapters to these devices. For example, there are pitchers from which various liquids may be drawn by setting the taps to different positions; pitchers from which hot, cold, or tepid water can be poured from the same spout; and pitchers that automatically discharge a set quantity of water. These effects were obtained by the ingenious use of siphons, floats, and valves and by empirical application of hydrostatic and aerostatic principles. Both works also describe fountains that change shape at regular intervals and automatic musical instruments whose construction is similar to that of the fountains.

It was al-Jazari's monumental clocks, however, that displayed the most impressive arrays of automata. Circles representing the zodiac, sun, and moon rotated at constant speed; birds discharged pellets from their beaks onto cymbals to sound the hour; doors opened to reveal small figurines. At regular intervals musicians—drummers, trumpeters, tambourine players, and so forth—performed on their instruments. Usually the automata were actuated by a float sinking at a constant rate in a water reservoir. A string attached to the top of the float passed around a large pulley wheel that was the main drive of the clock. Through other pulleys it rotated the zodiac circle and drew along, behind the face of the clock, a small wheeled vehicle to which was fixed a vertical rod that operated the tripping mechanisms. The musicians were actuated by the constant discharge of water from the reservoir; the water dripped into a vessel and was suddenly released at the required moment. It ran into the scoops of a waterwheel whose axle was equipped with cams that struck extension pieces fixed to the arms of the percussion players. From a trough beneath the scoop wheel the water discharged into an air vessel to which an automatic whistle, representing the sound of the trumpeters, was attached. When the water rose to the top of the air vessel, it was evacuated through a siphon into a cistern.

The successful operation of the water clocks depended upon achieving a constant rate of discharge of water. One method was to form a vertical, conical valve seat at the end of the outlet tap from the reservoir. Beneath this valve seat was a small float chamber, with the conical valve plug fixed to the top of the float. The outlet pipe was soldered to the lower end of the float chamber. When the tap was opened, water ran into the float chamber and the valve closed momentarily, only to reopen momentarily when water was discharged from the float chamber. The cycle repeated itself continuously until the water in the reservoir was exhausted, and there was thus only a very slight fluctuation of the head of water over the orifice.

This closed-loop system operated by feedback control reappeared in Europe during the Industrial Revolution. Conical valves were first mentioned in the West by Leonardo da Vinci, and they came into general use in Europe during the sixteenth century. A great deal of research still remains to be done before the sources of Leonardo's ideas can be fully established. It seems likely, for example, that he would have had access to some of the translations from Arabic made in Toledo in the twelfth century. A notable instance of the fruitfulness of Hispano-Arab sources is the incorporation of Muslim material in Dante's *Divine Comedy*, and technologists are usually at least as ready as poets to accept new ideas.

A common method of obtaining the sudden release of a known quantity of water at regular intervals was the tipping bucket, a special vessel balanced on half axles set in bearings. Water from a graduated orifice dripped at a constant rate into the tipping bucket. The tipping bucket tilted when full, discharged its contents, then returned to the horizontal position. In some models, the water was used to actuate automata directly; in other cases, lever arms attached to the tipping bucket actuated time-recording mechanisms. Tipping buckets re-emerged in Europe in the sixteenth century as essential components of rain gauges and other measuring devices and are still in use today.

There exists an important manuscript, written by an Andalusian Muslim in the eleventh century. The only known manuscript is badly defaced, but enough remains to enable us to know that the author was a certain al-Muradi and that he was describing water-clocks and large automata. It is clear from the text and illustrations that he used epicyclic and segmental gears to transmit power. Also in the Iberian peninsula, the *Libros del Saber* were compiled about 1277 under the direction of Alfonso X of Castile. The books were translations and paraphrases of Arabic works, and were expressly intended to convey Arabic knowledge of astronomy and other subjects to Europe. One of the devices is a weight-driven clock with a mercury escapement. Taken together, these two works demonstrate the probability of Arabic influence on the development of the mechanical clock.

ENGINEERING

The concept that "technology" and "applied science" can be used synonymously, implying that scientific developments must precede advances in engineering and industry, is comparatively recent. In the past, many phenomena were put to use before their scientific bases were properly understood. Equally modern is the assumption that engineering must be accompanied by rigorous mathematical analysis. Both these assumptions, although valid up to a point, omit the cross-fertilization between theory and practice that is essential to the realization of truly comprehensive engineering, not to mention the sociological, aesthetic, and environmental factors that only now are beginning to play their proper role in the evaluation of engineering projects.

Arab engineers of antiquity probably never gave much thought to such abstract considerations, nor would they have understood the modern concept of specialization. They needed to have at their command all the contemporary scientific and technical skills available in order to obtain the best possible results from the limited resources at their disposal. There is little doubt that the machines that they described were actually made; the designs are in most cases eminently practical, and the descriptions of constructional methods given by al-Jazari, for example, are very convincing. Besides, we know from Ibn Jubayr that the clock described by Ridwan was working in 1184, and the remains of two monumental water clocks can still be seen in Fez, Morocco. Arab engineers obviously took their work seriously and gave considerable thought, not only to achieving the required results, but also to ensuring that the finished machines would be easy to operate and maintain. There is undoubtedly an aesthetic motivation in invention, in providing elegant solutions to engineering problems. It is clear that Arab engineers experienced this motivation strongly and that they would never have reached their high standards without it.

Arab technology was essentially based upon the use of the effects of water pressure and air pressure. Of course, most of the mathematical relationships that underlie the physical phenomena had not then been identified, and engineers had to draw upon a large fund of practical experience. We can use a single example as an illustration: al-Jazari knew that the flow of liquid from an orifice varies with the head of water above it, but he was unaware that the exact relationship is $Q = K\sqrt{h}$, where Q is the rate of flow, K is a constant, and h is the head of water. He knew the required hourly discharge and, from previous experience, the approximate diameter of the orifice. He therefore made the orifice intentionally too narrow and then gradually enlarged it with copper wire and emery powder until he obtained the required discharge rate. Of course, not all the work of Arab engineers was so laborious; they had a clear understanding of arithmetic, plane geometry, and measurement, and they used these sciences to the full in the construction and assembly of their devices. But when a set of mechanisms

208

A vertical waterwheel at Hamah, Syria.

was particularly complex and delicate, final assembly and adjustment were done by painstaking trial and error.

Many of the methods used to obtain the necessary standards of accuracy and finish seem surprisingly modern to us, until we reflect that these methods were later transmitted from the Arabs into developing European technology. There are a number of notable examples. The plugs of valves and taps were ground into their seats with emery powder until the required tolerance was obtained. The different types of fit used in modern workshop practice (push fit, sliding fit, and running fit) were understood and differentiated. Large pulley wheels, sometimes made of laminated timber to minimize warping, were set up on lathes and rotated, small pieces of lead being added to their perimeters until they were in perfect static balance. Great care was taken to ensure that water containers, made from sheet copper, were of uniform cross section by hammering them around circular wooden templates; the insides of the containers were thoroughly tinned to prevent corrosion. For some of the more intricately shaped components, paper models were made to ensure that the components would fit correctly into the machines. Al-Jazari described a casting technique, using green sand with closed mold boxes, that was not known in Europe until the end of the fifteenth century.

MACHINES

Two types of mill have been known since classical times, one with a vertical waterwheel that drives the millstones through a pair of gear wheels, the other with a horizontal-vaned waterwheel with direct drive to the millstones. It has been computed that the second type could reach an output of ten horsepower with an efficiency of seventy-five percent. From the accounts of geographers and travelers, we know that both types of mill were widely used in the Islamic lands for grinding grain and for industrial purposes.

Naturally, machines for raising water have always played an important part in the economies of Middle Eastern countries, mainly for irrigation but also for supplying water to communities. The simplest of these, the *shaduf*, or sweep, is of ancient origin and is still in use today.

It consists essentially of a long pole balanced on a fulcrum, with a bucket at one end and a counterweight at the other. A second, more complicated machine, the *saqiyah*, or chain of pots, was known in classical times but probably did not come into widespread use until about the fifth century, when the addition of a ratchet-and-pawl mechanism improved its reliability. It is powered by an animal walking in a circular path. A shaft connects the animal to a horizontal gear wheel that engages a vertical gear wheel. The axle of the second gear wheel rotates the wheel that carries the chain of pots. After being immersed in the well, each pot discharges its contents into an irrigation channel or a reservoir when it reaches the top of the wheel. Like the *shaduf*, the *saqiyah* is still in use today. Although it is quite a complicated machine, with more than two hundred separate component parts, it can readily be maintained by a local craftsman, whereas a pump is expensive to buy and is not always easily repaired. In areas where a continuous water supply is literally a life-and-death matter, the *shaduf* and *saqiyah* have obvious advantages over the theoretically more efficient pump.

The five full-scale machines described by al-Jazari were all designed to raise water, and four of them incorporate features that are of great significance in the history of machine technology. The first of these used animal power to raise a flume-beam sweep, that is, a wooden channel with a large scoop at one end and a fulcrum at the other. The scoop dipped into a well, and when the sweep was raised above the fulcrum, the water ran along the channel and discharged into the irrigation system. Power was transmitted by a donkey tethered to a vertical axle, which rotated as the donkey walked around in a circle. The axle, through a pair of gear wheels, rotated a horizontal axle upon which was mounted a wheel with teeth on a quarter of its circumference. This wheel meshed with a lantern pinion that was located on the horizontal axle upon which the sweep was pivoted. While the donkey circled, the sweep rose and fell as the segmental gear wheel engaged with and disengaged from the lantern pinion. Segmental gears, which find many uses in modern engineering, first appeared in the West in Giovanni de' Dondi's astronomical clock, completed in 1364.

Al-Jazari's second machine was a refinement of the first. It had four sweeps, segmental gear wheels, and lantern pinions, which quadrupled the output. A further improvement, according to al-Jazari, was the smoother operation obtained by reducing out-of-balance forces.

His third machine also used a flume-beam sweep, and was powered by a donkey walking in a circular path. In this case, however, the end of a crank, driven through a system of gears, entered a long slot beneath the channel of the sweep. As the crank turned, the sweep rose and fell. Although cranks had been in use for centuries in hand mills and on contrivances such as winches and capstans, they were in all cases operated by hand. Al-Jazari's machine provided the first example in history of a crank being incorporated in a machine.

The fourth machine is of little importance, being simply a chain of pots driven by a concealed scoop wheel. It was apparently intended for use near an ornamental pool.

Al-Jazari's fifth machine, however, is of the greatest significance, since it has an important place in the development of the steam engine and pumping machinery. (A copy of al-Jazari's drawing and a diagram with roman lettering appears on the opposite page.) A reciprocating pump with two cylinders, it was designed to raise water to a height of about thirty-three feet

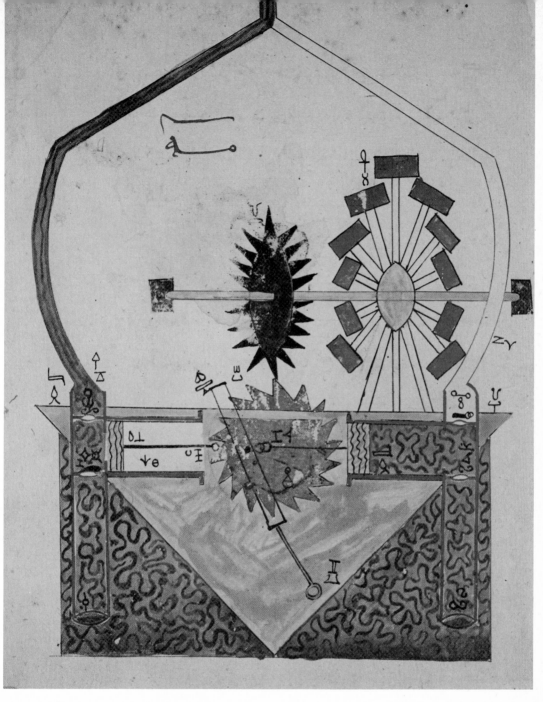

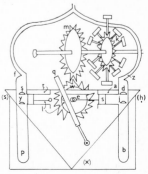

Illustrations of al-Jazari's mechanical devices were copied repeatedly in the Muslim world during the Middle Ages. The illustration of a reciprocating pump with two cylinders (above) is from a manuscript in the Fogg Art Museum in Cambridge, Mass. An explanation of the pump's operation may be found on pages 210 and 212, keyed to the diagram (right), which is based on a similar manuscript in the Bodleian Library, Oxford.

(ten meters). A large paddle wheel (k) was erected in a running stream. It carried on its extended horizontal axle a toothed wheel (m) that meshed with a second toothed wheel (w) mounted in a large box. Toward the outer rim of this second wheel was a peg, fixed normal to the surface of the wheel. This peg entered a slot rod (q), the lower end of which was pivoted at the bottom of the box. When the wheel turned, the peg moved up and down in the slot, and the rod oscillated from side to side. The connecting rods (e and l) were attached by ring-and-staple fittings to the sides of the slot rod, and to the end of each of these was fixed a piston, made from two circular copper disks with hemp packed between them. The pistons entered cylinders (a and t) that were fixed horizontally through the sides of the box. Each piston was provided with a suction pipe (p and b) that descended into the water. The delivery pipes (f and z) were reduced in diameter shortly after they left the pistons and were connected together to form a single delivery exit. Both suction and delivery openings were provided with one-way clack valves (d, s, j, and y). As the slot rod oscillated, one piston was on its delivery stroke. the other on its suction stroke. The pump, which worked on the double-acting principle, is a notable early example of the conversion of rotary to reciprocating action and is also remarkable for having true suction pipes, albeit rather short ones. In the Greek and Roman pumps that are known to us from treatises and from archaeological discoveries, the single cylinders rested vertically in the water, and the suction entry was a hole in the bottom covered by a plate valve.

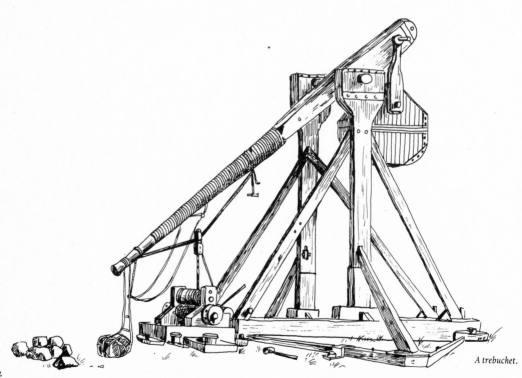

A trebuchet.

The siege engines used by the Arabs in their early conquests were probably similar to those developed by the Greeks and Romans: catapults that depended upon the resilience of wood or twisted fibers to produce their propulsive thrust. These machines discharged fairly light missiles and were rather unreliable, because the elasticity of the fibers varied with temperature, humidity, and age. By the end of the seventh century, however, a more powerful machine had been introduced into the Middle East from China, by way of Central Asia. This consisted of a beam, pivoted at a point that divided its length in a ratio of two to one, or more or less according to the size of the machine. A sling for carrying the missile was attached at the end of the longer arm. The missile was discharged by a team of men pulling on ropes attached to the end of the shorter arm. Much later, probably about the middle of the twelfth century, an even more powerful and accurate machine was invented somewhere in the eastern Mediterranean region. In this machine, called a trebuchet, a heavy counterweight replaced the team of men pulling on ropes. We do not yet know for certain where the trebuchet originated, in Christendom or in Islam, but we do know that the Arabs quickly became experts in its construction and use. Batteries of trebuchets were used by the Muslims at the siege of Acre in 1291, and two Muslim engineers are known to have constructed trebuchets for the Mongol leader Kubilai in 1272.

TOOLS

We do not have any precise descriptions of the tools used by Arab engineers, but from the work they did we can infer that the range of tools available to them was quite extensive. Their materials included wood, sheet brass, sheet copper, iron (usually for small fittings, nails, and axles), small quantities of gold and silver, glass, lead, and tin. They handled wood with great confidence. They grooved it, pierced it with circular holes, made it perfectly flat and smooth, and cut it to curved profiles. We may therefore assume that the craftsmen had hammers, chisels, augers and drills, a wide variety of saws, and at least one efficient type of plane. A solid workbench, together with some means of holding the work steady, would also have been standard equipment.

Sheet metal was beaten into intricate shapes, implying the use of a variety of metalworking hammers. Parts were joined together by soldering, and the insides of water containers were tinned, so that soldering irons of various shapes and sizes were certainly available. We have a little more information concerning other tools. Al-Jazari mentions the lathe several times, and it is probable that he used it for his more delicate drilling operations, as well as for turning circular components. Arab craftsmen used files for shaping the teeth of cogwheels and for removing surplus metal from castings, and they cleaned metal surfaces with a scraper before applying paint. They cut elaborate floral patterns in brass and copper with chisels, and they apparently sometimes used etching, a technique that was well established in the Arab world. Since small nuts, bolts, and woodscrews were not in general use until the Industrial Revolution, Arab engineers obviously did not have spanners or screwdrivers. For measurement and setting out they employed rules, straightedges, protractors, squares, compasses, and dividers. Divi-

Built on the island of Roda in 716, the nilometer, consisting of a square well with a graduated pillar in the center, measured the daily rise and fall of the Nile.

ders were used not only for marking out circles but also for cutting disks from sheet metal. Horizontals were checked with water levels, verticals with a plumb line.

There is ample evidence that knowledge of Arabic science, medicine, mathematics, and philosophy was transmitted to Europe in written form, but very little evidence that engineering ideas were disseminated in that way. It is most desirable, therefore, that a program of research be undertaken to discover, first, whether there are hitherto unknown Arabic manuscripts on engineering subjects and, second, whether there are any medieval translations of Arabic engineering documents in European languages. Even if such an investigation should prove fruitless, however, this would not mean that the mechanical technology of the Arabs was not spread abroad. There can be no question about this, since—as we have seen—European engineering incorporated many Arab concepts and techniques. Technological ideas have frequently been carried from one culture to another by travelers' reports, by the observations of commercial agents, and by direct contacts between craftsmen. Until modern times, such crossfertilizations were probably more frequent and more fruitful than written communications.

Historians have perhaps tended to concentrate overmuch on the wars between Islam and the West, to the relative neglect of the close commercial, cultural, and even political relationships that were established in various places during the period from the ninth to the thirteenth centuries—and beyond. Indeed, such relationships were so common that we can list only a few outstanding examples: the exchange of embassies between the courts of the Abbasid caliphs and the Carolingian rulers; the mingling of Arabs, Normans, and Hohenstaufens in Sicily; the trading arrangements between Italian mercantile cities and the Levant; and the intermixture in the Iberian Peninsula during the entire period. With careful research, it should be possible to establish the means by which engineering ideas were transferred in those areas where Islam and Christendom were in close contact. Similar efforts have already had some success in related disciplines; it has been shown, for example, that the pointed arch and vault, essential components in the developments of Gothic architecture, were transmitted early in the eleventh century from Fatimid Egypt to Amalfi, a city with many Egyptian connections at that time. It is less easy to trace the borrowings of engineering techniques and fine mechanisms, but properly directed investigations could surely achieve significant results.

Decorative detail from al-Jazari's water clock of the peacocks.

Badi' az-Zaman Isma'il bin ar-Razzaz al-Jazari

(Twelfth–thirteenth centuries)

In the once standard, original Oxford University Press volume, *The Legacy of Islam* (edited by T. Arnold and A. Guillaume), a work of some four hundred pages that is scarcely half a century old, the entire pre-modern legacy of Islamic technology, mechanics, and engineering is summarized in twelve lines. One author mentioned is Badi' az-Zaman Isma'il bin ar-Razzaz al-Jazari. His *Kitab fi Ma'rifat al-Hiyal al-Handasiyah* (*The Book of Knowledge of Ingenious Mechanical Devices*) has finally been made available in English, with high competence by D. R. Hill of London, and as a result all subsequent "legacy" works will have to devote more space to Arab and Islamic achievements in these fields.

Almost nothing is known of al-Jazari's life beyond a few brief facts adduced in the introduction to his work and whatever may be gleaned from it and from its subsequent fate in the manuscript tradition. His name indicates that he came from al-Jazirah (the island)—the land between the upper Euphrates and Tigris in what is today eastern Turkey, northeast Syria, and northern Iraq. His masters were the Turkman Artuqid dynasty, which was centered on Diyar Bakr in southeastern Turkey. He entered the service of this dynasty under Nur ad-Din Muhammad, who reigned from 1174 to 1185, served under his son and successor, Qutb ad-Din, who reigned from 1185 to 1200, and under Qutb's brother, Nasir ad-Din, who reigned from 1200 to 1222. He began his service about 1180 and completed his masterwork on mechanical devices twenty-five years later.

It is not clear in exactly what basic capacity al-Jazari served the Artuqids, but his account of how he came to write his book suggests that he may have been a kind of court engineer whose function was to produce amazing, beautiful, and useful devices for the delectation of the ruler and his circle.

> I was in [Nasir ad-Din's] presence one day and had brought him something which he had ordered me to make. He looked at me and he looked at what I had made and thought about it, without my noticing. He guessed what I had been thinking about, and unveiled unerringly what I had concealed. He said, "You have made peerless devices, and through strength have brought them forth as works, so do not lose what you have wearied yourself with and have plainly constructed. I wish you to compose for me a book which

assembles what you have created separately, and brings together a selection of individual items and pictures."

Whatever his exact function, al-Jazari's book in fact produced plans for intricate water clocks, amusing machines where robot serving girls place a drinking glass in the ruler's hand, mechanical flutes, utilitarian irrigation devices, and purely decorative items, such as a monumental door with one of the earliest descriptions of green-sand casting (the first European description was not written until 1540). In general, the techniques described in this book drew on al-Jazari's Hellenistic and Asian technological ancestors, but his treatise elaborates on those earlier models and makes some significant advances. One aspect of al-Jazari's work that is in marked contrast to Leonardo da Vinci's, whose mechanical devices inevitably invite comparison, is that al-Jazari's shows no examples of machines with a military application. No catapults, battering rams, rockets, or submarines are presented. Rather, he creates devices that will either please the affluent or benefit society.

One might imagine that al-Jazari's book was of interest only to him and his patrons; however, the manuscript was copied so often that we must assume Islam had a broad interest in the work. Fifteen copy manuscripts, fourteen of them in Arabic, are known to exist. The earliest is dated 1206; the latest, a Persian translation, is dated 1874. Some of these were copied in Syria and Egypt; at least one was of Mughal provenance. But, curiously, there is no evidence that *Kitab fi Ma'rifat al-Hiyal al-Handasiyah* became a part of the ongoing world cultural development. On the basis of available scholarship we are forced to believe that al-Jazari's work, with the various pictures and diagrams that profusely illustrate it, did not transmit such important advances as conical valves to the European cultural revolution known as the Renaissance. If this transfer did not, in fact, take place, one must wonder why it did not, since al-Jazari's work appeared relatively early in medieval Islam, at a time when cultural transference from East to West was at its height. No compelling solution to the mystery suggests itself. Revived interest in Arab/Islamic technology may, in time, produce one. Until then we are left only with the certainty that if al-Jazari, like Leonardo, had devoted some of his genius to constructing machines of war, his name would be well remembered in the West today.

R. B. WINDER

216

A musical beverage dispenser, shaped like a castle, designed by al-Jazari in The Book of Knowledge of Ingenious Mechanical Devices.

Trade and Commerce

Ragaei El Mallakh is a Professor of Economics, Chairman of the African and Middle Eastern Studies Program at the University of Colorado, and Director of the International Research Center for Energy and Economic Development. A former consultant to the World Bank, he is editor of the *Journal of Energy and Development* and author of three volumes on Kuwait as well as books on the economic development of Saudi Arabia, Qatar, and the United Arab Emirates. Dorothea El Mallakh is associate editor of the *Journal of Energy and Development*, holds a doctoral degree in history, and has received National Defense Rare Language Fellowships, a Rotary International Fellowship, and a Perrine Memorial Fellowship. She currently does editing, research, and writing on the Middle East, economic development, and energy affairs, including *Saudi Arabia : Energy, Developmental Planning, and Industrialization.*

Trade and Commerce

Ragaei and Dorothea El Mallakh

The place of trade and commerce in the Arab empire and their subsequent impact on Europe during the Middle Ages and the Renaissance were determined by three interlocking elements: geography, historical development, and the special input of Islam. A map of Europe and Asia indicates precisely why the territory encompassed by the Arab empire from the eighth to the early twelfth century forms a natural trading and commercial entrepôt. Most Western historians tend to rivet attention on the Mediterranean Basin and to fit the Arab influence in the Middle Ages into this framework. But equally important bodies of water—the Red Sea, the Gulf of Aden, the Arabian Sea, and the Indian Ocean—lie farther to the east. As ancient in the annals of trade as the Mediterranean and more vast and continuous, these waterways link the Arabian/Persian Gulf with the Indian subcontinent and East Africa, and they stretch eastward as far as Southeast Asia and the Straits of Malacca. Strategically located between these two maritime spheres of trade and commerce is the land mass of Arabia and the contiguous regions—a sea of sand, crossed and recrossed over the centuries by caravans of camels, the ships of the desert.

The ancient trading routes led to and from the centers of the Mesopotamian, Phoenician-Palestinian, Egyptian, and Indus Valley civilizations. Archaeology has contributed a clear view of some of the more trade-oriented cultures. The Nabatean culture, for example, which reached its peak about the third century, was centered at Petra and had outposts southward on the Arabian Peninsula along the coast of the Red Sea. During the Greco-Roman period, *Arabia Felix* ("Fertile Arabia"), the Roman name for the province on the southeast coast of the Arabian Peninsula, was the exchange point for many items; linen and glass from Egypt and Syria were traded for cotton, silk, and spices from India, China, and Indonesia. And as far back as 2000 B.C., the ancient kingdom of Dilmun—which may have been centered on the island of Bahrain—acted as intermediary between Mesopotamia and the Indus Valley and supervised the movement of copper from Makam (probably today's Oman) to Sumer.

Recent and ongoing archaeological work continues to expand understanding of just how vigorous and well established were the trade routes in the Arabian Peninsula prior to the Arab Empire. Excavation begun in 1972 by King Saud University and subsequently continued by the Saudi Department of Archaeology located and uncovered Qaryat Al-Fau. This city, flourishing between the second and fifth centuries A.D., was a major economic and commercial center in the heart of the Arabian Peninsula which lay on the trade route connecting the south of the peninsula with the north and northeast. At the height of its power, Qaryat Al-Fau was the capital of the State of Kinda, boasted palaces, temples, markets, and tombs, had a complex system of wells and surface canals to support agriculture, and even struck its own coins.

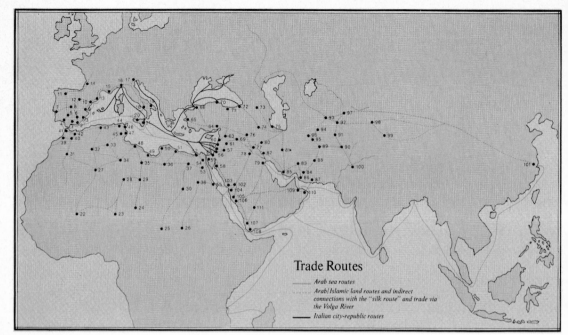

Trade Routes

— Arab sea routes

···· Arab/Islamic land routes and indirect
connections with the "silk route" and trade via
the Volga River

— Italian city-republic routes

● Major trading and commercial centers

Iberian Peninsula, Europe
1. Malaga
2. Almeria
3. Cartagena
4. Seville
5. Cordoba
6. Granada
7. Lisbon
8. Toledo
9. Valencia
10. Tortosa
11. Leon
12. Saragossa
13. Barcelona
14. Bordeaux
15. Marseilles
16. Genoa
17. Venice
18. Naples
19. Bari
20. Palermo
21. Syracusa

Africa
22. Timbuktu
23. Agades
24. Bilma
25. Abesehr
26. Al-Fasher

27. 'Ayn-Salah
28. Ghat
29. Marzug
30. Kufra Oases
31. Sijilmasa
32. Ghardaia
33. Touggourt
34. Ghadames
35. Jufra Oasis
36. Jalo Oasis
37. Siwa Oasis
38. Kharga Oasis
39. Rabat
40. Fez
41. Tangier
42. Tlemcen
43. Algiers
44. Bone
45. Kairouan
46. Tunis
47. Al-Mahdiyah
48. Tripoli
49. Sirte
50. Barqa
51. Tobruk
52. Alexandria
53. Fayyum
54. Cairo
55. Berenice

Eastern Mediterranean
56. Jerusalem
57. Damascus
58. 'Ayla
59. Al-Qulsum
60. Tripoli
61. Homs
62. Beirut
63. Aleppo
64. Tarsus
65. Smyrna
66. Constantinople
67. Sidon
68. Tyre
69. Palmyra
70. Sinop
71. Samsun
72. Trebizond
73. Tbilisi
74. Tabriz
75. Ardesil
76. Mosul
77. Baghdad
78. Kufah
79. Basrah
80. Kermanshah
81. Isfahan
82. Wasit
83. Kerman

84. Jiraft
85. Siraf
86. Hormuz
87. Tiz
88. Zaran
89. Herat
90. Kabul
91. Balkh
92. Samarkand
93. Bukhara
94. Merv
95. Nishapur
96. Meshed
97. Tashkent
98. Kashgar
99. Khotan
100. Multan
101. Hangchow
Arabian Peninsula
102. Medina
103. Al-Jar
104. Yanbu'
105. Jeddah
106. Makkah
107. San'a'
108. Aden
109. Oman
110. Muscat
111. Qaryat Al-Fau

Although the level of maritime trading activity has varied greatly in the Arabian/Persian Gulf region, it has gone on since earliest recorded history, and it has been highly instrumental in the spreading of culture. The Gulf traders, sailing their dhows, were proselytizers for their faith as well as merchants, and conversions to Islam in much of East and West Africa and Southeast Asia were effected mainly through trade. Today in the harbors of Kuwait, Dubai, Bahrain, and Abu Dhabi, among other Gulf states, the dhows, remarkably unchanged in design over the centuries, lie anchored between voyages. It should come as no surprise, then, that the Kuwaitis, Bahrainis, and others in the Gulf not only have retained their maritime skills but still possess a keen, almost uncanny mercantile mentality and ability.

ARAB TRADE ROUTES

The Mediterranean trade patterns of the Phoenicians, Egyptians, Greeks, and Romans are, perhaps, better known to Western readers. Whether or not it has been in the control of a single power, the Mediterranean has constituted a logical commercial entity. In Roman times trade extended as far as present-day Ceylon, but it was conducted through intermediaries. And chief among these intermediaries were the Arabs and the soon-to-be-"Arabized" peoples of the Middle East.

Into this background of history and geography, in which the Middle East functioned as a hub rather than a spoke, Islam injected a special attitude. Within the Arab empire, trade and commerce were allocated a unique role, largely because these economic activities had been prominent at the time and place of the birth of Islam. The prophet Muhammad earned his livelihood in commerce as a representative of the city of Makkah, which carried on a brisk caravan trade and organized small industries in the area from southern Palestine to southwest Arabia, with branches established as far away as East Africa. Islam arose primarily in a mercantile, not a nomadic or agricultural, milieu—although many early adherents to the faith were to come from the Bedouin tribes.

Among the recent discoveries at Qaryat al-Fau, Saudi Arabia, is this copper balance weight used to weigh grain. In the shape of a leopard or lion it carries ancient South Arabian inscriptions in relief.

223

No prohibitions were laid down against trading with Christians or nonbelievers in the Qur'an, the sayings of the Prophet, or the Muslim jurists' legal pronouncements, nor can any be found in the acts of the early caliphs of the Arab empire. Harun ar-Rashid (764–809), a successor of the Prophet, sent gifts to Charlemagne, and through their friendship an inn was founded for Christian pilgrims in Jerusalem and a market was established where the pilgrims could carry on business by paying an annual levy of two dinars.

By the end of the eighth century the Arab traders had developed routes from Mesopotamia, the new capital of Baghdad, and the port of Basrah, at the mouth of the Tigris and Euphrates Rivers, to India, Madagascar, Ceylon, Indonesia, and China. Overland, there was Arab or Islamic rule in Bactria (modern Balkh) and Chorasmia, or Khwarizm, and in the oasis cities of Bukhara and Samarkand. The area south of the Sea of Aral flourished under Arab suzerainty, and from here Arab caravans set out along the "silk route" to China over an arduous terrain that was made even more hazardous by the presence of fierce and uncontrolled desert tribesmen.

Gold Islamic coins: (left) Muwahhid coin from Seville, undated, (center) Umayyad coin from Damascus, 657 (right) Fatimid coin from Cairo, 1037.

In about 787 the first Arab vessel called at the port of "Kanfu," probably Hangchow, south of the Yangtze River. In China, according to an Arab merchant, the authorities would remove all the ship's cargo to warehouses, where it would be held for as long as six months. They would then take thirty percent of the goods as a "tax," returning the remainder to the merchant. Even considering the thirty percent cut of the Chinese ruler, Arab traders found the enterprise profitable, and for five centuries they virtually monopolized trade between China and Europe. It was not until the end of the thirteenth century that the Polo brothers of Venice made their famous trip.

Another trade route established by the Arabs can be tracked by the Islamic coins frequently found northward from the Caspian Sea, along the Volga River, through the eastern

Baltic region, and into the southern reaches of Finland, Norway, and Sweden. It will be recalled in connection with this evidence that the Scandinavians set up the commercial towns of western Russia, such as Kiev. In the tenth century, Chorasmia, south of the Sea of Aral, was a wealthy melting pot on the northeastern frontier of the Arab empire. Here European goods that had moved via the Volga River were delivered to Middle Eastern buyers—animal pelts, Slavic captives (from which the word "slave" is derived), cattle, sheep, arrows, wax, and special leather.

One wonders what kind of trade balance, to use modern economic jargon, the Arab empire ran with its trading partners to the East and West—possibly a deficit and a surplus, respectively. The number and variety of commodities flowing into and through the Arab empire can be gleaned from a mid-ninth-century list of imports into Iraq that appears in *The Investigation of Commerce*, a pamphlet ascribed to Abu 'Uthman 'Amr bin Bahr of Basrah, surnamed al-Jahiz (died 869). Among the sources and imports he lists are:

India—tigers, panthers, elephants, panther skins, rubies, ebony, coconuts
China—silk and silk stuffs, chinaware, paper, ink, peacocks, saddles, cinnamon, drugs, utensils of gold and silver, gold coins, engineers, agronomists, marble workers
Arabia—horses, pedigreed camels, tanned skins
The borders of Maghreb and Barbary—panthers, felts, hawks, *salam* leaves (used in tanning)
Yemen—incense, giraffes, gems, curcuma (used as a dye, condiment, and medicine)
Egypt—donkeys, suits of fine cloth, papyrus, balsam, "excellent" topazes
The land of Khazars—slaves, coats of mail, helmets, neck guards
The land of Chorasmia (Khwarizm)—musk, ermine, marten, fox and other furs, sugarcane
Samarkand—paper
Bactria (Balkh)—sweet grapes
Merve—zithers, zither players, carpets, suits
Isfahan—honey, pears, quinces, apples, salt, saffron, soda, syrups, white lead
Kirman—indigo, cumin
Fars—linen suits, rose water, jasmine ointment, syrups
Fasa—pistachios, rare fruit, glassware
Oman and the Seacoast—pearls
Mosul—quail, curtains, striped material
Armenia and Azerbaijan—felts, carpets, fine mats, wool, packsaddles

THE EFFECTS OF EMPIRE

Within the Arab empire, vigorous activities in trade and commerce led to a number of consequences: first, commodities produced in one part of the Arab world became available in others, so that a uniformity of consumer goods existed among a large, diverse population inhabiting a wide territory; second, the heart of the Arab empire, lying midway between East and West, served to disseminate technological innovations among the peoples of outlying areas; and third, advances were made in transportation, in applied and technical navigation, and in the allied fields of shipbuilding, cartography, and geography.

As the Arabs swept outward from the Arabian Peninsula, the material culture became more and more uniform. Never before, not even at the peak of the Greek and Roman expansion, had so many peoples spread over so vast a territory had such a large range of products available for their consumption. From the late seventh century to the end of the twelfth, the Arab empire functioned much like a free-trade area. The Arabs carried with them a standard of living based on the gracious, multifaceted life of their cultural centers. Thus, the Arabs of Spain wanted the same living conditions that were available in Baghdad and Damascus; and, of course, the indigenous populations in conquered territories sought the material advantages enjoyed by the Arabs. Like the Arab influence in science, literature, philosophy, art, and architecture, the commercial impact generally filtered into Europe through Islamic Spain and Sicily, or indirectly through Byzantium. Later, there was increasing direct contact with merchants from the great Italian port cities.

One of the most vigorous debates in historiography in this century concerns precisely this period and precisely these actors—the Arab empire and Western Europe (as distinct from the Eastern Roman Empire or Byzantium). A thesis advanced by the Belgian economic and social historian Henri Pirenne claims, in a generalized way, that it was not the invasions of the barbarian Germanic tribes (Goths, Ostrogoths, and Visigoths) in the fifth century that ended Rome's control of trade and commerce in the Mediterranean Basin but rather the creation of the Arab empire. The Islamic conquests, however, had positive as well as negative repercussions on the European continent. The wresting of North Africa and the eastern provinces of the Mediterranean Basin, such as Syria, from Byzantium by the Arabs forced Western Europe to turn inward upon itself and its own resources and eventually led to its cultural, economic, and territorial growth. Moreover, after an initial period of disruption in communications and trade in the Mediterranean, old contacts were resumed and new patterns established. This commercial relationship brought to medieval Europe a wealth of new products, techniques, and concepts. The Pirenne thesis has been modified by succeeding scholarship, but its contribution has drawn attention to the impact of Arab culture on the development of Western civilization, particularly in the economic sphere.

Arab naval forces completely dominated the Mediterranean only from the late seventh to the early ninth century, when they held all of North Africa, the Iberian Peninsula, Sardinia, Corsica, Sicily, Malta, Crete, and Cyprus and even had an outpost on the coast of France between Nice and Marseilles. Although the northern Mediterranean areas were retaken by the Christians, as in the Norman conquest of Sicily, Islamic rule left the native populations not only with Arab bloodlines but also with an expanded knowledge of commodities and a taste for a certain standard of living. Moreover, trading contacts, which had been established northward in Christian territory, continued even after Islamic Europe was no longer part of the empire.

The Arab merchant navy in the Mediterranean never rivaled that which plied the Indian Ocean, owing in part perhaps to the historical precedence of maritime activity in the east prior to the rise of Islam. The relative weakness of the Arab Mediterranean fleet led directly to the growth of the powerful Italian trading cities, which became crucial in the later Middle Ages

Dhows identical to those used by Arab merchants a millennium ago still ply the waters of the Middle East.

At a Moroccan market merchants sell produce introduced to North Africa and the West by the Arabs centuries ago.

and Renaissance. For it was not Arab vessels but the ships of Amalfi, Venice, Pisa, and Genoa that moved goods from North Africa, Spain, and the eastern Mediterranean. This trend was reinforced about the year 1000, when the Fatimids in Tunisia grew in power, broke with the Abbasid caliphs in Baghdad, conquered Egypt, and made Cairo their capital. Such expansion needed naval power; ships or wood for building ships and iron for arms had to be imported from Europe. The Italian merchants who had traded with the Fatimids in Tunisia now went directly to Egypt. Although the Italians carried goods between Egypt and Italy (and between one part of the Arab empire in the Mediterranean and another), they could not pass through Egypt to the Red Sea or the Sudan or otherwise penetrate into Arab land masses. A similar pattern was adopted by the Italians in regard to Byzantium and central Europe.

Perhaps the greatest service the Arabs rendered Europe was to introduce new goods from lands beyond the Mediterranean and to provide a continued flow of those commodities, such as spices, to which the Europeans had become accustomed. Most of these were expensive, often luxury items—at least by European standards; the high cost of long-distance transport made trade in bulky, heavy, or cheaper commodities unattractive. During the early centuries of the commercial revolution (beginning in the tenth century), when trade in Europe expanded faster than the output of coins, it was not uncommon for payments to be made in pepper and other exotic spices.

In China the Arabs found, not only silk and porcelain, but also gunpowder, saltpeter ("Chinese snow"), and paper. Europe had depended on papyrus for centuries, but its availability had decreased following the conquest of Egypt by the Arabs. It had never been a freely manufactured item; its production had been a state-controlled monopoly in Pharaonic, early Roman, and Christian Roman times. Invented about 105 A.D. in China, papermaking was brought to Samarkand by Chinese prisoners of war in 751. There the manufacture and export of this product were initiated. The vizier of Harun ar-Rashid, Yahya the Barmakid, built the first paper mill in Baghdad about 800. The use of paper spread through Syria, North Africa, and Spain; by 1190, Roger II of Sicily could issue a paper document. By contrast, it was not until the twelfth century that the first European paper mills were established.

Silk production also moved westward with the Arabs, who introduced the cultivation of mulberry trees at Gabes, south of Tunis. Similarly, the cultivation of cotton no longer remained an Indian specialty but was brought to North Africa and even Spain. Other Indian and East Asian crops were transplanted to the regions of the Arab empire: sugarcane to Egypt, Cyprus, and Spain and indigo to North Africa. In Spain the Arabs improved irrigation and introduced the cultivation of rice, oranges, lemons, apricots, eggplants, and artichokes, in addition to sugar and cotton.

Among the industries that the Arabs introduced to Spain are the manufacture and painting of ceramics, including tiles, and the manufacture of crystal, a process discovered in Cordoba in the second half of the ninth century. By the tenth century, the jewelry produced in Cordoba was equal in quality to that of Byzantium.

But it was in textiles that the Islamic empire excelled, and it is through the Arab merchants that Europe came to know a wide range of fabrics. Of the words derived from Arabic in European languages, especially in English, a significant number refer to cloth—for example, "gauze," "buckram," "chiffon," "satin," "tabby" (a cloth from 'Attabiyyah, a section of Baghdad), "mohair," "muslin" (from Mosul), "damask" (from Damascus), and "cotton." Aniline, a critical ingredient in textile dyes, was also introduced by the Arabs.

Although industry developed far earlier in the Islamic empire than in Europe, the very peculiarities of its development in the Arab-dominated lands eventually made it noncompetitive with European industry. In the Arab world, industry was, for example, wholly under the control of the ruler; it was characterized by a lack of capital and the failure of craftsmen to organize guilds.

COMMERCIAL DEVELOPMENTS

In Islamic Spain the Arabs introduced concepts of municipal administration and measures for control of commerce. Spanish words derived from Arabic in this area include *zocco* or *azoguej* "market," *almacen* "warehouse," *aduana* "customshouse," *almoneda* "public sale," *almojarife* "tax collection," *alcalde* "mayor," and *zalmedina* "magistrate," to cite but a few. This Arab heritage in Spain's city organization again underlines the urban element in Islam, an element associated with trade and commerce. Other words reflect the lasting Arab influence on these economic activities: "traffic" (Arabic, *tafriq*, meaning "distribution"), "tariff" (*ta'rifah*), "check" (*sakk*), "magazine" (*makhazin*, as in French *magazin*, meaning "store"), "mancus" (a term used for "coin" in the Middle Ages, from *manqush*), "almanac," "average," "caliber," "coffer," "cipher," "gabelle" (meaning a "tax," from the Latin *caballa* through the Arabic *qabala*), "nadir," "zenith," "zero," and "risk." Although some of these words can be traced to a Latin, Greek, or Persian source, they passed into European tongues through Arabic. The word "sterling," for example, has an ancient Greek base, but it was transmitted into English through Arabic.

In advancing the concept of the bill of exchange—*sakk*, or check—the Arabs made the financing of commerce more flexible. The second important contribution in this line was the development of joint stock companies, arrived at through the partnership of Muslim and Christian Italian merchants. Another significant Arabic contribution to European commercial development was expounded perhaps as early as the end of the ninth century in Damascus by Abu al-Fadl Ja'far bin 'Ali ad-Dimashqi in his work *A Guide to the Merits of Commerce and to Recognition of Both Fine and Defective Merchandise and the Swindles of Those Who Deal Dishonestly*:

> There are three kinds of merchants: he who travels, he who stocks, he who exports. Their trade is carried out in three ways: cash sale with a time limit for delivery, purchase on credit with payment by installment, and *muqaradah*.

The *muqaradah* in Islamic law is a contract in which one individual entrusts capital to a merchant for investment in trade in order to receive a share in the profits. The investor bears all the financial risks; the managing party risks his labor. The concept of *muqaradah* was certainly a precedent for the *commenda*, a legal, commercial device largely responsible for the expansion of medieval trade. It followed the general line of the *muqaradah* but had its own peculiarities, legally designating an association somewhere between a partnership and the lender-borrower relationship. It served as a crucial instrument by which capital could be pooled and investor and manager could be brought together in an enterprise.

The wealth of the Arab empire was not concentrated in only a few cities, such as Baghdad, Damascus, and Cairo. Aleppo remained a significant trading center, and North Africa boasted a number of flourishing commercial towns. Abu al-Qasim Muhammad bin Hauqal, in his *Book of Routes and Kingdoms*, recorded the conditions he found in three North African and two Italian municipalities he visited in about the year 977. Ajadabiya, near present-day Barce in Libya, was described as a modest town with a nonirrigated agricultural base. Being near the sea, it was a port of call for merchant ships and a jumping-off point for caravans to the south of the Sahara. Today, Ajadabiya does not even appear on the usual maps.

Farther west, Ibn Hauqal described the trade centers of Kairouan and Sijilmasa. The former, in Tunisia, still has religious significance, but the latter, located south of Fez in Morocco, has disappeared completely. At the end of the tenth century, however, Kairouan was, according to Ibn Hauqal, the largest municipality and seat of government in the Maghreb. Sijilmasa was the terminus for caravans to the gold-exporting areas of Senegal. The traveler told of seeing a private account book recording that one citizen of Sijilmasa owed another 40,000 dinars, and he further noted that when he "spoke about this later in Khurasan and in Iraq, the fact was regarded as unique." Small wonder such a figure astounded the listeners; it is one of the highest figures to be found in any existing records of private accounts in the Arab empire or in European records of the Middle Ages. In comparison with these tenth-century Arabic centers, the Italian cities of Naples and Amalfi were just beginning to expand commercially.

Concerned with the movement of goods to markets, the merchants of the Arab empire, *ipso facto*, made advances in the fields of geography and navigation. The commercial supremacy of the Arabs in the Indian Ocean and Red Sea was unchallenged for years before the rise of the

231

*An ancient map of Iraq
drawn by the fifteenth-century
geographer, al-Istakhri.*

Islamic empire, and that supremacy continued during the period under study, both at sea and on land. As these merchant-adventurers moved about, their experiences bore fruit in the form of geographical writings and descriptions of distant lands and peoples, information which seeped into Europe through Spain, Sicily, and Byzantium. The best-known author among them is probably the noted geographer al-Idrisi (1100–1166), resident at the court of the Christian Norman King Roger II of Sicily (1130–1154). Far better known, however, are the glorious adventure tales of Sindbad the Sailor, and for these, too, we are indebted to the maritime merchants of the Arab empire.

Among the Arab contributions to navigation and shipbuilding, one should probably include the compass. The Arabs were most likely the first to use it, though refinements were added almost at once by European seafarers. A more critical innovation was the lateen sail, which the Arabs introduced first in the Indian Ocean and then, via the lateen caravel, in the Mediterranean. Using this sail, the Arab vessels could beat against the wind, unlike the square-rigged galleons of the Mediterranean, which could sail only before the wind. The principle of the lateen sail was taken over and developed by European shipbuilders, especially by the Spanish and Portuguese between 1440 and 1490. During this period they adopted a design using mixed lateen and square-rigged sails that was applicable to much larger vessels than before. The English word "carrack," meaning "galleon," can be traced from the Spanish and Portuguese *carraca* to the Arabic *qaraqir*, meaning "merchant vessel." Other maritime words of Arabic origin dot the English language: "admiral," "bark," "barkentine," "cable," "sloop," "monsoon," "caliber," and "average."

232

Scholarship in this century has done much to place the Crusades in perspective by showing that trade, commerce, and intellectual contacts were significant and healthy between Europe and the Arab empire long before the Christian religious zeal brought about the drive to recover the Holy Land. The knowledge in the West of the riches, the high standard of living, and the commodities produced or available within the Islamic empire helped to spur the religious impulse. In about the year 1184 Abu al-Hasan Muhammad bin Jubayr, an inhabitant of Spain who traveled to all the Islamic countries on the Mediterranean as well as to the Christian communities of Sicily, Sardinia, and the Holy Land, noted somewhat cynically that Muslims and Christians in Palestine continued to trade despite the war between their forces. "The military men are busy in their wars, the peoples trade in peace, and the world belongs to whoever takes it," he said.

SUMMARY

From the eighth to the early twelfth century, the trade between Europe and Islam consisted chiefly of the exchange of raw materials from Europe (wood, iron, furs, slaves) for manufactured products and luxury agricultural items, such as spices, from the Arab empire. This pattern, it has been suggested, somewhat resembles the "colonial" trade of the nineteenth and twentieth centuries between European nations and their colonies or the trade patterns that currently exist between the industrialized and the underdeveloped countries.

The lasting Islamic impact on Europe did not result from the military confrontations of the Crusades but rather from the long years of Arab rule in Spain and Sicily. Through the innovations brought to these areas, new goods, processes, technology, and concepts were introduced into a Europe that was far less developed at that time than the world of Islam. That the debt of Europe and Western culture to Islam has been largely forgotten is evidence of how fully assimilated the Arab influence has been in the Western world. The Islamic contribution has become part and parcel of its heritage.

Abu al-Fadl Ja'far bin 'Ali ad-Dimashqi

(Eleventh century)

The identity of Abu al-Fadl Ja'far bin 'Ali ad-Dimashqi is known to us only through the circumstantial evidence gleaned from his lone work: *Kitab al-Isharah ila Mahasin at-Tijarah wa Ma'rifat Jayyid al-A'rad wa Radi 'iha wa Ghushush al-Mudallisin fiha* (*A Guide to the Merits of Commerce and to Recognition of Both Fine and Defective Merchandise and the Swindles of Those Who Deal Dishonestly*). Consequently, very little can be said about his life with any assurance. Two well-known European Orientalists, Helmut Ritter and Claude Cahen, have scrutinized ad-Dimashqi's book and give us the following tentative biographical information. Since ad-Dimashqi cites Ibn al-Mu'tazz (died 908) and al-Kindi (died after 870), he probably wrote no earlier than the end of the ninth century. Of the two extant manuscripts of his work, one bears the date 1174 and provides, therefore, a time by which the book had been completed. By interpreting other, more obscure references one may arrive at a more precise dating for his life. Ad-Dimashqi mentions, for example, an Indian coin bearing the likenesses of a horseman on one side and an ox on the other. He notes that a friend had seen such a coin in Ghazna and that he, himself, had observed one in Tripoli, on the Syrian coast. It might therefore be concluded that ad-Dimashqi lived in the eleventh century because both Ghazna and Tripoli were enjoying commercial prominence during that time, and the coin may still have been in circulation. Only on such tentative hypotheses can ad-Dimashqi's life be reconstructed.

The geographical milieu in which ad-Dimashqi moved is more certain. His name links him to the city of Damascus, and other information in his book indicates that he lived in the commercial center of the Islamic world—Egypt and the Syrian coast. From the tenth century, this region of the Islamic empire began to replace Baghdad and the Arabian/Persian Gulf ports as the hub of international commerce. As political strife in Baghdad worsened, merchants moved to Egypt and the Red Sea ports. With the establishment of the Fatimid dynasty in Egypt (969–1171) and the resulting political and religious rivalry with the Abbasids in Baghdad, trade took on even more significance. Ships embarked for Byzantium, Sicily, and the Levant from Egypt's Mediterranean ports. They returned loaded with slaves, furs, timber, and metals. Meanwhile, her Red Sea ports were entrepôts for goods from the Arabian Peninsula, India, Ceylon, and China. Precious stones and metals, textiles, spices, and other luxury goods arrived, were handled by middlemen, and then moved to the retail level or into export warehouses.

Ad-Dimashqi leaves little doubt that he was one of these middlemen. He makes reference to the retail trade and to manufacturing, but he clearly regards the import-export business as a superior occupation. Moreover, when he itemizes the best kinds of commodities, he shows an almost exclusive preference for luxury goods such as precious stones and expensive fabrics. Neither foodstuffs and grains nor finished products such as clothing and jewelry held any attraction for him. Investment in raw and partly finished materials was much more profitable and apparently less risky. Ad-Dimashqi was part of a commercial elite capable of raising large sums of capital and earning correspondingly sizable profits. Although his references to the sea and to various cities show that he himself had traveled on business, it appears that his journeying days were behind him by the time he wrote his book. Indications in his book suggest that he spent a good deal of his time investing his profits in real estate and other property that required a more sedentary life. He highly recommended urban or suburban property investments, and it may be assumed that he was speaking from experience. Undoubtedly wealthy and probably favored by the trade-conscious Fatimid rulers of Egypt, ad-Dimashqi appears an exemplar of the cultured, propertied merchant elite that emerged in the tenth and eleventh centuries.

His book, while representing only this elite minority of the business community, is nonetheless an invaluable record of business techniques and attitudes. By adopting a neo-Hellenic posture that praises wealth for its own sake, ad-Dimashqi manages to get by with no more than the obligatory citations of Qur'anic and Hadith maxims extolling the virtues of a commercial life. Since shrewd business transactions resulting in large profits are by definition meritorious and need no further justification, he is able to devote most of his *Guide* to practical advice.

His book begins with an essay on the true nature of wealth and then proceeds to discuss the necessity of money; how to test for the genuineness of money; how to evaluate commodities; their prices; how to discern good from defective merchandise; investment in real estate; handicrafts and manufactures; advice for salespeople; the advantages of business; the different types of merchants and their duties; how to avoid fraud; how to keep records; and the necessity of protecting one's wealth. Ad-Dimashqi concludes his book by admonishing the reader not to waste his wealth but to use it correctly.

Despite the uncertainties in dating ad-Dimashqi's life and work, his guide is an important source for understanding commerce in the Mediterranean world of the tenth and eleventh centuries.

ROBERT D. McCHESNEY

234

The Mediterranean port of Alexandria, Egypt, a center of import-export trade during the eleventh century.

Abu 'Abdallah Muhammad bin Muhammad 'Abdallah bin Idris al-Hammudi al-Hasani

(1100–1166)

The intellectual curiosity of the Arabs led them not only into abstract explorations of the human mind but also into concrete explorations of the geographical world.

In the Middle Ages geography was more an art than a science. Although astronomers by studying the universe were able to theorize about such general geographical subjects as the probable shape of the earth, geography was for the most part a product of the imagination, a collection of wondrous fables and marvelous tales. In the twelfth century, however, an Arab geographer and cartographer—Abu 'Abdallah Muhammad bin Muhammad 'Abdallah bin Idris al-Hammudi al-Hasani—began to apply scientific method to his studies of the known world.

Al-Idrisi was born in 1100 at Ceuta, Morocco, the son of a noble family, the Hammudites. As a direct descendent of the Prophet, Muhammad, he was privileged to use the title, ash-Sharif. During his youth he studied at Cordoba, the capital of Muslim Spain. He was a poet, a student of medicine, and an avid traveler. But despite his cosmopolitan background and his importance as a geographer and chronicler, al-Idrisi was generally ignored by Muslim historians and biographers in later years. This is perhaps explained by the fact that he spent most of his adult years in the service of the Norman king, Roger II of Sicily, at Palermo. His devotion to the Christian king and his separation from the world of Islam cost him the attention and respect of his contemporaries.

Before joining the court at Palermo, al-Idrisi had already led a legendary life. In his travels he had retraced the path of Islamic conquest. The warrior horsemen who had swept across the Mediterranean, spreading the new

faith, had vowed when they reached the Maghreb, "the place where the sun sets behind the water," that only the ocean waves would stop their horses. Al-Idrisi's spirit of adventure was equal to their own. He had voyaged westward to Madeira and the Canary Islands. Stopped in his geographical wanderings by the immensity of the unknown ocean, he turned eastward and visited Asia Minor instead.

It was al-Idrisi's fame as a scholar and traveler that won him an invitation from Roger II to visit Sicily, where he was received with all the honors due his noble birth. The monarch's insatiable curiosity about geography occupied all the time he did not spend administering the tiny kingdom that had been granted him by the treaty of Saint-Germain in 1139. It was this interest that bound al-Idrisi to him.

Before Roger II died in 1154 al-Idrisi had completed construction of a celestial sphere and a disk-shaped map of the known world. Both objects were made of solid silver provided by the king—with enough left over to cover al-Idrisi's reward.

The silver map was based on the encyclopedic work al-Idrisi completed under King Roger II's patronage: the *Kitab Nuzhat al-Mushtaq fi Ikhtiraq al-Afaq*, known currently as the *Book of Roger* or *Kitab ar-Rujari*. It was not until 1592 that the manuscript made its European appearance in an abridged version printed in Rome. It was translated into Latin in Paris in 1619, but it has yet to be translated into English in its entirety.

Al-Idrisi stayed on at the court in Palermo after the death of Roger II and wrote for his son, William I, another geographical treatise, *The Garden of Civilization and the Amusement of the Soul*. He died in 1166.

FLORENCE AMZALLAG TATISTCHEFF

236

A map of the world by al-Idrisi.

Muhammad bin 'Abdallah bin Battutah

(1304–1369)

The expanse of the mature Muslim culture, from the Atlantic Ocean to the borders of China, encouraged trade on a large scale over vast distances. A natural concomitant of this cultural and trading activity was the development of a group of writers who can more or less be thought of as professional travelers and who are known today because they authored books of "voyages" (singular, *rihlah*) that have survived. The breadth of Arab interest in related fields is indicated by the fact that one can with some precision distinguish travelers from geographers, cartographers, and compilers of geographical encyclopedias.

Of the travelers none is more celebrated than Muhammad bin 'Abdallah bin Battutah. Ibn Battutah was born in Tangier in 1304 and died in Marrakesh either about 1369 or in 1377. The comparison with Marco Polo, his Western counterpart and near contemporary (1254–1324), is interesting, for the Muslim traveler appeared as the sun was setting on the greatest period of Muslim creativity, whereas Polo introduced the rest of the world to the nascent Renaissance of the West.

Of Ibn Battutah's life Muslim scholars wrote little, but much can be gleaned from his accounts of his trips. His family tradition was the Muslim judiciary, and Professor H. A. R. Gibb, the English translator of Ibn Battutah, logically surmises that he received the classical training of a Muslim savant in religious, scholastic, and literary subjects. At the age of twenty-one, young Muhammad embarked on the pilgrimage to Makkah in order, firstly, to fulfill one of the "pillars of Islam" and also as a kind of grand-tour finishing school that would provide the cachet of study with scholars in the Muslim east to this western hopeful. Even on his first trip (eight are distinguishable), Ibn Battutah was a traveler, for he had already put into effect his rule, "Never, so far as possible, cover any road a second time." Using Makkah as a base, he managed to get as far east as Iraq and Iran, down both sides of the Red Sea to Yemen and Aden, thence down the East African coast, and back via Oman and the Arabian/Persian Gulf. On these later trips Ibn Battutah began to move in the company of princes and even had an entourage of his own.

Following another pilgrimage in 1332, Ibn Battutah wanted to go to Muslim India. He took a ship north and

238

went overland through Egypt and Syria. He traveled by ship from Latakia to Istanbul, crisscrossed Asia Minor, crossed the Black Sea to the Crimea, and made his way overland via the Golden Horde's territory, through Samarkand, Bukhara, and Afghanistan. He reached the Indus River frontier of India in September, 1333. In time he became chief judge of Delhi, and in 1342 he was sent by the sultan as his ambassador to the Mongol emperor of China. The trip took him to the Maldives, Bengal, Assam, Sumatra, and finally to the Chinese city of Zaytun (Ts'üan-chou) and possibly Peking. He returned to Morocco in 1349.

Forty-five years old, Ibn Battutah wanted to see new sights. First he crossed the Pillars of Hercules to the western European Muslim capital of Granada—a modest trip compared with his final major effort, which took him in 1352 across the Sahara to the Muslim empire of the Mandingos and back again across the great desert to his homeland a year later. On Ibn Battutah's return to Fez the Marinid sultan, Abu 'Inan, commanded him to dictate the story of his journeys to the scribe Ibn Jazayy. Thereafter, as Gibb notes, the intrepid traveler "passes from sight, and one can only guess at the manner in which he passed his last years as a *qadi* 'in some town or other.'"

Ibn Battutah finished dictating his account to Ibn Jazayy in 1357. It is impossible to tell where the author leaves off and the scribe begins. The style varies widely from the matter-of-fact to the euphuistic, and there are numerous difficulties in straightening out the chronologies of the trips. It seems clear that Ibn Jazayy exaggerated in general and that Ibn Battutah sometimes relied on his memory where his notes failed and perhaps on his imagination where his memory failed. Nevertheless, his account is one of the most valuable sources for early Ottoman history, the history of Muslim India, and the history of West Africa. Moreover, his narrative is fascinating. He explains how the city rice granaries worked in the midst of famine in Delhi. He comments on the fine bazaars and wide streets in the original Ottoman capital of Bursa and on the silk uniforms of the pages in Aydin. Like any foreigner in a strange land, he preferred to stay in the best quarter.

The *oikoumene* of the Muslims found in Ibn Battutah a traveler and reporter of unparalleled breadth and depth.

R. B. WINDER

Camel caravan, North Africa.

Conclusion

Dr. Ibrahim Madkour is the President of the Academy of Arabic
Language in Cairo. Previously he taught at Cairo University and the
Sorbonne. He has served in the Egyptian Senate and has
participated in academic conferences throughout the world. In 1972 he
received the State Prize in Social Science from the Egyptian
Government. Dr. Madkour's publications include *Islamic Philosophy*,
L'Organon d'Aristote, and *Terminology of Philosophy in Islam*.

Past, Present, and Future

Ibrahim Madkour

In any society, culture is the offspring of many factors: human potential, creative consciousness, intellectual and spiritual vitality, real achievement and progress, and freedom, among others. In the Arab society of the early eighth century, the potential for extraordinary cultural achievement clearly existed. The introduction of Islam into that society generated creative activity within the Arab consciousness. By providing new purpose and a new sense of direction, it unified a loose assemblage of tribes, inspired leadership, and unleashed collective and individual genius. In succeeding centuries, Arab society found and developed its own cultural identity, and in the process it rescued from near oblivion much of the legacy of pagan antiquity. Linking past with future, it helped pave the way for the European Renaissance.

The Arab world, like Western Europe prior to its Renaissance, experienced a "Dark Ages," however. During this period, which lasted some four centuries, an atmosphere of frustration and discouragement prevailed throughout the Arab lands. The days of conquest and glory were over. There were no new worlds to discover, no great achievements to be made. The prevailing mood of despondency and loss was summed up in a famous complaint: "The first have left nothing for the last!" Speculative thought was confined to increasingly narrow areas, scientific inquiry stagnated, and matters that had previously been studied and understood became obscure. Creative thinking and the spirit of discovery were replaced by sterile repetition and imitation, expressed in commentaries and studies of texts and stressing words rather than meaning. Cultural life was confined to a restricted group; the society at large fed on the past, ignored the present, and rejected any prospect of evolution or progress.

In the nineteenth century the Arabs once again began to be conscious of their own existence. This search for self-identity gave rise to a renewal of independent thinking, stimulated in part by intensive exposure to the thinking of others, particularly the scientists and scholars who accompanied the French expedition to Egypt early in the century. During the balance of the nineteenth century the Arab world, and particularly that part of it that borders on the eastern Mediterranean, was engaged in a process of absorption characterized by extensive contact with European scholars and teachers, doctors and engineers, architects and industrialists. Missions were sent to Europe to study mathematics, medicine, and the sciences, and large numbers of European and American scholars, businessmen, and technicians came to the Arab countries. Naturally, many problems resulted from this massive exchange of cultures and experiences, but the net effect was to stimulate in the Arab world a new desire for evolution and progress and to encourage its more remote areas to catch up with the Mediterranean regions, where the exposure to the industrial world was more advanced.

The twentieth century—a century of challenge and competition—is the real starting point of the contemporary cultural revival in the Arab world. Certainly there have been obstacles. Two world wars and numerous regional and domestic conflicts have taught the Arabs the high cost of violence in lives and treasure. If these sacrifices have meaning, it is to be found in their contribution to the development of a revitalized and meaningful Arab world, characterized not by isolation and self-doubt but by maturity, dignity, and solidarity in performance of its international responsibilities as one of the great contemporary civilizations.

If the Arab world is in general agreement as to its cultural goals, there remains much debate as to the best means to achieve them. If there is consensus that contemporary Arab culture must reflect the Arab personality and character, it is also agreed that the Arab world must not close its doors to the possible contribution of others. In other words, the goal of contemporary Arab culture is not only to revive the glories of its past but also to include the best aspects of the present, whatever the source. The past and the present, combined, give rise to the future—a future in which the Arabs will once again be able to speak proudly of their achievements in art, literature, science, and technology.

One of the principal areas of debate is that of language. During the Arab "Dark Ages" efforts were made by various colonial powers to substitute other languages—Turkish, French, English—for Arabic. As a result, the Arab world is bilingual and trilingual in many areas, but Arabic has maintained its primacy. The issue of "classical versus colloquial" Arabic has been largely resolved through the evolution of a modern classical form that, under the guidance of the several language academies, has proved to be both comprehensible to students and readily adaptable to educational needs. The Arabic language in general use today is noticeably different from that of the eighteenth and nineteenth centuries. Today's Arabic is a language that has been determined by the needs and the spirit of the times. It is an easier, more casual language, free of oddities, mannerisms, and conceits. It says what it means precisely, clearly, and directly. It is easily adapted to modern teaching and learning situations, and it is able to transcend class distinctions in an age that disdains such privileges. Modern Arabic has already helped to narrow the gap between the spoken and the written word, the common and the classic, and in time it will replace the various slang dialects that now divide the Arab world.

Essential as this development is in terms of nation-building, it by no means diminishes the importance of learning foreign languages. Arabs seem to have a particular aptitude for language study, and they have reason to recognize the importance of communication in the modern multinational world. In return, one hopes, more foreign countries will encourage the study of Arabic, as in fact appears to be happening, judging from increased enrollment in Arabic language and area programs in the Western countries.

The revival of the past, an essential part of the rediscovery of the Arabic heritage, has been accompanied by and has contributed to the flowering of contemporary letters. Modern literature reflects the challenge offered to the classic models by the new images of the present.

244

For example, poets influenced by the Western romantics have adopted some of the classical forms to give structure to their self-expression, while the "classicists" explore new rhymes and rhythms. The essay has been greatly expanded with the growth of the press and academic publications. (From the point of view of Arabic literature, the essay is simply an advanced form of the *maqamat*, modernized by journalists, politicians, and academicians, and as such it has had a significant role in social reform, political movements, literary criticism, and scientific analysis.) The novel and drama, on the other hand, express the hidden past or actual present of individuals and society. By revealing aspects of rural and urban life not generally known or observed, they often serve the cause of renovation and reform. But this does not mean that modern Arabic novels and plays have only regional significance. Many have been translated into foreign languages and are recognized among the world's masterpieces. In summary, contemporary Arabic literature, which began with imitation and progressed through inter-action between the classic and the modern, has now reached maturity and has developed forms and content of its own.

The revival of the arts has progressed in much the same way as has literature. This is especially true of music. The singing theater, radio, cinema, and television have opened new vistas for composers and singers and have helped to develop a common musical taste. The eastern Arab world has its purely oriental tunes and lyrics—of which Um Kalthum, a twentieth-century phenomenon, was the best-known exponent—while in North Africa no pains have been spared to revive the music known as "Andalusian."

Contemporary science and philosophy also reflect the new spirit of awareness, open-mindedness, and independence. This movement respects the rights and the integrity of the human being and provides room for speculative thought and reason. During the age of empire, the great rulers and thinkers were motivated by intellectual curiosity and scholarly acquisitiveness. Knowledge was revered, no matter what the source, and men who could contribute to the sum of human knowledge were honored, no matter who they were or where they came from. This spirit prevails today. The modern Arab world is open to the great Western achievements in research, exploration, and creative thinking. Remembering the long days of regression, it looks forward to an era of progress and renewal.

Arabs in the twentieth century know that they can never realize their ambitions without equipping themselves through education, and the spread of education has therefore been one of their primary aims. During the "Dark Ages" the Arab universities had dwindled to a tiny handful in which teachers isolated from the outside world monotonously repeated the lessons of the past. Today there are some forty universities in the Arab world. The study of Islamic sciences and civilization has been pursued under the guidance of world-famous professors, and modern research and analysis have opened up new realms of knowledge in such fields as contemporary sociology and psychology. In the natural sciences the Arab universities have moved rapidly to expand their activities. Modern laboratories, observatories, research centers, and teaching institutions have been established, and Arab scientists are now making contributions to the expansion of knowledge through original research, especially on problems of particular relevance to their region's material and human resources.

This brief summary of the development of contemporary Arab trends would be incomplete without a reference to the growth of popular culture. In the past, cultural activities tended to be confined to an elite group, but today Arab society rejects this concept as unfair and undemocratic. The various ministries, the mosques, the information media, the popular theater, and the schools and universities are working to further public understanding of the fact that the cultural heritage and ethical values of the Arab are in no way incompatible with national and individual progress and development.

As for the future, it seems probable that the Arab world will follow the precedents established in the more technologically advanced countries. By the end of the century illiteracy will be eliminated in most of the Arab countries, and the search for knowledge will be fully open to girls as well as boys. The new generation has already far outdistanced its predecessors in cultural awareness. In the future, one hopes, there will be less need to concentrate on the humanities and pure science and greater interest and opportunity in such shortage areas as agriculture, industry, and commerce.

The cultural isolation of the Arabs began in the fourteenth century when the empire began to shrink. It was replaced, at least partially, in succeeding centuries by various forms of dependence on foreign cultures, the outgrowth of colonialism. With the Arab world free once again to pursue its own destiny, cultural interdependence between Arabs and non-Arabs will continue to grow. The expansion of Arabic studies to Islamic Asia and Africa will increase, as will the number of Americans and Europeans attracted to Arabic studies by the expansion of economic and cultural relations between the Arab world and the industrialized countries. At the same time, the interchange of specialists and technicians among the Arab states will contribute to greater regional understanding and cooperation.

Islam is today, as in the past, the foundation stone of Arab culture. The Arab of today is respectful of religious obligations and has no patience with fanaticism or pedantry. He recognizes that science and faith are and always will be brothers. He will adhere to his principles as well as his responsibilities, believing that the precepts of religion are entirely compatible with the best behavior of mankind.

Arab culture today is developing and progressing without apprehension, confident of its ability to flourish in the larger world. It is reassured at its moment of rebirth by the knowledge that it has done this before. The legacy of greatness exists; the potential for future greatness is assured. By reaching outward for the knowledge needed to restore Arab culture to a position of prestige among the other great cultures of the world, the Arabs are, in a very real sense, beginning to share in the benefits of a gift they presented to humanity centuries ago.

A Guide to Further Reading

The faith of Islam, past and present, rests upon the *Qur'an*, and almost every facet of Muslim life has been shaped or touched by that book. No translation can do justice to the complex beauty of the original, but the reader of English has available an attempt to catch the poetic idiom by A. J. Arberry, *The Koran Interpreted* (New York 1970) and, since all translation is interpretation, a prose rendering by M. M. Pickthall, *The Meaning of the Glorious Koran* (rp. New York 1981), that is based on a traditional Muslim understanding of the text.

For scholars the *Qur'an* serves another important purpose: it is the chief document for the life, chiefly the spiritual life, of the Prophet of Islam, and when taken with another important source, the *Sirah* or *Life of the Prophet* written in the mid-eighth century (translated by A. Guillaume, *The Life of Muhammad* pb. New York 1970), provides the basis of most medieval and modern biographies of Muhammad. Western scholars have not been notably successful in interpreting the Prophet's life from a spiritual perspective, and if one excepts T. Andrae's *Muhammad, the Man and His Faith* (New York 1960), most Western biographies have attempted the simpler task of placing him in his social, economic or political context. Such is immediately apparent from M. Rodinson's survey of work on the Prophet's life ("A Critical Survey of Modern Studies on Muhammad" in M. L. Swartz (ed)., *Studies on Islam* (New York 1981) and in the two biographies that have gained some currency among English readers: W. M. Watt's *Muhammad, Prophet and Statesman* (London 1965) and Rodinson's own *Mohammed* (2nd ed. Cambridge 1971).

Islamic studies are still in their adolescence in the West, but the discipline has already produced a more or less authoritative, though not excessively technical work of basic reference in *The Encyclopaedia of Islam*, whose second edition is about halfway through its course of publication. "More or less authoritative" is likely the apposite phrase, though not for any lack of skill on the part of the contributors, who are generally the best in their fields and whose contributions do indeed reflect the "state of the art" on the subject, but for the more sobering reason that so much of what was written in Arabic, Persian, Turkish and Urdu remains still unread, unpublished and unstudied in modern times in libraries from Fez to Delhi.

Another standard work of reference, without pitfalls and nicely suited to both general readers and specialists, is *The Cambridge History of Islam* (2 vols., Cambridge 1970).

This is not simply history. The second volume in particular provides a number of excellent surveys of some of the same terrain covered in the present book. The same is true of Joseph Schacht's and C. E. Bosworth's new edition of *The Legacy of Islam* (Oxford 1973) and W. M. Watt's *The Influence of Islam on Medieval Europe* (Edinburgh and Chicago 1972), where the emphasis is on the Islamic cultural contribution to the West.

"Islam" is of course many things, a religion, a society and a culture, and the word "Islamic" has been applied to everything from literature and buildings to certain ways of thinking and acting. Not all such usages are legitimate, of course, whether they spring from Muslim or non-Muslim lips, but there are dense and complex realities that lie beneath the term. For a simple yet revealing entry into the religious dimension, the reader might well turn to the curiously mistitled *Muhammadanism* by H. A. R. Gibb (rp. New York 1971), which may then be broadened out into its comparative religious context in F. E. Peters' *The Children of Abraham: Judaism, Christianity and Islam* (Princeton 1982) and extended outward into society and more modern times in N. Keddie (ed.), *Scholars, Saints and Sufis* (Berkeley and Los Angeles 1978), D. Eickelman, *The Middle East: An Anthropological Approach* (Englewood Cliffs 1981) and R. C. Martin, *Islam: A Cultural Perspective* (Englewood Cliffs 1982). Finally for an *interpretation* of the traditional Islamic experience, there are two eccentric, sometimes opaque but almost always provocative books, *The Venture of Islam* by M. G. S. Hodgson (3 vols., Chicago 1975) and the briefer *Understanding Islam* by F. Schuon (Baltimore 1972).

The Muslim achievement in creating a high culture of ecumenical proportions was the product of a great cultural synthesis to which Arabs, Persians, Turks, Indians, Christians, Jews, Zoroastrians, Buddhists, Greeks, Romans and even the remote genius of Babylonia all contributed. It is simple minded, perhaps, to attempt to distinguish their individual roles in that rich compost of civilizations and cultures that made up the Islamic Middle Ages, but the historian, and particularly the cultural historian, works in simple-minded ways, and the medieval Muslim himself began the process of sorting out influences by distinguishing between the "Arab sciences" and the "foreign sciences" within his own legacy.

It is in the domain of the "Arab sciences", which derived by and large from the study, exegesis and legal elaboration of the *Qur'an*, that the original Arab contribution to

Islamic civilization is most clearly visible, and some sense of its complexity and sophistication can be gained from W. M. Watt's *Bell's Introduction to the Qur'an* (Edinburgh and Chicago 1970), in the authors' own words as they analyzed the sacred text in H. Gatje's *The Qur'an and Its Exegesis* (Berkeley and Los Angeles 1971), and in their elaboration of the great structure of Islamic law whose outlines are traced in J. Schacht's *An Introduction to Islamic Law* (Oxford 1964). Literature enters this configuration in a somewhat oblique manner: early on, the new Muslims judged that the best approach to the language and style of the *Qur'an* was through the poetry of their own bedouin past, that "time of ignorance" otherwise discredited by the coming of Islam. Thus blessed, Arab letters went their own way, though the poets at least continued to maintain conservative ties with their classical pre-Islamic roots.

Arabic poetry and poetics can be rocky terrain for the specialist and non-specialist alike, as a glance at M. Zwettler's *The Oral Tradition of Classical Arabic Poetry* (Columbus 1978) will quickly reveal, and perhaps the easiest introduction is through A. J. Arberry's *Arabic Poetry. A Primer for Students* (Cambridge 1965). The broad terrain of Arab letters is surveyed by R. A. Nicholson, *A Literary History of the Arabs*, first published in 1907 and now reprinted in paperback (New York 1969), and again on a more limited scale by H. A. R. Gibb, *Arabic Literature* (2nd ed., Oxford 1963) and I. Goldziher's *History of Classical Arabic Literature*, translated and revised by J. Desomogyi (Hildesheim 1966). All three of these works are surveys, longer on biography and description than on interpretation, and the reader in search of meaning and understanding might be better served by some of the chapters in G. von Grunebaum's *Medieval Islam. A Study in Cultural Orientation* (2nd ed., Chicago 1962) or the same author's collected studies entitled *Themes in Medieval Arabic Literature* (London 1981). Two convenient anthologies of translations are J. Kritzeck's *Anthology of Arabic Literature* (New York 1964) and N. Ullah's *Islamic Literature* (New York 1963).

The so-called "foreign sciences" appear anything but foreign to a Westerner. They are in fact, in their structure and methodology, a reproduction of the university curriculum in the faculty of philosophy in late Greco-Roman antiquity, and for instruction on what science was and how it was to be pursued, both Islam and the medieval West looked to the selfsame masters: Plato, Aristotle, Galen, Dioscorides, Ptolemy and Euclid. One need only to open F. Rosenthal's *The Classical Heritage in Islam* (Berkeley and Los Angeles 1975), an anthology of translations from Arabic scientists and philosophers, to appreciate Islam's scientific debt to Hellenism. How those Greek masters came into Islam in the ninth century and what use was made of them there is described by a contemporary in *The Fihrist of al-Nadim*, translated by B. Dodge (2 vols., New York 1970) and

traced in some of the central chapters of F. E. Peters' *Allah's Commonwealth. A History of Islam in the Near East 600–1100* (New York 1973).

What we call "science" the Greeks and Arabs regarded as one component in the broader category of "philosophy," a structured body of disciplines that began with logic and proceeded through the physical and mathematical sciences to the master science of "first philosophy" or metaphysics. All of this is laid out in detailed but clear fashion by Ibn Khaldun, Islam's premier scholar of the sociology of knowledge, in his monumental *Introduction*, available in English in a fully annotated version by F. Rosenthal, *Ibn Khaldun: The Muqaddimah* (3 vols., 2nd ed., Princeton 1967). Modern scholars are not, however, the polymaths their Arab predecessors were and so generally separate into "science" and "philosophy" what was so closely joined in late antiquity and Islam.

The student of Islamic philosophy is well served by either W. M. Watt's brief *Philosophy and Theology* in the series *Islamic Surveys* (Edinburgh and Chicago 1962) or the more detailed *History of Islamic Philosophy* (rev. ed., New York 1982) by M. Fahkry. For the taste of actual philosophical texts in annotated English translation, one from the beginnings of the philosophical movement in Islam and the other from near its end, there is A. L. Ivry's *Al-Kindi's Metaphysics* (Albany 1974) and S. van den Bergh's *Averroes' Tahafut al-Tahafut* (2 vols., London 1954). Equally revealing for both method and attitude is a rare autobiographical glimpse of one of the most eminent of the Islamic philosopher-scientists, the one known to the West as Avicenna: W. E. Gohlman, *The Life of Ibn Sina. A Critical Edition and Annotated Translation* (Albany 1974) and al-Ghazali's own personal quest for certitude in an Islamic world divided between the claims of faith and reason: R. McCarthy, *Freedom and Fulfillment: An Annotated Translation of Al-Ghazali's al-Munqidh min al-Dalal and Other Relevant Works* (Boston 1980).

Theology, that other partner in Ghazali's search for the truth, has been the stepchild of Western scholarship, and in Islam itself had an ambivalent though extravagantly rich career somewhere between the conservative pieties of the "Arab sciences" and the more blatant rationalism of the "foreign sciences." Watt's short book on Islamic philosophy and theology has already been mentioned, but for the more hardy and adventuresome, Watt has also written *The Formative Period of Islamic Thought* (Edinburgh and Chicago 1973). There is also M. M. Sharif (ed.), *A History of Muslim Philosophy* (2 vols., Wiesbaden 1966) which has the rare virtue of appreciating later Muslim theologians and the tradition of religious thought that has continued unbroken down into modern times, as witnessed, for example, by the Muslim theologians speaking or represented in C. K. Pullapilly (ed.), *Islam in the Contemporary World* (Notre

Dame 1980) and J. L. Donohue and J. L. Esposito (eds.), *Islam in Transition* (New York 1982).

The Western study of Arab music is far less developed than the comparable disciplines of language, literature, art and philosophy. For a very long time the standard treatment was historical/biographical, and from this perspective H.G. Farmer's *History of Arabian Music in the XIIIth Century* (rp. London 1973) is still a useful guide. The general reader might find it profitable to begin with a more synoptic view, like that provided by Owen Wright *et al.* in the article "Arab Music" in *The New Grove Dictionary of Music and Musicians*, vol. 9: 514–539, a survey that ranges from the medieval to the contemporary urban and folk traditions in music in the Arab world. Another, more technical and specialized approach is through Lois Ibsen al-Faruqi's *An Annotated Glossary of Arabic Musical Terms* (Westport 1981), which again covers the field from the medieval to the modern and includes material about theory, technique and the musical instruments that are a part of that rich and varied tradition.

The material available in English on science in Islam is scarce and uneven. There is biography in abundance and so the various entries devoted to Arab and Muslim scientists in the newly completed *Dictionary of Scientific Biography* are satisfyingly full. But this is the easiest part. The enormous manuscript resources on the sciences in Islam has scarcely been surveyed let alone read in modern times, and the differences in both annotation and attitude make their study a formidable task. Some idea of the methods and premises of Islamic science may be gotten from the texts translated in F. Rosenthal's *The Classical Heritage in Islam*, cited above, and for a modern Muslim perspective, which is marked by its own somewhat esoteric premises, the reader can turn to S. H. Nasr's *Science and Civilization in Islam* (New York 1970) and the same author's *An Introduction to Islamic Cosmological Doctrines* (Cambridge, Mass. 1964). More traditional is Pere G. Anawati's survey in Vol. II on *The Cambridge History of Islam* and the contributions by Plessner, Vernet and Wright to the new edition of *The Legacy of Islam* mentioned above.

If the reader wishes to proceed directly to some typical and important scientific texts, the following are readily accessible in English translation: L. Karpinsky and J. Winter, *Robert of Chester's Latin Translation of the Algebra of al-Khowarizmi* (New York 1972); B. Goldstein, *Al-Bitruji: On the Principles of Astronomy* (2 vols, New Haven and London 1971); E. S. Kennedy and D. Pingree, *The Astronomical History of Masha'allah* (Cambridge, Mass. 1971); R. Wright, *Elements of Astrology by al-Biruni* (London 1934); C. E. Sachau, *Al-Biruni: The Chronology of Ancient Nations* (London 1879; rp. Frankfurt 1969). For a comprehensive look at three major Islamic scientists through symposia celebrated in their honor, one should consult the various contributions to G. M. Wickens (ed.), *Avicenna: Scientist and Philosopher* (London 1952);

Hakim M. Said (ed.), *Ibn al-Haytham* (Karachi 1970) and the joint commemoration of al-Biruni and ar-Rumi: P. Chelkowski (ed.), *The Scholar and the Saint* (New York 1975).

The chief broad surveys of Arab medicine in English are by now quite old and badly in need of re-doing: E. G. Browne, *Arabian Medicine* (Cambridge 1921; rp. Westport, Ct. 1982) and D. Campbell, *Arabian Medicine and Its Influence on the Middle Ages* (2 vols., London 1926), the latter of which reveals by its very title why some aspects of Islamic science, medicine and philosophy, for example, have been relatively well studied, while others, like theology and applied mathematics, have received so little attention from Western scholars. Neither Browne nor Campbell nor even the more recent and professedly more ambitious *A Medical History of Persia and the Eastern Caliphate from the Earliest Times until the Year 1932 A.D.* by C. Elgood (Cambridge 1951) reveals the vast amount of detailed study currently being given to Arab Medicine. Much of it appears in journals and in languages other than English, but the interested reader can take some measure of the work in S. Hamarneh's *Bibliography on Medicine and Pharmacy in Medieval Islam* (Stuttgart 1964) and another volume in the series of *Islamic Surveys*: M. Ullmann, *Islamic Medicine* (Edinburgh 1978). The Muslim physician's concern for the more psychological aspects of the art of healing is well illustrated in A. J. Arberry's translation of *The Spiritual Physick of Rhazes* (London 1950), and the sophistication of the Arab-Greek-Indian pharmacopeia in Hakim M. Said's translation and S. Hamarneh's commentary on *Al-Biruni's Book of Pharmacy and Materia Medica* (2 vols., Karachi 1973).

The conversion of this knowledge into technology took what are to us somewhat unaccustomed forms. We can recognize the water wheel and the introduction of paper as utilitarian and profitable innovations, and we are just beginning to understand the level of mathematical sophistication that lies behind the religious obligation to establish the direction of prayer in correct orientation to Makkah or to divide inheritance shares exactly according to the provisions of Islamic law, but Muslim theoreticians, like their Hellenistic predecessors and Byzantine contemporaries were not beyond displaying their prodigious talents in the form of toys and gadgets, some of extraordinary imagination, like the ones on display in text and illustration in al-Jazari's thirteenth-century book of automata: D. R. Hill, *The Book of Knowledge of Ingenious Mechanical Devices* (Dordrecht-Boston 1974). Again, other efforts were in directions where we have ceased to march, in the application of chemistry to the "lifescience" of alchemy, for example, brilliantly described by both E. J. Holmyard, *Alchemy* (Harmondsworth 1957) and T. Burckhardt, *Alchemy. Science of the Cosmos, Science of the Soul* (Baltimore 1971), and the equally useful disposition of astronomical learning in what was for them the science of astrology.

The culture we call "Islamic" covered an enormous range of lands and people in the Middle Ages, united in their Islamic identity, diverse in their own ethnic, cultural and linguistic traditions. It was in a sense an "open" society, remarkably free of barriers to the exchange of either goods or ideas. Though profoundly agrarian even into modern times, the Islamic world of the Middle Ages boasted as well a high urban, commercial and technological tradition; its large cities were international not regional emporia and the rich merchants and upper bourgeoisie who lived in them enjoyed a comfortable and even a luxurious life supported not by conquest but by trade. There are witnesses, medieval and contemporary, on all sides, travellers like Ibn Jubayr (translated by R. J. C. Broadbent, London 1952) and Ibn Battuta (translated by H. A. R. Gibb, 2 vols., London 1959–1962) who crossed the length and breadth of the medieval "Abode of Islam" and experienced its material and spiritual marvels; modern scholars who are reconstructing the social and economic life of the Islamic city: I. Lapidus (ed.), *Middle Eastern Cities* (Berkeley and Los Angeles 1969); A. Hourani and S. M. Stern (eds.), *The Islamic City* (Oxford 1970); L. C. Brown (ed.), *From Medina to Metropolis* (Princeton 1973).

Little of this would have been possible without sophisticated mechanisms for both the acquisition and disposition of wealth. Traders long antedated Islam in the Middle East, of course, and Makkah had many commercial antecedents and rivals, as the archeological record continues to reveal in studies like G. Bibby's *Looking for Dilmun* (New York 1969) and A. al-Ansary's more recent *Qaryat al-Fau: A Portrait of Pre-Islamic Civilization in Saudi Arabia* (London 1982). But this was the faint dawn of the later splendor of Baghdad, Cairo, Damascus and Aleppo and the international network of which they were part. The breadth of that network and its links can be gathered from the selections in R. S. Lopez and I. W. Raymond (eds.), *Medieval Trade in the Mediterranean World* (New York 1955), but for the mechanics a closer view is required, like that provided by A. Udovitch, *Partnership and Profit in Medieval Islam* (Princeton 1970) and the essays collected by M. Cook (ed.) in his *Studies in the Economic History of the Middle East* (London 1970).

A great deal of this wealth collected through trade and taxation was redeployed in the society through the endowment mechanism known as *waqf*: the owner's allocation of the income of his property, which thereby became tax-free and inalienable, to some pious purpose. That pious purpose might mean feeding the poor or providing scholarships for students, but its understanding was broad enough that over the centuries *waqf* funds financed most of the great monuments of medieval Islam: mosques, law schools, convents, hospices and shrines; their construction, maintenance and staffing. Many of those buildings stand, in whole or in part, to this day, and their measure has been taken often and in detail, as is immediately apparent from K. A. C. Creswell's *Bibliography of the Architecture, Arts and Crafts of Islam* (Cairo 1961). Thus only a few of the major surveys will be cited here. J. D. Hoag, *Islamic Architecture* (New York 1977) and H. Stierlin, *Architecture of Islam* (New York 1980) generously cover the chief buildings, and those of Cairo have received particular attention, at the hands of Creswell, *The Muslim Architecture of Egypt* (Cairo 1952 and 1959), among others. The companion volumes on the monuments of Iran are A. Pope's *Persian Architecture* (London 1965). On painting there is T. Arnold, *Painting in Islam* (2nd ed., Oxford 1965), R. Ettinghausen's magnificent *Arab Painting* (Geneva 1962) and B. Gray, *Persian Painting* (Geneva 1961).

The richness of information implied by these surveys does not mean that all problems are solved nor that all avenues have been explored. Though the task has been taken up by some, like E. C. Dodd and S. Khairallah in their *Image of the Word: A Study of Qur'anic Verses in Islamic Architecture* (Beirut 1981) or the papers edited by P. Chelkowski and others, *Studies in Art and Literature of the Near East* (New York 1974), much of the work of integration still awaits. There are, moreover, new "discoveries" like the early Islamic city on the Syrian steppe excavated by O. Grabar, R. Holod, James Knustad and William Trusdale (*City in the Desert: Qasr al-Hayr East*, 2 vols., Cambridge, Mass. 1978) or old problems, like the Dome of the Rock in Jerusalem, which remain almost as intractable as when they were first posed. Many of them confront the investigator at the very beginnings of Islamic art and architecture, at the point of origins and essence, where the most reliable guide to both the problematic and the likely direction of solutions has been charted by O. Grabar in his *The Formation of Islamic Art* (New Haven 1973).

F. E. Peters

Credits and References

v Woodcut by Walter Ferro, based on the palmette on the decorative page of a Qur'an, copied by 'Ali bin Hilal, called Ibn al-Bawwab, Baghdad, 1000-01; Ms. 1431, folio 285r., Chester Beatty Library, Dublin.

xii Sultan Hasan Madrasah in silhouette, Cairo, 1356-63: Richard Wormser.

7 Page from a Qur'an written on vellum in Kufic script, Iraq, 9th c.; Or. 1397, folio 15v., British Museum, London.

9 Map, Byzantine and Persian Empires, 600: art, Walter Ferro; research, J. L. Dewar.

11 Map, Arab Empire at Greatest Extent, 700-850: art, Walter Ferro; research, J. L. Dewar.

13 Dome of the Rock, Jerusalem, 691: Alistair Duncan.

18 Page from Qur'an in Thuluth script, Egypt, mid-14th c.; 30.59v., Smithsonian Institution, Freer Gallery of Art, Washington, D.C.

23 Knights jousting, Kitab al-Baytarah (Book on Veterinary Medicine), Egypt, 14th c.; Inv. no. 18236, Abdel Fattah Eid, Museum of Islamic Art, Cairo.

27 Frontispiece, Qur'an of Sultan Baybars II, Egypt, 1304; Add. 22406, folios iv.-2r., British Museum, London.

28 The hare and the king of the elephants, Kalilah wa Dimnah (Kalila and Dimnah) Persian translation, 1343-44; Acc. 61, National Library, Cairo.

29 The lion and the jackal, Kalilah wa Dimnah (Kalila and Dimna), probably Syria, 1200-1220; Arabe 3464, folio 49v., courtesy of La Bibliothèque Nationale, Paris.

30 Funerary scene, Maqamat (The Assemblies) of al-Hariri, Iraq, 1237; Arabe 5847, folio 29v., courtesy of La Bibliothèque Nationale, Paris.

33 Abu Zayd before the governor of Rahbah, Maqamat (The Assemblies) of al-Hariri, Iraq, 1237; Arabe 5847, folio 26r., courtesy of La Bibliotheque Nationale, Paris.

38 Moroccan storyteller: Jay Maisel/Image Bank.

41 "The Story of the Fisherman," The Thousand and One Nights, a translation from Arabic with notes by Edward William Lane, engraving from original design by William Harvey, London, 1839; Columbia University Library, New York.

45 Qanun player, The Thousand and One Nights, a translation from Arabic with notes by Edward William Lane, engraving from original design by William Harvey, London, 1839; Columbia University Library, New York.

47 Giraffe, Kitab al-Hayawan (Book of Animals) by al-Jahiz, probably Syria, 14th c.; Ar. A.F.D. 140 Inf., folio 26r., Biblioteca Ambrosiana, Milan.

49 Ostrich, Kitab al-Hayawan (Book of Animals) by al-Jahiz, probably Syria, 14th c.; Ar. A.F.D. 140 Inf., folio 10r., Biblioteca Ambrosiana, Milan.

51 Enthroned ruler surrounded by court officials, Volume IV, Kitab al-Aghani (Book of Songs) by al-Isfahani, Iraq, 1217-19; Adab 579, Abdel Fattah Eid, National Library, Cairo.

57 A theology class at al-Azhar, Cairo: Richard Wormser.

62 The destruction of Jerusalem, al-Athar al-Baqiyah (Chronology of Ancient Nations) by al-Biruni; Arabe 1489, folio 147v., courtesy of La Bibliothèque Nationale, Paris.

67 "School of Athens" by Raphael, 1509-10; Vatican Palace, Rome.

69 Minaret of the Great Mosque of al-Mutawakkil, Samarra, 848/9-852: Shostal Associates/Kurt Scholz

71 Page from a Latin translation of Aristotle with commentaries by Ibn Rushd, 1562-74; Princeton University Library, Princeton, New Jersey.

73 Medieval city wall, Fez, Morocco: Michael Anguti.

79 The Treasury at Petra, Jordan, 2nd c. B.C.-106 A.D.: Thomas Walters.

80 Tin-glazed bowl painted in blue and green, Iraq, 9th-10th c.; Victoria and Albert Museum, London.

81 Luster-painted jar, Egypt, Fatimid period, first half of 12th c.; Victoria and Albert Museum, London.

83 Mihrab (prayer niche), Sultan Hasan Madrasah, Cairo, 1356-63: Michael Anguti.

85 Kutubiyah Mosque, Marrakesh, circa 1150: Michael Anguti.

87 The Great Mosque of Damascus, 705-715: Richard Wormser.

88 Muqarna in the Alhambra, Granada, 14th c.: Michael Anguti.

90 Arabesque detail, portal of the Great Mosque of Cordoba, 787-987: Michael Anguti.

93 Resting travelers, Maqamat (The Assemblies) of Al-Hariri, Iraq, 1237; Arabe 5847, folio 9r., courtesy of La Bibliothèque Nationale, Paris.

94 Detail, ivory casket inscribed with the name of al-Mughiza, Cordoba, 968; Inv. 4068, courtesy of Les Musées Nationaux, France.

96 Page from Qur'an of Sultan Uljaytu in gold Jalil script, Northern Iraq, 1310; Or. 4945, folio 36v., British Museum, London.

98 Detail, brass tray inlaid with silver, Syria, 13th c.; 45.386, Cleveland Museum of Art (Purchase from the J. H. Wade Fund and Gift of H. Kevorkian), Cleveland, Ohio.

99 Brass tray inlaid with silver, Syria, 13th c.; 45.386, Cleveland Museum of Art (Purchase from the J. H. Wade Fund and Gift of H. Kevorkian), Cleveland, Ohio.

101 Bronze figure of a lion, Egypt, Fatimid period, late 11th-early 12th c.; Inv. 4035, Museum of Islamic Art, Cairo.

103 Court of the Lions, the Alhambra, Granada, 14th c.: Michael Anguti.

105 Kairouan Mosque, Tunisia, 836-62: Michael Anguti.

107 Dome of the Great Mosque of Cordoba, 785-987: Michael Anguti.

109 Sultan Hasan Madrasah, Cairo, 1356-63: Michael Anguti.

111 Wood carving, Egypt, Tulunid period, 9th-10th c.; Inv. 6023, courtesy of Les Musees Nationaux, France.

113 Rock crystal ewer, Egypt, 10th c.; Treasury of San Marco, Venice.

115 Frontispiece, Kitab ad-Diryaq (Book of Antidotes) of Pseudo-Galen, probably Iraq, mid-13th c.; A.F. 10, folio 1r., Nationalbibliothek, Vienna.

117 Brass ewer inlaid with silver, made by Shuja' bin Man'a of Mosul; Blacas Collection, no. 66-12-29-61, British Museum, London.

123 Bowl, overglaze painted in golden luster, Iraq, 10th c.; 25.6, Smithsonian Institution, Freer Gallery of Art, Washington, D.C.

125 Ivory plaque, Egypt, 12th c.; cat. no. 80cF, Bargello Museum, Florence: Walter Denny.

126 Bayad singing and playing the 'ud, The Story of Bayad and Riyad, Spain or Morocco, 13th c.; Ms. ar. 368, folio 10r, Biblioteca Apostolica, Vatican Palace, Rome.

127 Drawing by Walter Ferro, based on a tenth century Abbasid coin, Arkeoloji Muzleri, Istanbul.

128 The Water Clock of the Drummers, Kitab fi Ma'rifat al-Hiyal al-Handisiyah (The Book of Knowledge of Ingenious Mechanical Devices) by al-Jazari, copied by Farruk ibn Abd al-Latif, Syria, 1315; 42.10v, Smithsonian Institution, Freer Gallery of Art, Washington, D.C.

133 Ivory Casket, Cordoba, 11th c.; Inv. no. 10.1866, Victoria and Albert Museum, London.

251

135 Bottle, glass enameled and gilded, Syria, 14th c.; 29.8, Smithsonian Institution, Freer Gallery of Art, Washington, D.C.

136 Musical instruments, sketches by Walter Ferro after Dr. Ali Jihad Racy.

143 Cylindrical inkwell, brass inlaid with silver, Syria or Iraq, 12th-13th c.; Metropolitan Museum of Art, New York.

145 The Alhambra, Granada: Tor Eigeland/Black Star.

151 Euclid's geometry expounded by at-Tusi, 1258; Add. 23387, folio 28r., British Museum, London.

153 Page from a treatise on mathematics and optics by Ibn al-Haytham; Acc. no. 2762, Süleymaniye Library, Istanbul.

155 Page from Nihayat as-Su'ul fi Tashih al-Usul (Solutions to Questions through Corrections of Traditions) by Ibn ash-Shatir; Arabic Ms. Marsh 139, folio 16v., Bodleian Library, Oxford.

157 Brass astrolabe, Baghdad, 1131; A-84, Adler Planetarium, Chicago, Illinois.

159 Draco, Suwar al-Kawakib ath-Thabitah (Treatise on the Fixed Stars) by as-Sufi, Samarkand, 1437; Arabe 5036, folio 33v., courtesy of La Bibliothèque Nationale, Paris.

161 Diagram from medieval Latin translation of Ibn al-Haytham's Kitab al-Manazir (Optics), 1269; Ms. CR. 3.3., folio 117r., Royal Observatory, Edinburgh.

163 Spherical astrolabe, probably Iraq, 1480-81; 62-25, Museum of the History of Science, Oxford.

165 Self-trimming lamp, Kitab al-Hiyal (On Mechanical Devices) by Ahmed bin Musa, Iraq, 9th c.; no. 5562, folio 137v., Staatsbibliothek, Berlin.

167 Page from a treatise on mathematics and optics by Ibn al-Haytham; Acc. no. 2762, Süleymaniye Library, Istanbul.

169 Astrological diagram from Almagestum seu magnae constructionis mathematicae by Ptolemy, 1528; Rare Book Division, New York Public Library, New York.

175 Portraits of nine physicians, Kitab ad-Diryaq (Book of Antidotes) of Pseudo-Galen, probably Iraq, mid-13th c.; A.F. 10, folio 15r., Nationalbibliothek, Vienna.

177 Frontispiece, Taqwim as-Shihhah (Maintaining Good Health) by Ibn Butlan, 1213; Or. 1347, folio 2v., British Museum, London.

181 Surgical instruments, treatise on surgery from at-Tasrif (a medical encyclopedia) by az-Zahrawi, Andalusia, 1000; Arabe 2953, folio 40r., courtesy of La Bibliothèque Nationale, Paris.

182 Man on horseback, Kitab al-Baytarah (Book on Veterinary Medicine), summarized from Ahmad bin al-Hasan bin al-Ahnas by 'Ali bin al-Hasan bin Hibat Allah, Baghdad, 1209; 8 Tibb f, alif Aga, Abdel Fattah Eid, National Library, Cairo.

185 A boy bitten by a snake, Kitab ad-Diryaq (Book of Antidotes) of Pseudo-Galen, probably Iraq, mid-13th c.; A.F. 10, folio 2v., Nationalbibliothek, Vienna.

186 Autumn crocus, Materia Medica of Dioscorides, copied by Abdallah bin al-Fadl, Iraq, 1224; 43.2v., Smithsonian Institution, Freer Gallery of Art, Washington, D.C.

188 Alchemical equipment, Sharh diwan ash-Shudhur (A Commentary on an Alchemical Poem) by al-Ansari; A65, National Library of Medicine, Bethesda, Maryland.

190 Pegasus, Suwar al-Kawakib ath-Thabitah (Treatise on the Fixed Stars) by as-Sufi, 1009; Arabic Ms. Marsh 144, Bodleian Library, Oxford.

191 Signs of the zodiac from the palace water clock, Kitab fi Ma'rifat al-Hiyal al-Handasiyah (The Book of Knowledge of Ingenious Mechanical Devices) by al-Jazari, copied by Farruk bin Abd al-Latif, Syria, 1315; 30.74v., Smithsonian Institution, Freer Gallery of Art, Washington, D.C.

193 Page from a treatise on the eye by Hunayn bin Ishaq, probably copied in 13th c.; 100 Tibb Taimur, folio 314, Abdel Fattah Eid, National Library, Cairo.

195 A stained glass window depicting ar-Razi, the narthex of Princeton University Chapel, Princeton, New Jersey: Shelby D. Phillips.

197 A page from a Latin translation of al-Urjuzah fi at-Tibb (Verses on Medicine) by Ibn Sina (Avicenna) with commentaries by Ibn Rushd (Averroes), 1562-73; Princeton University Library, Princeton, New Jersey.

199 Page from a 1531 Latin translation by Peter Argellata of a treatise on surgery by az-Zahrawi; National Library of Medicine, Bethesda, Maryland.

204 Mechanical boat with drinking men and musicians, Kitab fi Ma'rifat al-Hiyal al-Handasiyah (Book of Knowledge of Ingenious Mechanical Devices) by al-Jazari, copied by Muhammad bin Yusuf bin Osman al-Haskafi, Iraq, 1206; A3472, folio 98r., Topkapi Palace Museum, Istanbul.

209 Waterwheel, Hamah, Syria: Bruno Barbey/Magnum.

211 Reciprocating pump, Kitab fi Ma'rifat al-Hiyal al-Handasiyah (The Book of Knowledge of Ingenious Mechanical Devices) by al-Jazari, copied by Muhammad bin Ahmad al-Ismiri, 1354; Acc. no. 1965.476, James K. Ufford, courtesy of the Fogg Art Museum, Harvard University, Cambridge, Massachusetts.

211 Contemporary engineering line drawing of reciprocating pump based on al-Jazari's plans: Donald Hill.

212 Trebuchet line drawing: Walter Ferro.

214 The nilometer, Cairo, 716: Michael Anguti.

215 Detail from the water clock of the peacocks, Kitab fi Ma'rifat al-Hiyal al-Handasiyah (The Book of Knowledge of Ingenious Mechanical Devices) by al-Jazari, copied by Muhammad bin Yusuf bin Osman al-Haskafi, Iraq, 1206; A3472, folio 35v., Topkapi Palace Museum, Istanbul.

217 Castle wine dispenser, Kitab fi Ma'rifat al-Hiyal al-Handasiyah (The Book of Knowledge of Ingenious Mechanical Devices) by al-Jazari, copied by Muhammad bin Yusuf bin Osman al-Haskafi, Iraq, 1206; A3472, folio 88v., Topkapi Palace Museum, Istanbul.

222 Trade route map: research, Dorothea El Mallakh; art, Walter Ferro.

223 Copper balance weight, Qaryat al-Fau, 1st-5th c.; The Museum of King Saud University, Riyadh, Saudi Arabia.

224 Islamic coins: American Numismatic Society, New York.

226 A dhow sails towards Mombasa: Marion Kaplan.

228 Market scene, Morocco: Jay Maisel/Image Bank.

230 Earthenware containers: Michael Anguti.

232 Map of Iraq, Masalik al-Mamalik (Routes of the Dominions) by al-Istakhri, 15th c.; no. 199, Geography, Abdel Fattah Eid, National Library, Cairo.

233 A dhow sails on the Arabian Sea: Marion Kaplan.

235 Alexandria Harbor scene: Jonathan Blair/Black Star.

237 World map by al-Idrisi, 1533; Ms. Pococke 375, folios 3v.-4v., Bodleian Library, Oxford.

239 Camels: Richard Wilkie/Black Star.

Index

The Arabic definite article is disregarded in the alphabetizing of this index

PERSONS AND PLACES

Index

GENERAL